performance design
IN AUSTRALIA

performance design

IN AUSTRALIA

KRISTEN ANDERSON AND IMOGEN ROSS

WITH EAMON D'ARCY, DEREK NICHOLSON AND PAMELA ZEPLIN

CRAFTSMAN HOUSE

Australia | Council for the Arts

This project has been assisted by the Commonwealth Government through the Australia Council, its arts funding and advisory body.

The state of Western Australia has had an investment in this project through the Department for the Arts.

Fine Art Publishing Pty Ltd,
42 Chandos Street,
St Leonards, Sydney, NSW 2065
Enquiries: info@gbpub.com.au

ISBN 1 877004 04 9

Design: Kerry Klinner
Cover design: Caroline de Fries
Reprographics: Sang Choy, Singapore
Printing: Tien Wah Press, Singapore

page 1

Plate i **The King and I**
by Rodgers and Hammerstein
The Gordon/Frost Organisation
1991
venue: Her Majesty's Theatre, Sydney
director: Christopher Renshaw
set designer: Brian Thomson
costume designer: Roger Kirk
lighting designer: Nigel Levings
photographer: Peter Holderness
A concept rendering of Thomson's design for the *King and I* front-cloth by Sue Field.

pages 2–3

Plate ii **A Midsummer Night's Dream**
based on the play by William Shakespeare
music by Maurice Ravel
West Australian Ballet
1991
venue: His Majesty's Theatre, Perth
choreographer: Barry Moreland
set designer: Charles Blackman
costume designer: Anna French
lighting designer: Kenneth Rayner
photographer: Bill Plowman

page 4

Figure i **Sanctuary**
devised by Spare Parts Puppet Theatre
1995
venue: Spare Parts Puppet Theatre, Fremantle
director: Peter L. Wilson
set and costume designer: Tish Oldham
photographer: Chris Ha

page 5

Plate iii **A Midsummer Night's Dream**
by William Shakespeare
Sydney Theatre Company
1989
venue: Drama Theatre, Sydney
Opera House
director: Richard Wherrett
set designer: Brian Thomson
costume designer: Terry Ryan
lighting designer: John Rayment
photographer: Don McMurdo

Contents

Acknowledgments

Our sincere thanks to Gabrielle Bonney whose support, editorial skills and advice contributed greatly to this book in its early stages. She worked alongside both authors and was substantially involved in the discussion and creation of chapter formats and the initial shape taken by the book as a whole.

Many thanks to the Performing Arts Board of the Australia Council and the West Australian Department for the Arts for being the first to believe in our aims by providing us with the financial springboard from which to jump. With their combined financial assistance we were able to take the idea from basic interview transcripts to a finished manuscript ready to present for publishing. The undiminished and continuing support of Nevill Drury and Marah Braye from Craftsman House has also made this book a reality.

So many individuals and companies were involved in the creation of this book that it would take many, many pages to thank them all personally. As always, however, there were some people who stood out in their commitment and encouragement of the project. We would like to thank Tom Bannerman, Jeff Busby, Andrew Carter, Peter Cooke, Eamon D'Arcy, Laurel Frank, Anne Fraser, Branco Gaica, Ponch Hawkes, John Hoenig, Peter Holderness, Nigel Levings, Elise Lockwood, Robert McFarlane, Mary Moore, Derek Nicholson, Duncan Ord, Lynn Poole, Richard Roberts, Ian Robinson, Frank van Stratten, Jennie Tate, Brian Thomson, Rose and David Wilson, and Pamela Zeplin for helping us considerably during the four-and-a-half years of research and writing.

The following people were interviewed between August 1993 and February 1998 in the research for this book, and we thank them for allowing us to use their words and their work: William Akers, Ben Anderson, Michael A. R. Anderson, Tom Bannerman, Kym Barrett, Hilary Bell, John Bell, Antony Bibacci, Rachel Burke, Gordon Burns, Donn Byrnes, Kim Carpenter, Andrew Carter, Angela Chaplin, Judith Cobb, Geoff Cobham, Hugh Colman, Peter Cooke, Melody Cooper, Peter Corrigan, Derrick Cox, Teresa Crea, Stephen Curtis, Eamon D'Arcy, Rory Dempster, Glenn Elston, Bob Evans, Victoria Feitscher, Sue Field, Laurel Frank, Anne Fraser, Kristian Fredrikson, Anna French, Sue Grey-Gardener, Shaun Gurton, Bill Haycock, Judith Hoddinott, John Hoenig, David Hough, Mark Howett, Lindy Hume, Richard Jeziorny, Robert Juniper, Jenny Kemp, Robert Kemp, Tim Kobin, Barrie Kosky, Constantine Koukias, Justin Kurzel, Edie Kurzer, Allan Lees, Nigel Levings, Jo Litson, David Longmuir, Amanda Lovejoy, Graham Maclean, Catherine Martin, Louise McCarthy, Aubrey Mellor, Colin Mitchell, Patrick Mitchell, Graeme Murphy, Tim Newth, Derek Nicholson, Steve Nolan, Duncan Ord, Wendy Osmond, Moffatt Oxenbould, Trina Parker, William Passmore, Pamela Payne, Michael Pearce, Dan Potra, John Rayment, Richard Roberts, Ian Robinson, Andrew Ross, Kenneth Rowell, Nick Schlieper, Tess Schofield, Michael Scott-Mitchell, John Senczuk, Mark Shelton, Efterpie Soropos, Kathryn Sproul, John Stoddart, Jennie Tate, Pierre Thibaudeau, Mark Thompson, Brian Thomson, Karin Thorne, Tony Tripp, Lou Westbury, Richard Wherrett, Ken Wilby, Peter L. Wilson, Anne Wulff, Tony Youlden and Pamela Zeplin.

To all the photographers who allowed us to reprint their work within the book — we thank them for their overwhelming generosity, time and photographic skill.

Many friends were employed in the original typing out of interview transcripts — their help, humour and understanding pulled the manuscript into shape.

Companies from across Australia responded enthusiastically to our constant requests for visual material and information from their archives. We sincerely thank the publicity officers, marketing managers, archivists and technical production teams for allowing us into their files.

Lastly, we wish to thank our long-suffering flatmates, friends, partners and families for continuing to support us since we first began on this adventure. We could not have done it without you!

Foreword

'The rest is history'

I am delighted to have been invited to write the foreword to this long-overdue compilation of the work of Australian performance designers. The times have certainly changed for designers since I began in 1952.

Australians have always been theatregoers, from the earliest days of the gold rush to Friday nights at the Tivoli. In 1841 Melbourne's first theatre, the Royal Pavilion, was built in Bourke Street. Many theatres followed, including the Queen's, the Theatre Royal, the Olympic, the Haymarket, the Academy of Music, and the Princess — sadly, the only nineteenth-century theatre to have survived in Melbourne.

Wherever there were theatres there were theatre managements. J. C. Williamson co-founded what became known as 'The Firm' in 1882; later, under Sir George Tallis and the Tait brothers, it became one of the largest theatrical managements in the world, managing theatres all over Australia and New Zealand, and providing constant employment for hundreds of actors, singers, dancers and technicians. Sir Benjamin Fuller (and later Garnet Carroll) were at the Princess, and David N. Martin ran the Tivoli circuit. Their companies had their own workshops for costume makers, property makers, set builders and, of course, the scenic painters. The latter were constantly having to recreate sets from London or New York, creating their own designs if necessary. They were a world unto themselves, overseeing and painting the most beautiful scenery.

The late Dres Hardingham used to tell me that when he was an apprentice scenic artist the master painter would arrive at work in the morning dressed in a black morning coat, hat and gloves. The paint room had a polished floor (drop cloths were always put down to protect it), and at each end of the room there would be a large urn of flowers. This was at the Princess Theatre and I still remember that room — it had a lovely Georgian window at one end. It has all gone now in recent rebuilding. Another well-known scenic painter, William Constable, chose to combine scenic painting with his own artwork and designed many lovely productions for the Borovansky Company, which was the precursor of the Australian Ballet. I am fortunate to have worked with both gentlemen during my career in theatre, and consider them to be the forerunners to the scenic designers that came later.

For those who were interested in designing for the smaller local theatres, opportunities were presented by the many amateur companies in Melbourne. The Gregan McMahon Players, the Little Theatre (later St Martins), the Ballet Guild and the National Theatre all had strong followings. Those who wanted to be scenic designers — and wanted to earn a living — had to go to London to make their names. Loudon Sainthill, Kenneth Rowell, Warwick Armstrong and later Barry Kay come to mind.

I had always wanted to be an artist. My mother had been a fashion artist in New Zealand, where I was born. I had left school and was enrolled as a commercial art student — graphic art as it is now called — at the Royal Melbourne Institute of Technology (RMIT). During my time as a student I developed a strong interest in the theatre. A friend of my mother's suggested that I join the National Theatre School as a drama student under the guidance of Ruth Conabere. I did so, though I continued to study commercial art and, without knowing it, I changed the direction of my life.

In 1948 Melbourne was host to the Old Vic Theatre company from London. It presented three plays: *The School for Scandal* by Sheridan, *Richard III* by Shakespeare and *The Skin of Our Teeth* by Thornton Wilder. The company was led by Laurence Olivier and Vivien Leigh. It was magic, a joy to see and hear. I loved the costumes, the colours. It was modern — not dusty and old like some of J. C. Williamson's stock stuff.

I knew then what I wanted to see and do. But how? There were no colleges that could teach stage design, no schools, no NIDA — just the schools of experience, trial and error.

▲ Figure ii **Saint Joan**
by George Bernard Shaw
The National Theatre Movement
1952
venue: The Princess Theatre, Melbourne
director: William P. Carr
set and costume designer: Anne Fraser
photo: D. Nicholson archives
Fraser's stage setting for *St Joan*.

▲ Figure iii **Summer of the Seventeenth Doll**
by Ray Lawler
Union Theatre Repertory Company
1955
venue: Union Theatre, Melbourne
director: John Sumner
set and costume designer: Anne Fraser
photo: UTRC archives

The stage setting of the original production. The first production of Ray Lawler's classic play was in November 1955 at the Union Theatre, University of Melbourne. It was the first Australian play with a wholly Australian artistic input to tour England. Fraser's design recreated the look and feel of the small Victorian terraces that were common to Carlton. Lawler had specified many of the decorative features within the script, and had even suggested the ground plan. Fraser took her design cue from this, and created a small, naturalistic living room with the hint of a hallway, a kitchen beyond, a back garden, and an upstairs level. Sixteen kewpie dolls in glitter and gauze decorated the walls ...

Soon it was time for the National Theatre's 1952 arts festival at the Princess. My friend Ray Lawler told me that the management wanted to present George Bernard Shaw's *Saint Joan*. He suggested I submit some sketches to the board. I did so and they were accepted! Knowing that the National had limited funding and facilities, I had concentrated on settings that conveyed the strength and scope of *Saint Joan* (fig. ii) in as simple a way as possible: for example, suggesting the immensity of Rheims Cathedral by placing the action around the base of one enormous column and leaving the rest of the stage in darkness. On the other hand, I had designed costumes and props that made much use of heraldry and colour, and these gave a glowing richness to the sweep and movement of the play. I must in retrospect thank these people for having faith in me although I was a novice in this field. Happily it all worked and I had taken my first step as a set designer.

In the audience on the first night of *Saint Joan* was a young Englishman, John Sumner, who had come to Australia to manage the Union Theatre at Melbourne University. We did not meet on that occasion but, along with the rest of the Melbourne theatre world, I was intrigued when in 1954 he created the Union Theatre Repertory Company (UTRC — later the Melbourne Theatre Company), producing a different play every two weeks. Ray Lawler joined him there as an actor, as did many of Melbourne's thespian community.

I had a phone call from Ray about a year later — could he meet me in the foyer of the Athenaeum Theatre? He told me that John Sumner was leaving the company at the invitation of Hugh Hunt, who had been appointed artistic director of the newly formed Elizabethan Theatre Trust in

Sydney. Ray was to take over as artistic director of the UTRC and, as he had no technical skills, asked whether I would join him there as resident designer. Would I ever! At last I could give up my rather uninteresting job designing biscuit packets. This was an unusual and unique offer since no such position had previously existed in the local theatre companies. Little did I know I was to spend the next forty years of my life as a professional stage designer! My first UTRC production was Christopher Fry's *The Dark Is Light Enough*. It opened at the Union Theatre in September 1955.

Unbeknown to us, Ray had been writing a play. I was in the office when he received news that he had shared first place with Oriel Gray in the 1955 Playwrights' Advisory Board competition for his play *Summer of the Seventeenth Doll* (fig. iii, pls iv and v). Hugh Hunt suggested that John Sumner return to Melbourne and direct the play for the UTRC. He did. It opened on 28 November 1955 and was a huge success: at the invitation of Laurence Olivier, it travelled to London — and yes, I designed the set.

The rest is history.

Anne Fraser

Lawler's Doll Trilogy (*Summer of the Seventeenth Doll*, *Kid Stakes* and *Other Times*) takes place within the one house over a long period of time. The design challenge is to indicate the passage of time and characters within the constraints of a naturalistic stage setting. Subtle lighting and props changes take on great importance, as do costumes.

▲ Plate iv **The Doll Trilogy**
by Ray Lawler
Sydney Theatre Company
1985
venue: Drama Theatre, Sydney Opera House
director: Rodney Fisher
set designer: Brian Thomson
costume designer: Melody Cooper
lighting designer: John Rayment
set dresser: Robert Kemp
photo: STC archives
in photo: Harold Hopkins as Barney Ibbot and Heather Mitchell as Nancy Wells

▲ Plate v **Summer of the Seventeenth Doll**
by Ray Lawler
Australian Nouveau Theatre (ANThill)
1983
venue: ANThill Theatre, South Melbourne
director: Jean-Pierre Mignon
set and costume designer: Wendy Black
lighting designer: Trevlyn Gilmour
photographer: Jeff Busby

Mignon and his company radically reworked *Summer of the Seventeenth Doll* in order to present it as a play with classic and universal themes, referencing it to a heightened classical world reminiscent of Greek Tragedy. Inspired by the art of French surrealist painter Paul Delvaux, the actors appeared in stark relief against a blue warehouse background. The minimalist settings (complete with marble columns), challenged the audience's preconception of the play as a domestic working-class drama of the 1950s.

[notes — Katherine Sturak and Jean-Pierre Mignon, 1996]

Introduction

This book is about contemporary performance design as seen through the eyes of Australian designers, directors, choreographers and performance writers. By contemporary we mean the years from 1980 to 1995 (we have included photographs from that period), though many of the artists with whom we have spoken have been active in the field for much longer.[1]

◄ Figure iv **Burning**

developed by Natalie Weir and Bill
Haycock

Queensland Ballet Company

1994

venue: Queensland Ballet Studios

director: Natalie Weir

set and costume designer: Bill Haycock

lighting designer: David Whitford

photographer: Phillipe Hargreaves

in photo: Justin Rutzou

'Burning … it's about being alone and
then finding others to be close to. It's
about separation and loss, about that
closeness being taken away. It's about
looking for it again or living with its
memory. It's a work about being alive.'

[programme notes — Natalie Weir and
Bill Haycock]

How we began

The idea for the book began while we were still studying design at the Western Australian Academy of Performing Arts, in one of the many late-night dissections of the Australian theatre industry that tend to occur when one is young, idealistic, and at drama school. As undergraduate theatre designers we wanted to look for information beyond the old picture books about 'Russian theatre designers of the Revolution' and post-war European notions of theatre craft that barely filled the library shelves. We had so many questions. Who were the Australian artists who had helped to create the 'look' of Australian theatre? What names are recognised as being part of the theatre's design heritage? Who is currently setting Australian performance design standards, and what are the contemporary styles? Although we were being taught by practising and visiting designers, none seemed to have the time to document their own work, let alone the work of others. Though there have been many well-known Australian artists and designers working in the theatre, it is hard to access detailed information about them or their work since relatively few photographs or models have been kept in theatre, opera or ballet company archives. If one is interested in the performing arts, but does not live in a capital city, how is it possible to see and study the latest developments occurring on and off stage? What is specific to Australian performance? These questions led to broader ones about the entire industry and we soon realised that there is a dearth of publications aimed specifically at the Australian performance market. The articles and writings that do deal with live performance seldom look in depth at the impact of design in the performance making.

Our prime objective has been to create a platform for designers to explore their changing role in contemporary performance. We wish to encourage debate, criticism, celebration and public acknowledgment of design as a profession, a craft and a visual language. Since theatre and performance are collaborative artforms, where does the designer's role begin and finish? Do designers have the same status and impact on performance as directors and writers? Are designers working in peer collaboration or creating their environments in artistic isolation? To what extent are our directors, writers, performers and designers restricted by the availability of theatre spaces? Should critics review the role played by the designer as much as they do that of the director and the performers? How is design evolving in contemporary performance?

Australian playwrights, directors and choreographers are often interviewed or talked about in the media. Their opinions on the subjects of

▲ Plate vi **Banshee**

Meryl Tankard and the Australian Dance Theatre

1989

venue: Australian National Gallery, Canberra

director: Meryl Tankard

composer: Colin Offord

set and lighting designer: Regis Lansac

costume designer: Meryl Tankard and Dorothy Herel

paper costume artwork: Kathy Nix

photographer: Regis Lansac

in photo: Dancers of the Meryl Tankard Company (including Patrick Maguire and Roz Hervey)

Drawing on the Celtic myth of the Banshee, Tankard's artistic team created a performance which was as intricately composed as the prehistoric metals of the 'Irish Silver and Gold' exhibition at the Australian National Gallery, their source of inspiration. Lansac's method of projecting images onto moving figures was intrinsic to the choreography, which traversed primeval and modern Celtic lore. Designs from ancient Celtic artworks, abstract jewellery and sculpted stone friezes were projected onto the dancers' leather and paper costumes, giving the impression of primitive body paint.

Dancers moved in and out of front projections as if through a fluid medium of viscous colour. The dancers were wrapped in paper furls in shapes only 'tenuously related to their bodies so that their movements were partly independent of the costumes that surrounded rather than clothed them'.

[Marion Halligan, 'Focussing on dance: the Meryl Tankard Company', *VIVE* (Ansett Inflight Magazine), June 1990, p. 17]

▲ Figure v **Cowboy Claw**

devised by Anthony Babicci in association with the Brisbane Fringe Festival

1993

venue: The Performance Space, Sydney

director and production designer: Anthony Babicci

photographer: Christobelle Baranay

in photo: Anthony Babicci behind the screen in performance

theatre, dance and music can be read about in programme notes, prefaces to drama anthologies and in the seminar rooms of the many universities and conferences that deal with the evolution of Australian performance. The transient, unstated nature of performance design precludes this kind of documentation.

Performance design is absorbed by those who see it, then disappears. The visual legacy remains in the evolution of ideas that occurs between artforms, each new production bringing forward new interpretations based on what has gone before. Performance design cannot be bought or collected in the way that public artworks, sculptures and paintings are. There are no galleries to house the more splendid examples. The usual life span of a stage set is a few months; a couple of years if it is touring; or a decade with a classical ballet or opera repertory. Costumes are worn and washed and taken apart again. The coloured lights that sculpt the stage are simply turned off and taken down.

What is 'performance design'?

Performance design occurs when the physical space, the personal space and the atmospheric space are consciously manipulated to create an environment for live performance — be it physical or emotional. The environment created comes to life when both performer and audience enter within its boundaries. Under this definition, performance design stretches from the nearly empty stage of a carefully minimal modern dance to the Broadway musical extravaganzas with pink-on-pink lighting gels, exploding cakes and revolving floors. It can include opera in a barn and stilt walkers in drag. It is often the production team's treatment of the space that differentiates between interpretations of the same play, and provides the chosen illustration of theme and direction.

Babicci is a trained theatre designer as well as a performance artist. He has developed a performance technique using giant claws dipped in oil, with which he paints and writes. Performing as a grotesque shadow from behind a paper screen, his lines of oil become translucent, glowing as if made of liquid light. The set and lighting requirements are very tourable and Babicci has successfully performed *Cowboy Claw* in many theatres, nightclubs and dance party venues.

Design skills are similar across all live performance mediums — it is the scripts, budgets, time frames and venues that affect the final treatment. We have included interviews and photographs that document performance of all forms, including circus and acrobatic theatre, grand opera, modern opera, street theatre, classical ballet, modern dance, puppetry, theatre for young people,

▲ Figure vi **The Magic Flute**

Wolfgang Amadeus Mozart

Victoria State Opera

1994

venue: Playhouse, Victorian Arts Centre

director: Gale Edwards

set and costume designer: Roger Kirk

lighting designer: Jamieson Lewis

photographer: Jeff Busby

musicals and performance installations. The common link is that these all incorporate live performance within a given environment. To begin dividing into genre may institute a hierarchy that is unnecessary.

The term 'performance design' allows us to go beyond the traditional delineation between theatre, opera and dance, and into the world of multi-faceted performance forms. In most instances we have used the term 'design' to describe the work of artists in all production areas — sets, costumes and lighting. Depending on the needs of a particular production, these design areas achieve differing levels of prominence and impact. The traditional term 'set design' excludes costume and lighting, whereas 'theatre design' excludes dance, opera, musicals and non-mainstream modes of performance. The term 'production designer' remains most commonly used in film and television, not live theatre.

In order to more fully document live performance we have not covered film and television design. Production design for film and television is an extensive area with a huge range of designers and styles from which to choose. Although many Australian designers cross over and find work in film and/or television (Catherine Martin, Stephen Curtis and Brian Thomson are good examples of this), the requirements and structure of the industry are very different from those of live performance. The restrictions (and possibilities) of space are solved very differently via the camera. Fortunately for the design historian, a design is automatically archived because productions remain on permanent record within the film or video medium.

Similarly, we have not tackled the growing area of sound design. The sound pictures created for a performance play an integral part in the overall concept, but tend to operate independently of the other design elements — sets, lighting and costume. For this reason we felt it best not to combine both visual and aural design work.

Live performance is a transient medium. The initial impact is absorbed and stored in an audience's memory. It is the sensory aspects of theatre that lift a script from its page and give it three dimensions. The performers create action, sound and space around the ideas. An environment is formed around the action. The dramatic space of the work is scenically defined within a stage space. A video recording of live performance is often only of historical and educational value; it cannot accurately describe the energy of being within that environment. A photograph cannot recreate the atmosphere that was caused by subtle lighting, nor describe the interaction of performers within a defined space. The photographs reproduced here work most effectively as cue cards for the audience's memory, and are not fully representative of a production's achievements.

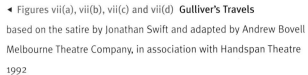

◄ Figures vii(a), vii(b), vii(c) and vii(d) **Gulliver's Travels**

based on the satire by Jonathan Swift and adapted by Andrew Bovell

Melbourne Theatre Company, in association with Handspan Theatre

1992

venue: Playhouse, Victorian Arts Centre

director: Terry O'Connell

puppet direction: David Baird

set and costume designer: Angus Strathie

puppet designer: Phillip Millar

lighting designer: Jamieson Lewis

photographer: Jeff Busby

in photo: Andrew McFarlane as Gulliver encounters strange beings on his travels
— the Lilliputians being but the first of many

'Tate's hauntingly beautiful set is a feast for the eyes; a high, stone wall,

weathered to muted autumnal hues, augmented by a frieze with a biblical

quote in gold lettering and rent by a crack that runs from top to bottom.'

(Bob Evans, 'A dramatic act of faith', *Sydney Morning Herald*, 15 April 1991, p. 8)

▲ Figure viii **Racing Demon**
by David Hare
Sydney Theatre Company
1991
venue: Wharf Theatre, Sydney Theatre Company
director: Rodney Fisher
set and costume designer: Jennie Tate
lighting designer: Nick Schlieper
photographer: Branco Gaica
in photo: (foreground, left to right) Bruce Myles, John Gregg and Robin Ramsay, with remaining cast behind

▼ Figure ix **The Game of Love and Chance**

by Marivaux

Royal Queensland Theatre Company

1991

venue: La Boite Theatre, Brisbane

director: David Bell

set and costume designer: Bill Haycock

lighting designer: David Walters

photographer: Sesh Raman

in photo: Christen O'Leary in performance

The stages of research

In compiling this book we interviewed sixty practising designers, as well as many other theatre artists, including writers, directors and critics. All printed quotes have come directly from those edited transcripts, previous interviews published in the media or published reviews of productions. Many reviews were sourced from the *Australian and New Zealand Theatre Record* (*ANZTR*).[2] Articles concerning design were found in the Denis Wolanski Library for the Performing Arts[3] and the Australian Production Designers' Association (APDA) files.[4] We collected programmes and season brochures, gathering individual curricula vitae and biographies. By cross-referencing between different designers and directors we discovered many varied and long-term collaborations. Along the way we contacted many thinkers, teachers and writers on the subject of performance design. Generous contributors to the text of the book have been Tom Bannerman, Gabrielle Bonney, Peter Cooke, Eamon D'Arcy, Derek Nicholson and Pamela Zeplin. Their interest, enthusiasm and support continues to inspire us.

Since our aim was to provide a forum for debate, we have chosen to combine many of the interviewees' responses under certain topic areas. Differing opinions are placed side by side. Where necessary, we have written the links between arguments and topics. A couple of interviews have been reprinted in their entirety because of their clear illustration of ideas.

Photographs and illustrations were chosen either because of their relevance to the text or because they illustrated certain aspects of contemporary design. A large number of important productions were unfortunately unable to be included, since the visual documentation was either non-existent or had been lost. Many companies were unable to respond to our request before the deadlines, and are sadly unrepresented here. Of the six hundred slides, drawings, plans and photographs we were given, we had space for only two hundred and twenty. Therefore the images reprinted here are by no means a full representation of the body of Australian performance design work.

The logistics of contacting and interviewing so many talented designers across Australia on a limited budget and then compiling the mountains of information into a readable and entertaining form has been an education in itself. Most importantly, it has reinforced our original belief that a book that documents and highlights the contribution of designers to the Australian performance industry is of great significance. It is a means of opening up for discussion, criticism and forum an artform that is not often publicly acknowledged.

There are many talented designers who could not be included for reasons of space and time. Our sincerest apologies to them. Another book or two would be required fully to cover the amount of work that has been done in the twentieth century in the area of performance design. It is our hope that this book is only the first of many documenting the gamut of Australian performance, both visually as well as in words.

And finally ...

This book began from the wish to give performance designers a voice or, rather, many voices. It has also become an extended biography of the many artists who are helping to shape our current notions of performance. Many of them are involved in other areas of performance, be it through writing, teaching, directing, filmmaking or the use of new technologies in design such as computer-animated lighting. In linking them together we have hoped to encourage a broader support network for designers based on common ideas and experience.

Imogen Ross and Kristen Anderson

1   Our photographic images date from 1980 onwards, though we have focused on images from post-1985 as being illustrative of the contemporary period.
2   *ANZTR* was based in the Department of Theatre Studies, University of New South Wales. This quarterly periodical reprinted theatre reviews from all major daily newspapers in every state.
3   The Denis Wolanski Library for the Performing Arts housed a substantial collection of designs, costume drawings, costumes and model boxes from the Sydney Opera House archives. It ceased to operate as a public library in 1995, and much of its collection is now curated by the National Institute of Dramatic Art.
4   The APDA files are currently held in the library of the National Institute of Dramatic Art.

A brief history

Another example would be the sudden appearance of a fabricated Being, made of wood and cloth, entirely invented, corresponding to nothing, yet disquieting by nature, capable of reintroducing on the stage a little breath of that great metaphysical fear which is at the root of all ancient theatre.

ANTONIN ARTAUD[1]

◄ Plate 1 **The Display**

Australian Ballet

composer: Malcolm Williamson

1964

venue: Princess Theatre, Melbourne

choreographer: Sir Robert Helpmann

set designer: Sir Sidney Nolan

costume designer: Adele Weiss

lighting designer: William Akers

photo: AB archives

in photo: Kathleen Gorman and Barry Kitcher

'I think there is less grey and less black in a lot of Australian work. There is a … "lightness". Years ago the Australian Ballet did a ballet called *The Display*, designed by Sir Sidney Nolan, and there it was — the colour [of Australia] and a real feeling of distance.'

[Graham Maclean, interview with author, 9 March 1995]

Design in performance has followed, and sometimes led, the development of theatre since the first actor donned a mask and addressed an audience.

Masks and make-up, fire and water, circles, platforms and unusual costumes form the historical basis of all performance design. For the many cultures that continue to link theatre with ritual and religion, the visual elements of performance are often the strongest storytelling elements, and as such are designed for the greatest effect. In non-European theatre, the development of design is strongly linked to the development of performance forms and, as in the case of the Kabuki and Noh theatre of Japan, a complex and highly elaborate visual language has developed over centuries of traditional performance. As western theatre venues developed from stone amphitheatres to travelling wagons, from bare boards to decorated tennis courts, from proscenium arch theatres with trapdoors and wings to studio spaces, so too have the theatrical conventions governing direction and design developed. It is in the application, be it spectacular, naturalistic, surreal or other, that contemporary design can present itself as something new. Through artistic collaboration with other artists, the designer interprets and devises new visual meanings according to the times.

◄ Figure 1 **Our Country's Good**

by Timberlake Wertenbaker

Royal Court Theatre Company

1989

venue: Wharf Theatre, Sydney Theatre Company

director: Max Stafford-Clark

photographer: Branco Gaica

in photo: Julian Wadham and Nigel Cooke

Since the history of design is so closely linked to the development of theatre, it is impossible to give a full and accurate account of it in one chapter. There are many detailed texts that deal with the history of both western and non-western theatre, and they provide much insight into how performance and writing styles are closely linked to the venues, costumes and staging practices of the time. The following simply places Australian performance design within a historical context.[2]

In Australia the development of scenic styles was slow as audiences remained dependent on imported theatre from England, musicals from the United States and classical ballet and opera from Europe. Between the late 1700s and the late 1800s the new colony's theatrical fare was a mixture of amateur productions performed by convicts and freemen, or imported artists travelling from settlement to settlement recreating English melodramas, farces and music hall favourites.

The first recorded play to have been performed in Australia was *The Recruiting Officer* by Englishman George Farquhar, performed by convicts to an audience of officers in 1789. The design, if any, would have focused on costume requirements (easily accessible military uniforms) and the making of a rough stage within a mud-brick hut. None of this was to matter very much to the appreciative audience which, by all accounts, was delighted to relieve the boredom of colony life by being witness to 'the novelty of a stage-representation'.[3]

In 1825 the first 'theatre' was built and performed in at the convict settlement at Emu Plains, 61 kilometres from Sydney. The following description, written to the *Sydney Gazette* by an audience member, gives an indication of the lengths to which the convict actors went in their adaptation of costume and setting:

> The scenery, which is painted in good taste, the dresses which were in part furnished by some of the ladies in the neighbourhood, together with the performances of the *dramatis personae*, won the admiration, and excited the joyful exclamations of the delighted spectators.[4]

▶ Figure 2 **The Recruiting Officer**
by George Farquhar
Melbourne Theatre Company
1989
venue: Playhouse, Victorian Arts Centre
director: Kim Durban
set and costume designer: Tony Tripp
lighting designer: Jamieson Lewis
photographer: Jeff Busby
in photo: Richard Piper as Kite

The early Australian penal settlements provided some of the first imports of English theatre. Wertenbaker's *Our Country's Good* was drawn from the novel *The Playmaker* by Thomas Keneally, and is based on the first play to be performed in Australia, *The Recruiting Officer* by George Farquhar in 1789. In an ironic parallel, both plays were produced by the Royal Court Theatre (in association with the Sydney Theatre Company) and brought out from England to be performed in repertoire in 1989. The design adhered fairly closely to the script's original intentions.

In a more humorous description, taken from a fictionalised account of convict life by ex-prisoner James Tucker, the Emu Plains theatre is shown to have had a very impressive approach to design, using whatever materials came to hand:

> The theatre, as before stated, had few external charms. It was formed only of slabs and bark, yet the interstices of the walls being filled in with mud, and the whole of the interior being whitewashed with pipe clay … it produced no despicable effect by candlelight.
>
> The canvas necessary was obtained in fragments of bags, prisoners' duck clothing, bed ticks, etc., and painted in distemper with pipe clay, charcoal and various coloured earths. Lamps and candlesticks were fabricated from worn out tin pots and dishes. Materials to light the theatre were supplied by voluntary contributions of the officials.
>
> But the wardrobe! Oh, the wardrobe! No powers of language can enable me to do justice to a description of the wardrobe.
>
> In the first place, to survey 'King Artexomines' in the solemn extravaganza of *Bumbastes Furioso*: his glittering crown was composed of odds and ends of tin and copper, brightly furbished, most of it garnished with pieces of window glass set on parti-coloured foils of a flowing wig fabricated of bits of sheepskin, the wool being powdered with bone ashes; a gaudy fringe of fur bedecked a regal mantle that in the days of its pristine freshness had been a purple stiff cloak with cape and hood, and belonging to 'Mother' Row, the wife of the camp constable; which splendid fur trimming had once covered a native cat, in the glossy spotted coat of which *indulgent* observers *might* detect a very faint resemblance to the imperial ermine; and to complete the truly magnificent ensemble of this August monarch, his boots of russet hue had assumed their present form from the legs of an ancient pair of duck trousers … dyed to that colour by the juice of wattle bark.[5]

Throughout the 1800s there was a growing demand for entertainment and many small companies formed, touring between settlements or playing seasons in the new wooden theatres that were being built in the larger towns.[6] Sydney had its first professional performance in 1832, establishing the Theatre Royal in a converted saloon. The Hobart Town Theatre opened in 1833 and Melbourne's first theatre, the Royal Pavilion, was built in 1842. Although these playhouses were able to accommodate painted sets that could be moved on and off set along wooden grooves, the travelling companies still made do with much simpler settings. Painted backcloths and movable screens were easy to set up in rented halls or tents. A company would usually have only one or two stock sets to perform in front of, so generalised scenes, either a townscape or 'the bush', were considered the norm.

Like many other social commentators of the time, Neild constantly called for the development of an indigenous colonial theatre, both in form and content. There was a growing demand for representational realism on stage, which soon showed itself through the use of recognisable Australian landscapes and archetypal costuming of characters.

With the establishment of large theatres in the mid-1800s came the growth of professional theatre managements. These managements were responsible not only for the introduction and touring of many international performers, but also for the setting up of huge carpentry, painting and costume workshops

In theatre reviews of the period the settings, costumes and scenic devices were often the focus of comment, taking up as much written space as the actual performance. One popular arts columnist of the 1860s and 1870s, James Neild, criticised the common transplanting of English conventions and localities onto the Australian stage as being unrepresentational of the landscape that audiences found themselves in. In his regular column in *The Australasian* he wrote:

> Did Mr [John] Hennings,[7] or whoever painted the scene in the fifth act, really believe that ridiculous picture represented the abode of an Australian settler? It looks like something between an English barn, an Australian cowshed, and the fancy abode of Robinson Crusoe. It might pass muster in London, where they do not know much about Australian bush homesteads; but for an Australian artist to present it as a possible picture of a Victorian squatter's habitation is diverting. It proves what I have many times before asserted, that the major part of what is done upon the stage is done without thought. Actors, painters and costumiers — all are alike. They do what has been done before, and think everything right which has the warrant of any sort of traditional authority.[8]

within the bigger cities. Hundreds of Australian craftspeople and artists were employed in the creation of elaborate scenery, special effects and wardrobes, which then became part of companies' stock sets. Lighting developed in its illuminating functions, moving on from the traditional yet dangerous oil lamps to gas lights and dimmers. Auditoriums remained lit by overhead and wall lights, and performers worked to the front of the stage, addressing the audiences, whom they could see. Scenery was based on the styles most popular to the tastes of the Victorian era, and as such employed a full range of illusory devices and magnificent painted backgrounds. For many audience members these settings were the only chance they had to experience developments in European painting styles, as well as satisfying popular perceptions of 'exotic' locales.

The theatre artists were talented amateur painters involved elsewhere in the theatre, commercial artists or imported professional scene painters. A good painter was highly valued, and scenic competition between companies was fierce. The use of design at this time, however, was still restricted to illustrating the scene or providing spectacular moments that lifted the production into the realms of popular fantasy. The same sets and costumes were often re-used or rented out to smaller companies, providing basic visual backgrounds that usually had little to do with the particular needs or themes of the play. The terms 'decor' and 'set decorator' were used to describe the work of designers, keeping the concept of design fixed as a background decoration. Very little innovation was encouraged, and the theatre managements retained major creative and financial control over the making and usage of the decor. This trend was continued right up until the 1950s by commercial managements such as J. C. Williamson, whose stock sets and costumes were constantly recycled in productions around Australia (fig. 3).

The popularity of domestic melodramas in the late 1800s moved the use of scenery from vast backcloths depicting epic scenes to the box setting, which defined a room (or series of rooms) within which the action occurred. Two-dimensional backgrounds and exotic locales were no longer suitable for much of the work being written and performed. Three-dimensional elements such as doorknobs and cornicing began to appear, particularly as electric lighting developed, allowing audiences to see further and further beyond the footlights. By the late nineteenth century the lights had dimmed and then been turned off completely in the auditorium, allowing the stage to become the focus. Performers retreated behind the proscenium arch, and the 'fourth wall' between the audience and the stage became an accepted convention in western theatre.

At the turn of the twentieth century, theatre and its design embarked on a new relationship based on the visual interpretation and expression of contemporary issues. Smaller companies dedicated to exploring theatre, dance and opera as a kinetic artform, rather than as an entertainment, sprang up and gained loyal audiences. In Europe the gradual rise of the director over the actor-producer as the dominant artistic voice within a company, encouraged theatre artists to discuss the expanding role of design in contemporary theatre and to seek an intellectual collaboration between directorial and designer visions. These ideas were taken up and explored in Australia by those theatre artists who had trained or worked in Europe between the wars, and by the increasing numbers of post-war immigrants who brought with them a knowledge of the latest theatre and art movements.

Just as the new writing of the twentieth century turned its themes away from melodrama and the spectacular, so the concept of stage decor being illustrative gave way to the need for function and meaning. Although not all areas of performance and management responded to this shift in thinking, the companies that did respond began to encourage three-dimensional design to play an integral part in new productions.

From the 1930s onwards a growing demand for locally produced theatre resulted in hundreds of plays, skits and comic operas being written. Although most were of a debatable quality, it brought Australian issues, colloquial language and 'Aussie' actors to the fore. Amateur companies became interested in producing new work as well as the European classics, providing theatre artists with an opportunity to explore their ideas on stage within an Australian context. It must be recognised, however, that many of the ideas of this time were copied from the work of touring overseas artists, and that Australians still looked self-consciously to the Northern Hemisphere for inspiration. Designers were looking at the work of other designers and reading the work of pre-war theatre innovators such as Adolphe Appia and Edward Gordon Craig.[9] These men, independently of each other,[10] called upon all those who termed themselves 'theatre artists' to revolutionise the ways in which costume and scenery were used, and pushed lighting to the fore as the contemporary tool for theatre.

In keeping with a general design shift towards clean, elegant lines, and in possible response to the elaborate and fantastical stage pictures of the Victorian era, modern designers from the 1930s onwards simplified the stage, and worked on creating a maximum of visual meaning with a minimum of spectacle. As arts researcher and critic Pamela Zeplin points out in her summary of Australian stage design history:

> The stage designer took the inherent formal properties of the setting — colour, space, shape, massing, light — as raw materials. Sculptural units, not necessarily referring directly to the world beyond the stage, replaced the illusionist backdrops of specific time and place ... the designer's brief was broadened to encompass some of the skills of architect, mathematician, painter, sculptor, carpenter and dressmaker.[11]

At the same time, smaller companies were moving away from the conventional proscenium arch theatres made popular during the nineteenth century and using other spaces such as halls, tents, warehouses and pubs. This took away the 'picture frame' staging that had separated the audience from the stage, and placed the action very close to the audience. Settings became increasingly sculptural; the dramatic space was used *around* them, rather than in front of them. This interaction related strongly to the changes in the art world of the time, where distinctions between forms were being broken down and artists were exploring all possible dimensions for their work.

The traditional 'high culture' arts such as ballet and opera were still being imported from overseas by the larger production companies, but

▼ Plate 2 **Coppelia**
music by Léo Delibes
Australian Ballet
1979
venue: Palais Theatre, St Kilda, Melbourne and Opera Theatre, Sydney Opera House
choreographer: Dame Peggy van Praagh
mime director: George Ogilvie
set and costume designer: Kristian Fredrikson
lighting designer: William Akers
photographer: Peter Holderness
Fredrikson's costume rendering of Dr Coppelius and his magical cloak of eyes.

DOCTOR COPPÉLIUS
ACT-II Coppélia

they brought with them the latest European design innovations in the form of simplified settings and backdrops by modern painters such as Natalia Goncharova, Léon Bakst, Pablo Picasso, Giorgio de Chirico and Jean Miró. The influence of Constructivism, Cubism, Surrealism and Expressionism was very strong. Ballet in particular was responsible for challenging audience expectations and design conventions. During the 1920s Anna Pavlova's Russian Ballet company toured twice, introducing Australians to simple, integrated visions that combined the design with the dance. Colonel de Basil brought the Ballet Russe de Monte Carlo out to Australia on several occasions in the 1930s, and was responsible for encouraging several Australian painters to become involved in designing for the ballet. The work of Sidney Nolan and the Martin sisters, Kathleen and Florence, was taken up by de Basil in productions of *Icare* and *Lutte Eternelle* respectively. Although the designs were still in the form of large backdrops behind the action, the emphasis was on the artists' individual interpretation and style, rather than on creating recognisable settings. Costumes and lighting worked together, in the same vein as the settings, to give audiences 'a total sensory experience'.[12] Advances in lighting technology enabled dancers to use light as an expressive tool, utilising its abstract qualities far in advance of mainstream theatre.

In 1943 Edouard Borovansky (who had toured previously with Anna Pavlova in 1929) established the Borovansky Ballet in collaboration with J. C. Williamson's company. He toured throughout Australia, presenting versions of European dance classics. While utilising the Williamson company's scenic departments he developed a close working relationship with its leading scenic artist, William Constable. Constable was responsible for designing the settings for nearly all of Borovansky's ballets before leaving Australia for a successful design career overseas. The Australian Ballet's former production director William Akers worked with both men during that time as the Borovansky company's stage manager-director.[13] He recalls what it was like to watch them work together in the theatre:

> Mr Borovansky did great big glamorous productions of ballets and the public absolutely adored them. They were done as soft scenery mostly, because it was a touring company and very little scenery was built. William Constable was a very fine painter as well as being a theatre designer, and Mr Borovansky was also a painter — though rather more inclined to portraiture than the other types of painting. On a number of occasions I stood on the stage of Her Majesty's Theatre and they would sit in the stalls and shout and scream at one another. Packets of cigarettes would be smoked — Camels mostly — and millions of cups of coffee

drunk while they lit the production, and I stood on the stage and wrote down what they said ... The ballet was always done with washes of coloured lighting, very beautifully painted by Mr Borovansky ... He would say: 'This is integral; if you give an actor words it doesn't make a play, if you give a singer notes it doesn't make an aria, if you give a painter paint, he paints a picture — but on the stage that picture has to come to life. You have to paint the picture until it is alive. Then you look for balance. Everything in life and in lighting is balanced'. [14]

When Borovansky was dying he asked Akers to design the lighting for his production of *The Sleeping Beauty*. At the time the lighting was always done by the director or choreographer, but Akers took on the challenge, inspired by Borovansky's artistic treatment of light. He went on to become Australia's first publicly acknowledged lighting designer (pls 1, 2 and 3), remaining resident as a production and lighting director with the Australian Ballet from its inception in 1962 until his retirement in 1995.

In the world of opera, international designs and designers were consistently imported for productions, keeping Australian artists at a

▲ Plate 3 **Coppelia**

music by Léo Delibes

Australian Ballet

1979

venue: Palais Theatre, St Kilda, Melbourne and Opera Theatre, Sydney Opera House

choreographer: Dame Peggy van Praagh

mime director: George Ogilvie

set and costume designer: Kristian Fredrikson

lighting designer: William Akers

photographer: AB archives

in photo: Ray Powell (Dr Coppelius) and Ann Jenner in performance. Fredrikson's fantastical set illustrated the mechanical toy world of Dr Coppelius

distance from practising the form right up to the mid-twentieth century. The establishment of the Australian Elizabethan Theatre Trust (AETT) in 1954 led to an increased number of operas being produced by an Australian-managed company on a national scale. Though this encouraged many talented artists and craftspeople to find creative employment in the opera workshops, like much of the AETT's work, however, most of the designers and directors were still brought in from elsewhere. Not until the Australian Opera was created from the AETT in 1972 (coinciding with the finishing of the Sydney Opera House) were successful expatriates such as Kenneth Rowell invited back to design opera in Australia.

During the 1940s and 1950s, while amateur theatres were embracing more and more of the ideas coming out of Europe, commercial theatres were busy reproducing the hugely popular American musicals and creating work for theatre artists by having them copy what was being seen on Broadway. In this way theatre technology and design skills continued to develop both in the large-scale venues (with access to machinery, lighting, huge costume departments and special effects) and in the smaller unpaid theatres with improvised lighting rigs, simple sets and imaginative low-budget costumes. Artists and craftspeople with an interest in design could find many avenues for their skills, though few could forge a living. During this time many talented and experienced artists went to London in order to

▲ Figure 4 **Fitzroy Crossing**
by Phil Motherwell
La Mama
1987
venue: La Mama, Melbourne
director: Denis Moore
set and costume designer: Peter Corrigan
photo: La Mama archives
in photo: Vince Gail, Gina Riley, Greg Carroll and Joe Drake
Corrigan played with audience perceptions of the tiny La Mama space, using cyclone wire with a deep perspective point to create the sense of a large desert beyond. This distancing effect was enhanced aurally by using body microphones on some of the actors.

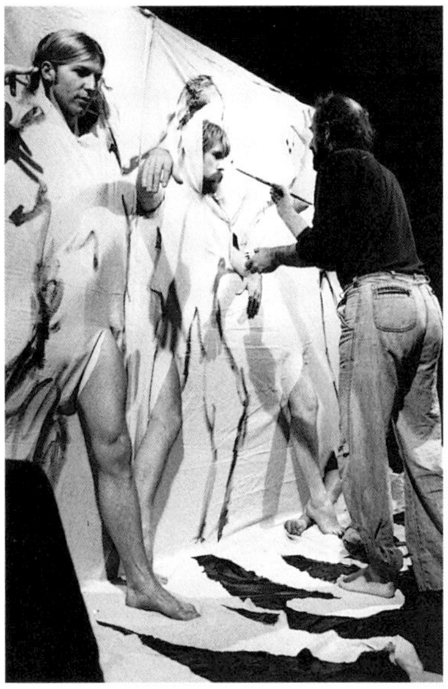

▲ Figure 5 **Bastraction One**
performance developed by Lloyd Jones
La Mama
1977
venue: La Mama, Melbourne
director and designer: Lloyd Jones
lighting designer: Fred Wallace
photographer: Anthony Figallo
in photo: Lloyd Jones painting performers on canvas. At the time of researching this book, Lloyd Jones had performed, created and directed new works for La Mama since its inception in 1966.

'For some, La Mama provides a first step towards going on to commercial arenas in the theatre world. For me, La Mama "is" the top. I honestly believe there is nowhere better.' — Lloyd Jones 1987.

[Betty Burstall, Liz Jones & Helen Garner, *La Mama: The Story of a Theatre*,

McPhee Gribble/Penguin, Ringwood, Victoria, 1988, p. 48]

follow a career in design. Some of the notable designers who left Australia were William Constable, Loudon Sainthill, Florence and Kathleen Martin, Don Finley, Kenneth Rowell and John Truscott.

Between the 1940s and the 1960s Australian theatre developed in response not only to international theatre movements but also to the growing call for nationalism in the arts. Semi-professional and amateur theatre companies around the country took on the challenge to create a recognisable Australian theatre, training directors, designers, writers and actors in the process, who then went on to form the mainstay of Australia's professional theatre in the 1970s. Fuelled by the popular amateur and university scenes in Melbourne, companies such as the Melbourne Little Theatre Guild (later St Martins Theatre Company), the New Theatre Movement (also strong in Sydney, Adelaide, Perth and Brisbane) and, later, Wal Cherry's Emerald Hill

'The design farewelled the Pram Factory by beginning the work of its anticipated demolition. The windows smashed, partition walls stoved in, floor littered with piles of broken bricks, and the whole mess splashed with left-over paint, it appeared initially that Corrigan had been very drunk or very angry ... The bleak despairing tone of the performance, although seething with eroticism and punctuated by humour, was made more plangent still by the physical battlefield in which Corrigan placed it. The nihilism of *Bold Tales* found the scarred and brutal landscape it needed.'

[M. A. R. Anderson, 'Pressing against ideas', in *Cities of Hope*, ed. Conrad Hamann, Oxford University Press, Melbourne, 1993, p. 156]

▶ Figure 6 **Bold Tales**
based on stories by Peter Carey and Frank Moorhouse
Australian Performing Group
1981
venue: Pram Factory, Melbourne
director: Peter King
set and costume designer: Peter Corrigan
photo: Peter Corrigan archives
For the APG's last play in the Pram Factory (before the building was pulled down) Corrigan utilised the already partly demolished space in his design, adding further elements of chaos, and subsequently highlighting the central themes of corruption, licentiousness and destruction.

▲ Figure 7 **Macbeth**

by William Shakespeare

State Theatre Company of South
Australia

1977

venue: Playhouse, Adelaide Festival
Centre

director: Colin George

set and costume designer: Hugh Colman

lighting designer: Nigel Levings

photographer: David Wilson

in photo: Edwin Hodgeman as Macbeth
and Daphne Grey as Lady Macbeth

'Colin gave me the brief that his
inspiration for [this production] had been
Akira Kurosawa's *Seven Samurai* [1954],
but he didn't want to reproduce it.
He wanted to look at the play in terms
of a warrior society that had resonances
of eastern spareness within the whole
design of the set and costumes, and that
was something very close to my
interests.'

[H. Colman, interview with author,
18 August 1993]

▲ Figure 8 **Vocations**

by Alma De Groen

State Theatre Company of South Australia

1984

venue: Playhouse, Adelaide Festival Centre

director: Ros Horin

set designer: Geoffrey Gifford

costume designer: Amanda Lovejoy

lighting designer: Nigel Levings

photographer: David Wilson

Gifford's set design successfully merged
the stage space between two adjoining
apartments, reinforcing the play's questioning of gender roles and expectations
within the home.

Theatre all actively promoted and produced new work. Doris Fitton's Independent Theatre in Sydney was also a landmark in the development of Australian theatre practice, as was the National Theatre in Perth. Designers who received their early training during this time learnt to use a minimum of resources effectively in a variety of ad-hoc venues. Warwick Armstrong, Desmonde Downing, Vane Lindsay, Cedric Flower and Elaine Haxton were among those who worked consistently during this time.

In 1954 the Union Theatre Repertory Company (UTRC) was established in Melbourne, and for the first time an Australian designer, Anne Fraser, was employed as resident within the company. She was not expected to build and paint the sets, nor to sew the costumes, but to work in close collaboration with the director in determining the look and shape of a production (see Foreword, fig. iii). This significant step marked a change in the way the designer's role worked within a company, in its opening up of design as a paid career and in encouraging women to seek professional employment in the area of theatre design. Fraser continued to work for the UTRC, and then with most of the major theatre and opera companies in Australia, throughout her long career. She was soon followed by many others.

From the 1960s onwards it became possible for designers to find regular paid work with the newly formed permanent companies, supported in part by the Australian Elizabethan Theatre Trust (AETT). New Zealand artists Richard Prins, Kristian Fredrikson, Allan Lees and Desmond Digby all arrived in the 1960s and forged their careers in production design, first with the UTRC and the AETT, and then with companies such as the Nimrod Theatre Company and the Old Tote. Stage and lighting designer Stanislaus Ostoja-Kotkowski emigrated to Australia from Europe in 1949 and inspired many by exploring the design potential of electronic technology (sound, lighting and projection), integrated into performance. Younger designers such as Wendy Dickson, Hugh Colman and Anna French were encouraged and employed by the UTRC, and went on to design in all areas of the performing arts — theatre, dance and opera, film and television.

▲ Figure 9 **Much Ado About Nothing**

by William Shakespeare

Nimrod

1977

venue: Nimrod Theatre, Sydney

director: John Bell

set and costume designer: Larry Eastwood

photographer: Peter Holderness

in photo: (clockwise from top)
The full cast on stage: Alan Tobin, Ivar Kants, Dennis Scott, Tony Llewellyn-Jones, Robert Alexander, Drew Forsythe, Deborah Kennedy, Tony Sheldon, Peter Carroll, Anna Volska, Gordon McDougall and Maggie Blinco

▲ Figure 10 **Travelling North**

by David Williamson

Nimrod

1979

venue: Nimrod Theatre, Sydney

director: John Bell

set and costume designer: Ian Robinson

lighting designer: Peter Holderness

photographer: Peter Holderness

Robinson's set model for *Travelling North*.

A brief history

► Figure 11 **Hancock's Last Half-hour**

by Heathcote Williams

Hoopla Productions, in association with
Nimrod

1977

venue: Nimrod Theatre, Sydney

director: Graeme Blundell

set and costume designer: Peter Corrigan

photographer: Robert McFarlane

in photo: Denis Moore as Tony Hancock

'The play mapped a fictitious episode
from the drunken and decrepit twilight
lurchings of the British comedian Tony
Hancock, the action never leaving his
hotel room ... Corrigan's design placed
the tiny hotel room in the middle of the
space, with the audience on all sides. To
enclose and confine the action clear
plastic walls separated the stage from
the audience all around ... the character
of Hancock assumed tragic dimensions,
all the more so because the audience
was forced to address his face from the
"other" perspective, the point of view of
voyeurs ... Corrigan's setting, by placing
the actor in a waterless aquarium, served
only to magnify the pathos of the action,
and contribute to its audience's
discomfort.'

[M. A. R. Anderson, 'Pressing against
ideas', in *Cities of Hope*, ed. Conrad
Hamann, Oxford University Press,
Melbourne, 1993, pp. 154–5]

The establishment of the National Institute of Dramatic Art (NIDA) in Sydney in 1958 marked the beginning of formalised theatre teaching in Australia. From 1962 technical production was taught, training students as stage managers, stage directors, carpenters, painters and lighting technicians. In 1972 design as a distinct area of study was included on the NIDA syllabus under the guidance of British designer Arthur Dicks, who used English theatre design schools as his teaching model. Since that time many of Australia's professional designers have emerged from the three-year training diploma (now a four-year degree), enabling theatre companies to employ 'ready-made' designers rather than encourage long-term apprenticeships. Dicks, Robin Lovejoy, Allan Lees and Peter Cooke have headed the course since its inception. Other states have since responded by creating accredited design streams within their own vocational theatre schools. Their graduate impact on the Australian performing arts is growing, despite their design departments still being in developing stages.

The Australian Performing Group (APG) formed an influential theatre collective in 1968 that worked first from the tiny theatre space called La Mama, and then from the Pram Factory (1970–81), both in Carlton, Melbourne. Much innovative and bold new writing developed there, and because of the restrictions of space imposed upon the company, new ways of dealing with space were explored (figs 4, 5 and 6). Design as a separate form was not a priority, and those who did choose to design did so within the rules of 'poor' theatre, where the performers created much of the space by their actions, not properties. Peter Corrigan was one designer who was very involved with the workshopping and staging of APG work from 1974 onwards, operating on the strength of improvisation and makeshift budgets. In a theatre biography by Michael A. R. Anderson, Corrigan's early work is recalled, impressing upon the reader what it must have been like to be sitting in the cramped space of the Pram Factory, watching the first production of John Romeril's *The Floating World*:

Entering a new era of Australian identity in the theatre, this production was a firm reminder of new temptations and eternal corruption. Set in the lavish Sydney apartment of the Bosanquets, Thomson's popular set design captured the assumed elegance of the pre-yuppie 1970s, highlighting the characters' preoccupation with size and quantity. It made such an impact on audiences, that one *Sydney Morning Herald* interior design writer urged his readers to go and see the play to gain decorating tips: 'All the floor is a thick shag beige, the colour we still love, rich and flattering — and in a practical sense, a colour that goes with many schemes ... A clever point in the actual set is the way the dramatic backdrop lettering of the play's name, *Big Toys*, slides away to reveal the coveted magnificence of a harbour view — one of the real status symbols of life in Sydney'.

[L. Walford, 'Trendy bedroom for play's bitter couple', *Sydney Morning Herald*, 26 August 1977, p. 10]

▲ Figure 12 **Big Toys**
by Patrick White
Old Tote Theatre Company
1977
venue: Parade Theatre, Sydney
director: Jim Sharman
set designer: Brian Thomson
costume designer: Victoria Alexander
lighting designer: Jerry Luke
photographer: Robert McFarlane
In a review, Dorothy Hewett observed: 'Kate Fitzpatrick as Mag Bosanquet lounging on a huge centrepiece circular bed, dressed in a white satin robe, balancing a giant red balloon on the tip of one impossibly elegant ankle-strap red shoe, cooing into a red telephone "I'm concerned about people darling".'
[D. Hewett, 'Big Sydney toys', *Theatre Australia*, Sept./Oct. 1977, p. 44]

The audience, enclosed in a large cage, were seated in two long narrow banks either side of a thin central acting strip. At either end raised stages sported a prow-like projection, upon which was painted the grimacing sabre-toothed smile of a Spitfire fighter plane. Complete with curved metal balustrading, rounded door-ways, circular dots for windows, and banded stripes of colour, the setting presented a wealth of nautical imagery through connotative means. The ship upon which much of the action was placed was never described so much as implied.[15]

At the same time as the APG many new theatre companies were moving into newly built or unconventional theatre spaces, bringing with them designers and directors keen to push theatre staging in new directions, including the Ensemble Theatre (1958 – present), the Old Tote (1962–78) and the Nimrod Theatre Company (1970–87) in Sydney; the Hole in the Wall Theatre in Perth (1965–92); the State Theatre Company of South Australia (1965 – present) and Troupe (1976–87) in Adelaide; and Hoopla (1976, later to form Playbox) in Melbourne. Many of the professional designers working today cut their teeth working for companies such as these in the late 1960s, 1970s and 1980s, when what are regarded as the first and second waves of Australian playwriting were washing over the theatre industry. It was from the new directions in playwriting that many modern concepts for design sprang, for the form often required quick changes, dream sequences and epic journeys of its characters. Much of the new writing was rooted in identifiably 'Aussie' locations, even though this was often the target of lampooning and irony. Design responded by loosening its need to describe the environment in specific ways, focusing instead on a central concept that could be explored in surreal and non-naturalistic ways. The early work of Kim Carpenter (fig. 14), Hugh Colman (fig. 7), Peter Corrigan (figs 4, 6 and 11), Peter Cooke, Larry Eastwood (fig. 9), Roger Kirk, Brian Thomson (figs 12, 13 and 15), Nigel Triffitt, Victoria Feitscher, Tom Lingwood, Michael Pearce, Ron Reid, Ian Robinson (fig. 10), John Stoddart, Yoshi Tosa and Tony Tripp dates from these decades. Many designers freelanced between

classics by Shakespeare, Sophocles and Shaw to the work of young writers such as David Williamson, Jack Hibberd and John Romeril.

Under the influence of American protest theatre and guerrilla street theatre, much of the new work produced in the 1970s moved further away from traditional venues, utilising the design possibilities offered by open-air spaces and streetscapes. Costumes and special effects dominated, as did puppetry techniques. The Australian Marionette Theatre was established, Nigel Triffitt's *Yellow Brick Roadshow* and *Momma's Little Shop of Horrors* (1976) took Australia (and the world) by storm, Circus Oz (1977) and the Flying Fruit Flies (1979) began their all-human, no-holds-barred circus cabarets, and puppeteers such as Peter L. Wilson began introducing Japanese and Asian forms of puppetry to the country. Subsidised theatre-in-education companies travelled the states, giving many designers the chance to develop imaginative low-budget touring sets. Toe Truck (1976–93) in Sydney and Magpie (1978—97) in Adelaide were two of the longest-running companies. Arts festivals began to encourage and subsidise open-air performance, thus developing unique forms of travelling street theatre.

In the commercial arena, the musicals *Hair* (1969) and *Jesus Christ Superstar* (1972) were produced by Harry M. Miller and directed by young director Jim Sharman for audiences of more than one million. The fruitful collaborations between Sharman and his designer Brian Thomson (figs 13, 15, 16 and pl. 32) were responsible for many of the ground-breaking productions in Australia and London at that time. Their productions were boldly staged and showcased the latest in staging wizardry. Audiences were overawed by the spectacular effects, which helped maintain 'the musical' as a very popular form of entertainment and pushed Australian

▲ Figures 14a and 14b **Slice**
developed by Kim Carpenter
Nimrod
1981
venue: Nimrod Downstairs, Sydney
director and designer: Kim Carpenter
choreographer: Tony Strachan
lighting designer: Jonathan Ciddor
music: Michael Carlos
photographer: David Parker
in photos: 14a (left to right) George Shevtsov, Simon Eddy, Christine Mahoney and Su Cruikshank are the 'crowd' in the impersonal metropolis — the surreal environment in which *Slice* is set. In *Slice*, the words were subordinate to the visual imagery. In interview, Carpenter described his vision as 'working from the view of cartoon-strip sets of images, as told through colour and sound'; 14b Simon Eddy
[S. Molloy, 'Slice ... with a dash of menace', *Sydney Morning Herald*, 16 July 1981, p. 8]

designers into further exploration of theatre technology. The powerful and colourful lighting promoted by international rock-and-roll concerts began to be fully adopted by theatre technicians. Lighting as an artform gained significant recognition in all areas of the performing arts, with many companies placing lighting above settings in their budgets and programme credits. It became a distinct professional role for a 'lighting designer', moving away from that of stage manager or electrical technician. Roger Barratt, Donn Byrnes, John Comeadow, Nigel Levings (figs 8, 20), David Longmuir, David Murray, Duncan Ord, John Rayment, Ken Rayner and Tony Youlden all began their careers as lighting designers during these years.

The 1980s tended to cement the existing state companies within their permanent venues, though smaller companies such as Doppio Teatro (1983—present) and Red Shed Company (1986—1998) in Adelaide and Australian Nouveau Theatre (also known as ANThill, 1981–94) in Melbourne (pl. v and fig. 20), to name but three, continued to work in improvised theatre spaces such as school halls, warehouses and old factories. This gave designers the chance to develop an understanding of local venues while developing personal methods of dealing with particular stages. Fewer designers were imported from overseas, although the Australian Ballet and the Australian Opera still gave preference to international directors and allowed international directors their choice of designer.

◄ Figure 15 **Jesus Christ Superstar**
by Tim Rice and Andrew Lloyd Webber
produced by Harry M. Miller
1972
venue: Capitol Theatre, Sydney
director: Jim Sharman
set designer: Brian Thomson
costume designer: Rex Cramphorn
lighting designer: Jules Fisher
photo: H. M. M. archives
'The curtain rose on a stage of scaffolding and curtains dominated by a huge, slowly revolving dodecahedron (a twelve sided globe). It broke apart, the top disappearing upwards into the roof and the sides unfolding like petals of a flower. The action of the evening flowed around this piece of equipment, which assumed many different shapes in the course of the night.'
[John West, *Theatre in Australia*, Cassel Australia, Sydney, 1978, p. 238]

▲ Figure 16 **Death In Venice**
by Benjamin Britten
State Opera of South Australia, in association with the Adelaide Festival Theatre Trust
1980
venue: Adelaide Festival Theatre
director: Jim Sharman
conductor: Myer Fredman
choreography: Ian Spink
set designer: Brian Thomson
costume designer: Luciana Arrighi
lighting designer: Rory Dempster
photographer: Don McMurdo

'For the athletic beach scenes, there falls a dazzling white curtain made of material with the consistency, translucence and lively surface of parachute silk. Its appearance, as it drapes itself in seemingly random loopings and gatherings, quivering and trembling with ceaseless eddies of self-caressing movement is one of the most sensuous moments in the history of Australian theatre ... It is a genuine theatrical symbol and image, working at every level of understanding.'
[R. Covell, 'Sharman scores with this production', *Sydney Morning Herald*, 10 March 1980, p. 12]

This critically acclaimed festival opera was praised for its discretion, consistency and bold elegance of design. This was Thomson's first opera and he said of his inspiration for the design: 'It was all in the music so there was no point in visually evoking Venice, no need for detail. I'm not at all interested in naturalism, I've never done a box set and I never will. Even with *Big Toys*, *A Cheery Soul* and *Pandora's Cross* there was no need.'

(R. Page, 'The evolution of a designer', *Theatre Australia*, July 1981, p. 27)

When describing the design style of Tony Tripp, theatre reviewer Jo Litson said, 'He's looking for that one simple statement — to use one metaphor to speak for the whole play. When you think of *High Society* for example ... he found the wedding cake which was absolutely perfect; this whole family in the grip of wedding fever. The huge cake then opens up and the house is inside!'

(J. Litson, interview with author, 15 March 1995)

▲ Figure 17 **High Society**

music and lyrics by Cole Porter, adapted by Carolyn Burns

Melbourne Theatre Company, in association with State Theatre Company of South Australia, Royal Queensland Theatre Company and Sue Farrelly Productions

1994

venue: Playhouse, Adelaide Festival Centre

director: Simon Phillips
choreographer: Ross Coleman
musical director: Ian McDonald
set and costume designer: Tony Tripp
lighting designer: Karen Norris
photographer: Jeff Busby
in photo: (left to right) Charmaine Gorman, Jeremy Stanford, Helen Buday, Bob Hornery, Lorrae Desmond and Kevin Miles

▼ Figures 18a, 18b, 18c and 18d **High Society**

Melbourne Theatre Company

1994

see fig. 17

photographer: Robert Colvin

Tripp's costume designs for *High Society*:
18a — Liz, Act 1
18b — Caroline, Act 2
18c — Tracey, Act 2
18d — Margaret, Act 2

The establishment of government-funded theatre companies has also affected the professional status of designers by giving some the opportunity to work as resident designers within a company, thus maintaining artistic collaboration between themselves and directors. Shaun Gurton's role as associate director and designer at the STCSA (1990–96) is a good example of this. However, it is interesting to note that despite the success of having resident designers within a company, fewer companies were willing to do so in the 1990s, making freelance design professionals the industry norm. In 1997 the only state theatre company to have had full-time designers continuously on its payroll was the Melbourne Theatre Company (MTC) — an interesting fact, since it was the UTRC (MTC's predecessor) that was the first funded theatre company to employ a resident designer in 1954. It may also be the last.[16]

1   A. Artaud, *The Theatre and its Double,* Grove Press Inc., New York, 1958, p. 44.

2   For a fuller chronology and design history, please refer to Pamela Zeplin's 'Stage design and effects', in *Companion to Theatre in Australia*, ed. Phillip Parsons, Currency Press, Sydney, 1995, pp. 545–50.

3   W. Tench, A *Complete Account of the Settlement at Port Jackson, in New South Wales*, London, 1793, p. 25; cited in *The Australian Stage: A Documentary History*, ed. Harold Love, University of New South Wales Press, Sydney, 1984, p. 13.

4   *Sydney Gazette*, 21 July 1825; cited in *The Australian Stage: A Documentary History*, op. cit., p. 14.

5   C. Roderick (ed.), *Ralph Rashleigh or the Life of an Exile*, Angus & Robertson, Sydney, 1952, pp. 92–6.

6   For a fuller history of the development of Australian theatre buildings see Ross Thorne's interesting and concise history 'Theatres', in *Companion to Theatre in Australia*, op. cit., pp. 589–95.

7   German-born scene painter John Hennings was responsible for much of the design and settings created at The Melbourne Royal in the mid to late 1800s.

8   J. Neild, 'Entertainment, theatres and culture' column, *The Australasian*, 19 March 1870, p. 370.

9   Craig wrote many books and articles on the subject of theatre. For an abbreviated study of his work and writings see J. Michael Walton (ed.), *Craig on Theatre*, Methuen, London, 1983.

10 Craig (1872–1966) and Appia (1862–1928) did not meet until 1914, despite promoting and publishing similar ideas regarding the theatre.

11 Zeplin, op. cit., p. 548.

12 ibid.

13 See Akers' fuller description of how he began as a lighting designer in chapter 7.

14 W. Akers, interview with author, 8 March 1995.

15 M. A. R. Anderson, 'Pressing against ideas', in *Cities of Hope*, ed. Conrad Hamann, Oxford University Press, Melbourne, 1993, p. 153.

16 The MTC ceased to employ a resident designer in 1999.

▶ Figure 19 **Long Day's Journey into Night**

by Eugene O'Neill

Playbox

1982

venue: CUB Malthouse, Melbourne

director: Ken Boucher

set and costume designer: Anna French

lighting designer: David Murray

photographer: Henry Jolles

◀ Figure 20 **The Misanthrope**

by Molière, translated by Richard Wilbur

Australian Nouveau Theatre (ANThill), in association with the Sydney Theatre Company

1985

venue: The Gasworks, South Melbourne and the Wharf, Sydney Theatre Company

director: Jean-Pierre Mignon

set and costume designer: Wendy Black

lighting designers: Mark White (Melbourne) and Nigel Levings (Sydney)

photographer: Branco Gaica

in photo: (left to right) Verity Higgins, Robert Meldrum, David Goldstraw, David Jobling and Julie Forsyth

'Walls partly covered with mirrors accentuated the narcissism of the characters; the chessboard floor their emotional manipulations. Modern chairs hinted at the contemporary relevance of the work.'

[notes — Jean-Pierre Mignon and Katherine Sturak, 1995]

▲ **Greek**

by Stephen Berkoff

Chamber Made Opera

1991

venue: Merlyn Theatre, CUB Malthouse,
Melbourne

director: Douglas Horton

set and costume designer: Trina Parker

photographer: Trina Parker

photo-collage of Parker's set within the
studio environment of the Merlyn Theatre

Performance politics

moving from microcosm to macrocosm

An interview with Pamela Zeplin

Within the microcosm of each production, the designer has a powerful position, aligning himself or herself with the director and choreographer as an initiator and facilitator of the visual language supporting performance. It is worth noting, however, that designers' roles in the long term have been, and may still be, largely forgotten if they do not ensure that their individual and collective input into the theatre culture is recognised by writers and historians.

Performance design straddles the fence between the visual arts and the theatre arts. As such, the political and historical role of the designer is often sidelined, resulting in a lack of serious writing and discussion on the artform itself. In the broader arena of performance appreciation, that of audiences, academics and reviewers, the design is not often seen as worthy of critique or study.

As an Australian 'pioneer' of serious research in this field in the 1980s, Pamela Zeplin was an outspoken advocate for designers to become politically responsible for forging new directions in the Australian theatre. Although not a designer herself, she has been involved (through academia and her own art practices) with many aspects of performance and design. The following is an extract from an interview with Zeplin regarding the need for a pro-active professional stance from Australian designers:

I've always been puzzled by the idea that the arts in western culture have been arbitrarily divided up and colonised. What leaks out between boundaries (as you say, under the 'fences') can be tremendously exciting — often because these leakages are ephemeral. They are also 'moving' in both a literal and metaphorical sense. My training as a visual arts writer, however, focused upon inanimate objects and individual egos so, in the late 1970s, I began research into the interdisciplinarity and collaboration of Russian avant-garde art, most evident in stage design and performance art. Then in 1980 I visited my first Adelaide Festival from Melbourne and was seriously moved by Peter Brook's *Ubu* in the quarry; I suspect it changed my life. At that time, Australian theatre research was dominated by an academic, text-based approach, rather than the study of live performance, so I saw an opportunity for interdisciplinary research in Australian theatre.

In beginning my MA thesis in 1980, I went to see John Sumner (who directed the Melbourne Theatre Company for about thirty years), and he informed me — in declamatory tones — that there was no theatre in Australia before 1953! I couldn't resist the challenge!

Firstly, Sumner was wrong. The historical base of Australian theatre from about 1900 to the 1960s was vibrant, thriving and innovative — mostly done by talented and dedicated amateurs. It is important here to consider that the only other alternative at the time was the J. C. Williamson commercial sphere. Artists and theatre people worked together, they collaborated and cross-fertilised as unpaid 'professionals', inspired by the Diaghilev period. Women designers like the Martin sisters and, later, Anne Fraser, were right up front here, too, despite their subsequent invisibility.

Another major realisation was how Australian (and western) culture moved from a nineteenth-century emphasis on visual spectacle to a twentieth-century preoccupation with literature, words and the narrative play. The role of designer, therefore, moved from providing extravagant decor (audiences frequently applauded stage design) through Realism, to a more integrated and conceptual relationship with the entire production; designers retreated into the background while directors took centre stage. Because the records of this period were in oral history, personal scrapbooks and fragmented writings of designers, artists and critics, etc., the task of recording became urgent. As older designers (and directors) left Australia, retired or died, the tangible means for the new generation to access this experience — an entire era of Australian design — was becoming lost. Much valuable work in salvaging this material was done by underfunded theatre museums around the country, in particular the Performing Arts Museum in Melbourne and the Denis Wolanski Library for the Performing Arts in Sydney.

How did this knowledge lead you to analyse and critique the performance industry as it was then, in the 1980s?

It seemed to me that not a lot had changed; most contemporary designers with whom I spoke were still complaining about industry and academic acknowledgment, conditions, status and, most of all, training, despite strong lobbying by the Australian Production Designers Association [APDA] across Australia throughout the 1980s. Indeed, they were still occupying a marginal position in both theatre and the visual arts.

I found artists and designers, rather than institutions, were interested in my ideas so at the 1989 OISTAT[1] conference in Sydney I decided it was time to harangue designers to get off their bums, get organised and get theorised, instead of being passive victims of history. The whole OISTAT event was a paradigm shift in Australian designers' political consciousness because it offered the first major opportunity for designers, theatre workers and academics throughout Australia to come together with international designers. This international perspective allowed a sharing of experience and strategies, heightened morale, a chance to organise and, I suppose, some necessary 'bonding'.

In the 1980s postmodernist cultural theory hit Australia. The new theory suited hybrid artforms because it encouraged a broader social, cultural and political context for understanding the arts — and popular culture — and placed particular emphasis upon interdisciplinary modes of practice. Suddenly, art didn't have to be quite so serious because irony, pastiche and play became fashionable.

What were the most significant factors undermining the recognition of a designer's role in the industry?

As well as the factors I mentioned earlier, like a lack of historical/theoretical knowledge about one's genealogy, probably the key issue would be the professionalisation and specialisation of an industry which was dominated in terms of status by playwriting and opera as the authoritative forms of theatre art. There was no room for a 'between artforms' to flourish.

I'm fascinated by the visual arts' sense of puritan paranoia about theatre as 'tainted' because of its collaborative (read compromised) character, rather than being a 'pure' artform. This puritanism goes back, of course, to Plato's hierarchies of the senses and to seventeenth-century pulpit preachers fulminating about the evils of entertainment. About the worst description an artist can get about his/her work is that it's 'theatrical'.

Despite some brilliant and innovative collaborations by artists, designers and theatre workers, and a recent trend towards multimedia and interactive installations, much of this achievement remains 'colonised' within a visual arts–gallery frame of reference. It is rare for visual people (mainly administrators and academics, but artists as well) to either attend or support the contemporary theatre and dance industry. So ignorance still exists about these common intersections and the wheel keeps being reinvented.

On the other hand, in our society artists are regarded as precocious adolescents, so the theatre culture still carries some of that baggage in its treatment of designers. However, we shouldn't underestimate the public's hunger for stimulation and its capacity to recognise and support intelligent, exciting collaborations. In the past two decades we have seen such work occurring within companies such as Danceworks, Meryl Tankard's Australian Dance Theatre (now ADT), the Sydney Front and ANThill — the latter two companies no longer being in existence.

I believe there are some fascinating similarities between the position of contemporary performance designer and performance artists. The latter tend to work somewhere between the visual arts ghetto and more conventional theatre and dance, often eschewing traditions of direction, acting, etc. but privileging the visual aspects (it's sometimes called visual theatre). The Performance Space in Sydney has been a key institution in encouraging such work. It is precisely because the field is so ill-defined that enormous opportunities for expressive autonomy are opened up, and designers are heading into this field.

Of what importance is the need for political space and research into the design role?

Rather than discuss relative industrial comparisons between text versus directing versus the design profession, I suggest we need to build audiences for a wide variety of performance, even purely visual or purely aural performance. Educating all high school students, as well as theatre, dance and visual arts students about the bigger picture framing the arts in this country, including the hybrid, multimedia forms that emerge, would be a good start.

If designers wish to improve their level of influence, they'll need to be better informed. Marginalisation can also contain great potential for creativity which, ultimately, means power. I would hope by now that 'proto-designers' are being plugged into a relevant theoretical and historical genealogy of art, dance, film and theatre. If not, designers, through a national/international forum, will have to change this themselves. You cannot hope to understand your profession if you don't understand the issues of your wider culture.

Since the 1989 OISTAT conference that Zeplin attended, along with many leading designers and theatre architects, there have been some changes, but not many.[2] Few links exist between theory-based and vocational design training, though there are individuals who move between the two. The numbers of training institutions that teach performance design as an accredited subject are growing. Their design graduates are coming into the industry with higher expectations of industry acknowledgment and political status. Since Australian designers are non-unionised and tend to work freelance, however, it is not easy for them to come together and discuss professional issues on a nationwide level. Indeed, it could be argued that performance design will persistently be referred to as a 'craft' rather than as a profession if designers do not unite to promote themselves as a professional body.

Despite this, the design role is constantly expanding. The design crossovers between television, film and live performance are increasing, with many designers freelancing between mediums. Increasingly, too, many designers are finding commercial work in the non-theatre arena, using their skills honed in theatre to create environments and effects for the broader public. This is serving designers well, in terms of pushing their profile beyond the closed ranks of the performance industry. As more alternative performance styles begin to enter the mainstream, designers with the ability to move freely between mediums will be in demand. Designers are increasingly working in decision-making roles with artistic managements, writers, other specialist artists and government-funding bodies. As designers take control and push forward their professional status, the histories, theories and achievements of performance design will also come to light.

1   International Organisation of Scenographers, Theatre Architects and Technicians.
2   The conference was convened by the Sydney chapter of the Australian Production and Design Association (APDA) and invited speakers from around Australia. The conference theme revolved around Australian theatre spaces and encouraged dialogue between theatre practitioners, academics and architects.

   A compilation of many of the keynote lectures was published by the APDA, titled *Australian Theatre Design*.

Designer role-play

Y ou as a designer have to understand that you are not just designing beautiful things. I think that era has gone. Design is an actor.

DAN POTRA[1]

Y ou change your style to whatever they want. Entertainment can be any form. It could be glove puppets, it could be ballet; it could be anything. It does not mean that it is any less serious, and it does not mean that the more serious you get, the more conservative you become with your design approach. It is just to make it entertaining. You need a certain amount of restrictions to design anything; it has to be designed for some purpose. The whole point about design is that there is some intent, whether it is just for three people or whether it has a cast of forty. It is about whether it succeeds and whether people are moved or entertained by the things that you threw up there.

WILLIAM PASSMORE[2]

◄ Plate 4 **Kafka Dances**

by Timothy Daly

Griffin Theatre Company in association with the Sydney Theatre Company

1994

venue: Wharf 1, Sydney Theatre Company

director: Ros Horin

set and costume designer: Stephen Curtis

lighting designer: Geoff Cobham

photographer: Robert McFarlane

in photo: Lech Mackiewicz as Franz Kafka

(quote from programme notes)

The play is constructed around Kafka's absorption and interactions with the Yiddish Theatre Troupe during 1912. Kafka's dreams of the actors begin to merge with his waking life. Curtis highlighted the surreal aspects of Kafka's dreams, presenting a 'vulgar cabaret' within a dull world. The false perspective backcloth elongated the Griffin stage (where it was initially performed) to create a highly stylised room. This backcloth was adapted when the production was restaged in the larger Wharf 1 theatre.

Expectation

Live performance is an immediate artform — it breathes in the audience and feeds on its expectations. Design plays a substantial role, part performer, part director and part dramaturge, in an audience's understanding of a performance event. The design does not stand on its own; it must support the action, enhance our understanding and fuel our imagination. Design elements collaborate with the performance just as designers collaborate with their choreographers, directors, writers and one another. Peter Corrigan once described design as providing 'something like, in architectural terms, the superstructure … or in literary terms, the grammar and punctuation' of a production.[3] If this were not so, if the designed elements were the main focus and reason for watching, we should call it an art installation, a *son et lumière*, an exercise in object manipulation. This is not theatre. Theatre is about performance, and design must perform a role in pushing forward audience understanding.

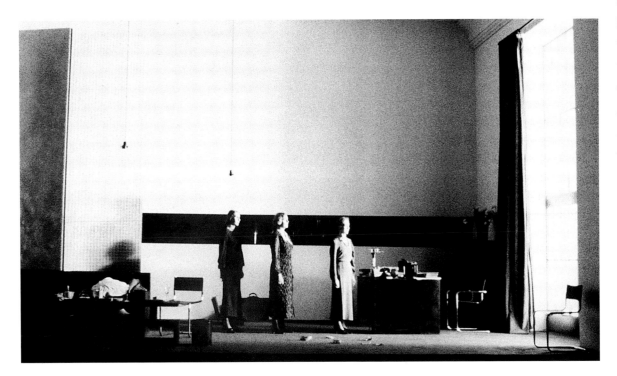

▲ Figure 21 **Mrs Klein**

by Nicholas Wright

Royal Queensland Theatre Company

1991

venue: Queensland Performing Arts Centre, Brisbane

director: Sue Rider

set and costume designer: Bill Haycock

lighting designer: David Walters

photographer: Sesh Raman

in photo: (left to right) Jennifer Flowers, Jennifer Blocksidge and Sally McKenzie

◄ Figure 22 **Ghosts**

by Henrik Ibsen

Belvoir Street Theatre

1988

venue: Belvoir Street Theatre, Sydney

director: Neil Armfield

set designer: Brian Thomson

costume designer: Jennie Tate

lighting designer: Mark Shelton

photographer: Robert McFarlane

in photo: Julia Blake and Robert Menzies

◄ Plate 5 **Interface/Interplay**

devised by Stelarc

1992

venue: La Mama, Melbourne

direction and production design: Stelarc

photographer: Anthony Figallo

in photo: Stelarc in performance. In the programme notes he explained: 'The performances at La Mama will use an interactive video installation in which the amplified body (with a third hand attached) will compose and choreograph its visual and acoustical rhythms — counterpointing improvised gestures, involuntary motion and programmed machine sequences'.

Manipulation

There is always some conscious manipulation of the performance space in order to focus audience attention. From the earliest days of theatre, the gathering of an audience to focus on a performance has indicated an image of some kind, even if it is simply the small rostrum placed in the centre of the crowd, the bright colours of the street performers' clothing and make-up, or the fires held up high. This is raw design, but design nonetheless, using spectacle to capture an audience's interest. Yet even a performer standing in the light of one lamp on a bare floor is utilising the space to his or her advantage. Within such an environment it is a designer's role to highlight the essence of the performance as simply as possible, while still honouring the work's original intentions.

'The result was a cacophony of searing lights and jarring sounds as Stelarc's body twitched and jerked under the stimulus of muscular electronic shocks, which were then fed back into the light and sound system by means of respiratory, cardiac and muscular sensors attached to his skin.'

[Richard Wright, *Performance Magazine*, London, 1991]

As part of the Museum of Victoria's exhibition of large-scale insects, Ante Matter performed this acrobatic-aerial piece while floating down the Yarra River during the Melbourne Moomba festival. The 'float' was designed to fold down as it passed under the numerous city bridges. Most of the performance occurred on a large 'web', requiring precision timing by the performers and technicians to unhook themselves each time the cantilever rig collapsed under a bridge.

Reaction

Performance is a reaction to and an interpretation of diverse stimuli. The contemporary performance designer is not a painter of canvas backdrops and wooden flats, though that is still a part of the skills required. This is an age of computer-generated images, satellite communications and multimedia presentations. The designer must find an appropriate means of interpreting and supporting a particular performance work. This may take the form of a bare black room, a sculptured costume, a series of moving sets that form part of the action or the choice of colours best suited to a particular venue.

Situation

Good design is problem solving and choice making. The need for dancers to hang from ropes and swing back and forth across a stage can be solved by good design. The heights of the borders and the position of the lights are often calculated according to where the audience is sitting. The weight of a fabric and the choice of a costume silhouette affects a performer's ability to move in character across the stage. The reflective differences between matt and shiny paint can create depth and texture. Performance design responds to the needs of a particular production, and the options

◄ Plate 6 **Gargantuans**
devised by Ante Matter
1992
venue: Yarra River, Southbank, Melbourne
director and designer: Sally Forth
lighting designer: Phillip Lethlean
design of cantilever structure: Phillip Lethlean
photo: Moomba Festival archives

are endless. The constant factors are the venue and the shape of the stage, the eventual position of the audience to the stage space, the desired relationship between the performers and the audience, and the initial concept — be it a script, a score or a workshopped idea. It is the ways in which these considerations are manipulated which engender, resolve and produce an environment specific to the performance.

Robert Kemp aptly described his design role as

someone who finds things that are appropriate for a particular situation. Oddly enough it means that I'm not that interested in 'design for design's sake'. My role is in telling a story and finding the truth. The design part for me is making something work for a production. Designing is taking something that you want on stage and making it fit. Which means a set can become a bit like a machine. It functions in order to make the play move forward.[4]

▲ Plate 7 **Medea**
based on the play by Seneca
Chamber Made Opera
1993
venue: Athenaeum Theatre, Melbourne
director: Douglas Horton
composer: Gordon Kerry
librettist: Justin McDonnell
set and costume designer: Trina Parker
lighting designer: Efterpie Soropos
photographer: Ponch Hawkes

Facilitation

The designer's role is one of initiation and facilitation; to develop ideas into a functional reality. Since collaboration is the backbone of theatre, the roles assumed by the artistic team are often blurred.

Trina Parker (pl. 7) sees the design role changing between different collaborations, depending on the style of the director:

Douglas Horton from Chamber Made Opera has a very strong visual sense and because he is often the instigator of a production my job as a technician and a professional designer can help him realise his particular view. And because in his work the visual is so strongly connected to the way he directs, that [role] is fine. I am able to supplement the ideas that he's got and make them happen for him. In another case it may be that a director will be very vague and I feel as though I'm doing all the work of going through the script

Parker chose to create a suffocating grey set as a foil to Medea's anger. Her passion and inability to become a part of her husband's controlling environment was visually represented through the use of intense colours and crisp textures in her costume.

working out scene by scene what the process is and trying to find what I call 'the metaphor' — a concept of what it is that makes that shape. So much of it is done before you actually decide whether something is pink or blue.

Initiation

Although the conventional role of design is to support a director's (or choreographer's) vision of a performance, in many productions the design leads the action, particularly in cases where the developed visual language provides as much meaning and clarity as the text.

Barrie Kosky is one director who works very closely with his designers and sees their input as being fused with his own:

> I get enormously frustrated, in terms of the Australian arts media, when they separate the work of the director and the designer. They will talk about the direction being 'this and this', and the design is 'this and this', and compliment or [denigrate] one particular element. To me it is virtually impossible to separate the roles between director and designer … Yes, the designer is in charge of the visual impact of a piece and the director is actually responsible for getting it on, but in terms of the conceptual framework behind a piece, the role of the director/designer is very much a collaborative process for me.[5]

He agreed that it is his visual response which inspires his direction of a production:

> I would say that text is only a trigger … I don't think text itself can make theatre. For me the starting point for any production or process is a combination of visual imagery and music.

Kosky's productions are well known for their strong, and sometimes startling, use of symbol and metaphor in the design. His production of *Nabucco* for the Australian Opera in 1995 was booed by some and applauded by others for its confronting direction and design.[6] On the other hand, his *Exile Trilogy*[7] (pls 8, 9), which was performed in disused warehouses and railway sheds with a minimum of functional props, lights and costumes, was much praised for its theatricality and powerful symbolic imagery. All four productions were collaborations with the well-known Melbourne architect Peter Corrigan.

▼ ▶ Plates 8a–8i **Exile Trilogy — The Dybbuk**

by Anski; based on traditional Jewish folk tales of the Dybbuk

Gilgul Theatre Company, in association with Company B

1993

venue: Town Hall Motors, St Kilda, Melbourne, and the Engine Shop, Eveleigh Railway Yards, Sydney

director: Barrie Kosky

set and costume designer: Peter Corrigan

lighting designer: Robert Lehrer

photo: Peter Corrigan archives

in photos: The cast of *The Dybbuk* (Elisa Gray, Michael Kantor, Yoni Prior and Thomas Wright), performing at the Eveleigh Railway Yards

The first play of a trilogy, *The Dybbuk* was performed on concrete floors in large abandoned warehouses. The audience sat on narrow, high-banked seating rows, stretched out along a thin corridor of light that led the actors into the space. Using a limited palette of set elements that were repeatedly transformed by their usage, Corrigan's grotesque setting resonated deeply with Judaic references and unspoken moments of joy and horror. Anderson described the constancy of Corrigan's 'symbolic juxtaposition of barbarous glinting hooks in the background, and tiny flickering candles in fragile glasses in the foreground, both united by the broken concrete floor beneath, painted a sort of maroon, the colour of dried blood' as being instrumental in making the whole disturbing experience coherent.

[M. A. R. Anderson, 'Pressing against ideas', in *Cities of Hope*, ed. Conrad Hamann, Oxford University Press, Melbourne, 1993, p. 157]

'*The Dybbuk* contains the fractured and displaced recollections of four dead, wandering theatre souls ... the potatoes of the ghetto kitchens, the dressing room of the old Yiddish theatre in North Carlton, the fans gathered outside the backstage doors, the closed gates at Ellis Island, the cut-out cardboard scenery waiting in the wings, the entrance of Warsaw Centralna Station, the colour of the sky at night in Poland, a Marx Brothers Film, the ritual of marriage, burial, exorcism and kosher slaughtering, the Bundist Utopia, the nostalgic television documentary, the road to hell, the shop window of the tailor in Balaclava Road, the road out of purgatory, the shattered shop window of the tailor in Ring Strasse, the Kabbalistic road to beauty and wisdom, the faded foyer photographs, the reconstructed film print, the Zionist Utopia, the empty orchestra pit, the garish make-up of performance and memory. Shifting, blurred, unfocused.'

[programme notes — B. Koskyl

Designer role-play

For the second play of the trilogy, Kosky
and Corrigan placed the audience around a
dark and earthy space, a makeshift bar,
around which the air seemed thick with
smoke. They created a small dark world,
void of external life, where performers
became small sparks of light, fighting for
survival. With the help of a travelling group
of vaudevillian actors, lost souls confronted
their hungry demons.

Interpretation

Design affects how the audience will understand or interpret a production. By updating the imagery associated with a classic script or libretto, a design can contemporise and illuminate themes, revitalising its relevance to the modern audience.

Artistic director of the Bell Shakespeare Company, John Bell, believes that the most important function of the designer is to structure metaphorical meaning through a visual subtext. He is most interested in developing a clarity of design, admitting that it can often be a long process of decision making and collaboration:

> I have to go through a lot and throw out a lot to achieve the essence of something. It is easy to throw money at a production and put a whole lot of stuff on the stage, but it is much more difficult to prune away and end up with something very simple but resonant.[8]

Few directors and designers consciously wish to overpower an existing script with inappropriate imagery. Design (in all its forms) must work very hard to support the central motifs without dictating the direction. Though

◄ Plate 10 **Julius Caesar**
by William Shakespeare
State Theatre Company of South Australia
1991
venue: Playhouse, Adelaide Festival Centre
director: Simon Phillips
set designer: Shaun Gurton
costume designer: Bronwyn Jones
lighting designer: Nigel Levings
photographer: David Wilson

Moore described *The Winter's Tale* as being a play of two worlds in which the 'worlds were gendered to reflect the narrative structure of the text. In monochrome Sicillia, the "masculine world", a series of symmetrically placed phallic poles cut diagonally through the circular mass of the horizontal plane. Behind the poles, caryatids (drawn from classical Greek sculpture) symbolised women acting as the supporting structures of their own oppression. In colourful Bohemia, the "feminine world", the vertical bars were curved in the shape of a rainbow to harmonise with the circular floor. On the return to Sicillia in the final act, the caryatids were replaced by famous icons of women contained within the vertical poles'.

(Mary Moore, 'Sexing the space', in *Converging Realities*, ed. Peta Tait, Currency Press, Sydney, 1995, pp. 227-33)

not always completely successful in its realisation, the Bell Shakespeare Company has always striven to place its work within a relevant design context, presenting a new world, complete with social customs and fashions pertinent to the story. Bell consciously works with many different designers, and tailors the 'look' to each production (pls 13, 14, 15).

Opera Australia (previously the Australian Opera)[9] is another company that is constantly updating classic works within its repertoire. Though often constrained by perceived conservative audience expectations, Opera Australia has been responsible for some very interesting design collaborations in recent years. Moffatt Oxenbould (formerly the artistic director of Opera Australia) strongly believed that design is a major part of the operatic experience and spoke of the 'unity of approach' needed between the conductor, director, designer and major performers. He actively encouraged collaboration between younger and older artists and pushed Opera Australia's support of Australian design into new areas through the employ-

ment of recent design graduates from training institutes such as NIDA.[10]

One example of this was the 1990 production of *La Bohème* (pl. 16, fig. 23). This production attracted much media attention because of the way in which director Baz Luhrmann and his design team, Catherine Martin and Bill Marron, completely reworked the nineteenth-century setting of Puccini's tragic opera into the neo-Bohemian world of Paris in the 1950s. The design played a significant role in highlighting the modern themes and relationships within the opera. The singers were young, the costumes bright and primary, and the sets constructed with visible scaffolding. A huge, red fluorescent 'amour' glowed from the roof above the bohemians' attic, somewhat akin to the glittering Coca-Cola sign in Kings Cross, Sydney. The production attracted a new, younger audience to Opera Australia and has further encouraged state opera and ballet companies to trust and employ younger Australian designers and directors wishing to reinterpret classical works.

▶ Plate 12 **The Mikado**
by Gilbert and Sullivan
Esgee Productions
1995 — national tour
director: Craig Schaeffer
set and costume designer: Graham Maclean
lighting designer: Nigel Swift
photo: Esgee Productions archives
in photo: (left to right) Jon English, Drew Forsythe, David Gould and Geraldine Turner

▲ Plate 13 **Richard III**
by William Shakespeare
Bell Shakespeare Company
1993 — national tour
director: John Bell
set designer: Michael Scott-Mitchell
costume designer: Sue Field
lighting designers: Nigel Levings and
Geoff Cobham
composer: Nigel Westlake
photographer: Sue Field
Field's concept painting of the battle
scene and costumes in *Richard III*.

'The production is an odd mixture of historical and period elements: modified chain mail and armour for the final battle; a throne that resembles a tennis umpire's chair; and rich and extravagant costuming, eye-catching at times and silly at others ... the early scenes in red and black tonings are striking. So is the funeral of Henry VI with its ghoulish pall-bearers with blood-red faces. So is the scene with the citizens and the Lord Mayor of London, in which the men wear long coats, the women tailored suits with long skirts, and everyone is decked out in tall black hats. The battle of Bosworth is strikingly choreographed and staged, with Richmond's army in orange and gold.'

[Leonard Radic, 'Despite quirks an engrossing Richard III', *Age*, 6 June 1992, p. 12]

▶ Plate 14a **Richard III**

Bell Shakespeare Company

1993 — national tour

photographer: Branco Gaica

in photo: John Bell (left) as Richard during the battle of Bosworth

▼ Plate 14b **Richard III**

Bell Shakespeare Company

1993 — national tour

photographer: Branco Gaica

in photo: Susie Doherty as Queen Elizabeth, with her advisers — Lord Rivers (Simon Arlidge), Lord Grey (Marian Dworakowski) and Lord Dorset (Sean O'Shea)

by William Shakespeare

Bell Shakespeare Company

1994 — national tour

director: David Fenton

set designer: Michael Scott-Mitchell

costume designer: Rodney Brunsdon

lighting designer: Mark Shelton

composer: Nigel Westlake

photographer: Branco Gaica

in photo: (left to right) Essie Davis, Camilla Ah Kin and Darren Gilshenan as the three 'Weird Sisters'

Fenton and designers Scott-Mitchell and Brunsdon chose to cast *Macbeth* into a futurist 'aliens' world: 'Ultimately we see chaos suppressed, but in the process *Macbeth* celebrates the glorious heights of rebellion.'

[programme notes — D. Fenton]

Unfortunately the production was not well received, and the design in particular was seen to have overpowered the message. Pamela Payne summed it up by asking: 'What sense is there when three witches whiz in on their silver dragon rockets and start on their "eye of newt, hand of bat" bit?'.

[P. Payne, interview with author, 22 March 1995]

Catherine Martin (pl. 16, fig. 23) described her design collaboration as being a conscious reaction to what had been seen before:

I come from a history of great and fantastic designers like Brian Thomson who come from a minimalist school of approach. Basically our work (Baz Luhrmann's, mine and Bill Marron's) is a reaction, I suppose, to the minimalism that has come before us. Our theatricality or use of colour has exactly the same effect as when Bertolt Brecht, after years and years of there being lots of scenery and heaps of make-up, went for no scenery and no make-up in order to wake his audience up. Theatricality is a convention that shocks or enlivens the audience and I think that was a word used a lot in references to *Strictly Ballroom*. It is basically about exploiting a whole lot of things that have been used in theatre before but not seen for a long time. So it has more impact and we are more interested in it ... Whether you're in the theatre or you're watching an opera or you're watching a movie, everything is an illusion. It's not about the style in which you present something, but the way that you express it. It is the 'language' that you decide to tell your particular story in. You decide that our story about this world will have more impact if we treat it in this particular style.[11]

Lindy Hume cannot believe that there are audiences who still think that classical opera is only done in big dresses and grand palatial settings and invites all those who do to see more opera. Her style of opera direction is followed closely by that of her designers, resulting in witty, well-conceived environments that reflect much of the contemporary world. She has worked with designers as diverse as Peter Long, Mary Moore, Dan Potra, Richard Roberts, William Passmore and Angus Strathie. As her comments regarding *La Perichole* (pls 17, 18) indicate, she is committed to finding the right designer for the opera in hand, as each work requires a different interpretation:

I am not sure that it is the same in Europe, or even in America where people are enormously conservative, but I think that in Australia people expect an interpretation which is an interpretation. I don't think people expect any reference to traditionalism any more ... the emphasis is not a new look versus an old look. It is 'What are we doing with this piece?'.[12]

▲ Plate 16 **La Bohème**
by Giacomo Puccini
Australian Opera
1990
venue: Opera Theatre, Sydney Opera House
director: Baz Luhrmann
set and costume designers: Catherine Martin and Bill Marron
lighting designer: Nigel Levings
photo: OA archives
in photo: (left to right) Colline (Stephen Bennett), Schaunard (David Lemke), Benoit (Graeme Ewer), Marcello (Roger Lemke) and Rodolfo (David Hobson) in Act 1

◄ Figure 23 **La Bohème**
Australian Opera
1990
see pl. 16
photo: OA archives
Martin's set model of Act 1.

▸ Plate 17 **La Perichole**

by Jacques Offenbach

Australian Opera

1993

venue: Opera Theatre, Sydney Opera House

director: Lindy Hume

set designer: Inspiration (William Passmore and Axel Bartz)

costume designer: Angus Strathie

lighting designer: Rory Dempster

photo: OA archives

in photo: Artists of the Australian Opera in performance

Hume, Inspiration and Strathie drew heavily on the world of cartoon for this highly stylised interpretation of the mad world of *La Perichole*. Hume's vision of the world she wished to create for her production of *La Perichole* eventually led her to Passmore's design company Inspiration. She knew exactly what she wanted the designer to express visually: 'I wasn't talking about reality. I wasn't talking about a building here or there. I was talking about an energy and a madness, an anarchy. One person's anarchy is not necessarily another's'.

(L. Hume, interview with author, 20 March 1995)

◂ Plate 18 **La Perichole**

Australian Opera

1994

see pl. 17

photo: OA archives

Act 1: The opening set — the exterior of the town — with a gauze dropped in front.

Question

Mary Moore consciously uses design as a means of altering an audience's relationship to the performers and the performance

'The sound of lapping water could be heard. A rhythm emerged from the sound of the water and the bodies began to move ...'

space. In a paper given to the 1989 OISTAT[13] conference in Sydney, Moore spoke of using design to 'engage in a spatial dialogue with the audience'.[14] She saw a strong link between space and its use in performance, and the ways in which an audience perceive gender and power issues. Design can alter the perspective of the viewers, either raising or lowering them from the action, forcing them to confront the performers (or one another) in a space that is no longer what they had at first assumed. The use of engendered shapes, colours and lines physically affects our view of the space and strengthens underlying themes and tensions in the text, while also playing with popular or symbolic associations. The role of design thus becomes a sociopolitical one, assuming that 'in order to change the way that people think, it is necessary, quite literally, to change the way they see'.[15] Moore's work on *Under Southern Eyes* (pl. 19) in 1988 led audiences around a boatshed in Port Adelaide, becoming enmeshed in each chamber, viewing the action from above, beneath and within. Her work with Red Shed and the State Theatre Company of South Australia (STCSA) has constantly challenged the audience perspective of the 'theatre space'.

◀ Plate 19 **Under Southern Eyes**

developed by the Flinders University Drama Centre

commissioned by the Adelaide Festival 1988

venue: No. 2 Shed, McLaren Wharf, Port Adelaide

director: Julie Holledge

composer: Robert Lloyd

choreographer: Michael Fuller

set and costume designer: Mary Moore

in photo: One of the drowning bodies seen suspended above the audience as they moved between installations in the 'Ghost Ship'

The performance piece was based on stories surrounding the history of Port Adelaide and performed in a disused wharf shed as part of an experimental workshop developed by Flinders. The aim was to use a non-traditional theatre space and engage in what Moore described as 'a spatial dialogue with the audience ... playing all the time with notions of power and looking'. The audience moved around the space, 'lost in a labyrinth of images with constantly changing positions'.

[Mary Moore, 'Performance for non-theatre spaces', in *Australian Theatre Design*, ed. Kim Spinks, Australian Production and Design Association, Sydney, 1992, pp. 141–6]

Agitation

Dan Potra agreed with Moore that design needs to have a sociopolitical intention and function. Since his early experiences as a designer and artist in Romania, Potra (pls 20a, 20b) has believed very strongly in the designer playing the role of agitator and

troublemaker because you really stir up ideas … I believe that having a response to something that stirs you is a positive step … It invites debate, ideas and opinions … I think the mechanism of my design has changed since arriving in Australia. Back in Romania one had to think much more in visual metaphors, because you were not allowed to say certain things. Therefore, there was a secret language that was growing between the theatre and its audiences. Film and TV were heavily censored, but theatre was not because you could always find another way of expressing things: in the way you pronounced a phrase, the way you used an object, or the way the setting was used. Audiences revelled in that and flocked into the theatres. We shared a common enemy. It was a moment of crisis for me when I first landed here in Australia and studied design at NIDA. I realised that I did not have to hide any more. Romanian theatre went into a similar crisis [after the fall of the government] when they started losing their audiences. How can we be different if we don't have that secret language any more? It was easier before — you knew what to avoid and how to get around censorship. It was the challenge that you needed to make you more inventive. It took me a few years to realise what I have to say in today's society in Australia … it is in the ways we edit or 'say' something. I always go back to the Jewish religion, which believes that you should never draw the image of God

▲ ▼ Plates 20a and 20b **Faust**

by Goethe; translated by Robert David MacDonald

Melbourne Theatre Company

1993

venue: Russell Street Theatre, Melbourne

director: Barrie Kosky

set and costume designer: Dan Potra

lighting designer: Rory Dempster

photographer: Peter Holderness

Potra's collaged and painted costume renderings for *Faust*.

'Potra's design was a complex twisted space, made of interlocking steel bridges and luminous orange roots. The Russell Street proscenium was broken as actors as gorillas charged up and down the auditorium aisles. Overhead television screens played out war footage and crazed commentaries. The set moved from its grungy and claustrophobic beginnings, reminiscent of an old man's soiled mattress, to a deep, yawning black space described by one reviewer as being "a remarkable series of levels and layers which seem to go on and on in all directions, constantly shifting the sense of the abyss …" .'

[John Larkin, 'Flamboyant Kosky has a devil of a show in *Faust*', *Sunday Age*, 15 August 1993, p. 7]

— just say the word and the word will recreate in your imagination. You recreate the entire part, you deal with your inner fears and it is therefore more personal and frightening. If you just touch the audience, if you just give them half words or images, you will awaken their curiosity to join in. Even if they took a little question from the show and it still echoes for a while in their mind. That's good. Next time they will come and enjoy it even more because they have already asked a few questions.[16]

Revelation

It is in the realm of costume that the designer's role becomes most involved with that of the performer. Character analysis and knowledge of that character's movements or progression through performance form the basis of good costume design. The effect may be spectacular, as in grand opera, street theatre or circus; it may be subtle and only hint at its theatrical form; it may be primarily functional; or it may be elaborate and descriptive of psyche.

A costume designer consciously engages in the analysis of character. Amanda Lovejoy summed up the role of costume design as being 'all about the revealing or concealing of different parts of people's natures, as well as working with whatever the plot of the play might be'.[17] Her work with the actors in *On Parliament Hill* (fig. 24) was a complete collaboration in that she had time 'to allow their costumes to grow with their characters ... Having the time to try things in rehearsal with both actors was a luxury and so productive. I consider them to be two of the most successful and enjoyable costumes I have worked on'.[18]

An understanding of movement is vital as it underpins the way in which a performer will be able to use the costume. Acutely aware of this, Kristian

◄ Figure 24 **On Parliament Hill**
by Noel Grieg
Belvoir Street Theatre
1987
venue: Belvoir Street Theatre, Sydney
director: Robyn Archer
set and costume designer: Amanda Lovejoy
photographer: Robert McFarlane
in photo: Paul Blackwell and Geoffrey Rush as corpses
'Paul became the corpse of a refined effeminate Scotsman who had been "made-up" before burial at a mortician's ... Geoffrey was a rotting corpse, with a flavour of vaudeville, who picked his flesh off and flicked it at the audience! He delighted in wearing real cow-bones under latex-covered pantihose, which I had to leave out in the sun to be cleaned up by an ants nest for over a week. The effect was worth it!'
[notes — A. Lovejoy, 26 March 1996]

◄ Figures 25a, 25b and 26 **Salome**
based on the play by Oscar Wilde; adapted by Graeme Murphy
Australian Opera
1993
director: Graeme Murphy
set and costume designer: Kristian Fredrikson
photographer: Peter Holderness
in photo: 25a Slave; 25b Naamena the executioner; 26 Herod
Fredrikson always makes detailed costume drawings, working first in pencil, and then pen-and-ink.

▲ Figure 27 **Circus Oz**

1994 — national and international tour

director: Sue Broadway

set designers: Ben Anderson and Louise McCarthy

costume designer: Laurel Frank

photographer: Ponch Hawkes

in photo: (left to right) Lisa Small and Nicci Wilks in 'Plate Spinning!'

▲ Figure 28 **Circus Oz**

1994 — national and international tour

director: Sue Broadway

costume designer: Laurel Frank

photographer: Ponch Hawkes

in photo: Tanya Lester performs 'The Web Rope'

▼ Figures 29 and 30 **The Old Woman at the Window**

developed by Elizabeth Paterson

1980 — national and international tour

director and production designer: Elizabeth Paterson

photographer: Gary Willis

in photo: Paterson as the old woman, encased within an architecturally inspired bodysuit

Fredrikson constantly attends dance rehearsals when working with Graeme Murphy (Artistic Director of the Sydney Dance Company), because of the need to adapt his designs to fit Murphy's choreography. He literally fits the cloth to the specific needs of the performers (figs 25, 26).

Similarly, Anna French has long been sought after as a costume designer because of her personal affinity with performers, fabrics and colours. Tony Award-winning designer Roger Kirk[19] understands the heightened role of costume and has as an example often utilised glamour and high camp in musicals to create accessible character 'types' that push forward the theatrical story, as has Angus Strathie in his opera and film designs (pls 17, 18).

Juxtaposition

Circus Oz has always exploited the design potential for visual humour, juxtaposing traditional and contemporary circus imagery while inverting social stereotypes. Costumes in particular have formed the basis of its design style. Men in tutus and spangly costumes jostle women in strong-man outfits; the clowns are punks and the animals are made from fake fur (figs 27, 28). Laurel Frank has worked with Circus Oz since its inception in the early 1970s[20] and believes that

> the design [style] evolved from the notion that we were turning circus on its head ... I suppose in the politics of the time we were very concerned to show that women were equally important and had strengths, and so we developed a style of [costuming] that didn't get much comment here in Australia, but overseas got heaps of comments in reviews — neuter gender ... We always enjoyed playing with the visual politics of gender. One act had six boys in pink cocktail frocks which were initially made for the girls ... transgender and cross-dressing is already being explored openly, so [this] is not so shocking to us anymore.[21]

Performance artist Elizabeth Paterson creates costumes that become the central metaphor for her work. Since she often works solo her soft, sculptured costumes are designed to become her performance environment. In one piece, *The Old Woman at the Window* (figs 29, 30) Paterson transformed herself into a window and wall, as well as the wrinkled old woman leaning out. In another, *Suburban Rhapsody* (fig. 31, pl. 21) she moved between free-standing set elements that became part costume as she stepped into them, incorporating herself into the mailbox, the kitchen screen door and the bath. In all her work the design is part of the action, on occasion subjugating the human to serve the inanimate.

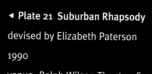

◄ **Plate 21 Suburban Rhapsody**
devised by Elizabeth Paterson
1990
venue: Ralph Wilson Theatre, Canberra
director: Ellen Cressey
set and costume designer: Geoff Cobham

photographer: Neil Roberts
in photo: Paterson as a patchwork
garden in her brightly coloured, flower-
appliqued skirt. During the performance
she also became one with the mailbox,
the street sign and the red gingham
kitchen door

Cobham's lighting captured the mood as Paterson

cast out a net from her costume bathtub in order to

pull in dreams from the

deep waters around her.

► Figure 31 **Suburban Rhapsody**
developed by Elizabeth Paterson
1990 — national tour
photographer: Neil Roberts

▲ Figure 32 **From Here to There**
devised by Legs on the Wall
Legs on the Wall
1995
venue: Wharf 2, Sydney Theatre Company
director: Rodney Fisher
set and costume designer: Jennie Tate
lighting designer: Shane Stevens
photographer: Robert McFarlane

Spatialisation

Design for non-text-based performance often evolves directly from the rehearsal room process, and plays a pronounced role in the creation of visual language and action. Whether it is for different forms of dance, the more experimental, environmental theatre pieces that are based on group devising, or non-theatre-based forms such as circus and cabaret, design is often the unifying element that links a series of ideas and scenes.

Design plays a strongly supportive role for acrobatic theatre companies such as Legs on the Wall, who must use their performance environment in creative yet practical ways. The walls become climbing frames and costumes have safety features which attach them to ropes or chains. The designer works closely with the company at every stage to ensure that the environment remains functional, adapting to new developments as soon as they occur in the rehearsal process. When Sue Field designed *All of Me* (pl. 22), she added ladders, ropes and scaffolding levels to the existing 'warehouse' features of The Performance Space, literally turning the theatre into a child's oversized playground. The company was able to tell the story on many levels, either distancing the audience or in among them. Similarly, *From Here to There* (fig. 32) was a clever distortion of the usual stage space. Jennie Tate literally turned the stage on its side, allowing the performers to spend much of their time on a vertical plane, rather than on the ground.

Designer-director Pierre Thibaudeau worked closely with his company Entr'acte (1979–99), developing the design in response to suggestions made by performers as they rehearsed, as well as by the directions that the work began to take. The movement-based work undertaken by Entr'acte usually demanded an open floor, so Thibaudeau focused more on creating an environment — an installation — than a built setting within the space.

He often presents different focal points and levels within his designs, altering the audience's perspective depending on where they are placed within the space. Much of his work has involved projected images, kinetic lighting and video effects. His design for *Possessed/Dispossessed* (pl. 23) utilised the large floor space and high ceilings of The Performance Space, allowing him to create images floating above the audience and the performers.

▶ Plate 22 **All of Me**
by Nigel Jamieson and Mary Morris
Legs on the Wall
1993 — national and international tour
venue: The Performance Space, Sydney
director: Nigel Jamieson
set and costume designer: Sue Field
lighting designer: Geoff Cobham
photographer: Sue Field
Field's concept rendering for the set of
All of Me.

▼ Plate 23 **Possessed/Dispossessed**

devised by the company
Entr'acte

1991–92 — international tour

venue: The Performance Space, Sydney

director: Elisabeth Burke

composer: Paul Charlier

dramaturge: Sarah de Jong

set designer: Pierre Thibaudeau

costume designer: Mary Ellen Flannery
with Mr and Mrs Molino

lighting designer: Pascale Baxter and
Simon Wise

photographer: Corrie Ancone

in photo: (left to right) Pierre
Thibaudeau, Katia Molino and Bruce
Keller in performance

'The set design for *Possessed/Dispossessed* is that of a world off-balance, poised on the edge between the interior and the exterior.'

(programme notes — P. Thibaudeau)

Dance reviewer Jill Sykes described Thibaudeau's design as giving 'an eerie feeling of the lid being lifted off our everyday life, of our innermost feelings being exposed, or perhaps even our planet being observed from some other world ... A sail-like white trapezoid shape hovers over the performing area of a glossy black floor, enclosed by a white border which seems to belong to the sail roof, as though it has been cut from it'. Thibaudeau's design was later displayed at the 1991 Prague Quadrennial (for theatre design) as part of the Australian exhibition.

(J. Sykes, 'Multi-layered vignette of life after someone lifted off the lid', *Sydney Morning Herald*, 2 February 1991, p. 42)

Illumination

The role of lighting in performance is multi-layered. As Rachel Burke (formerly resident lighting designer for Playbox) (pl. 24) describes it

> Its first function is to illuminate, so you are seeing something. Then it also provides shadow on the stage, so you're working with two kinds of opposites. You can put a light on the stage specifically to create a shadow for someone to work in — that's the functional side. Then [lighting] is also working as an emotional tool; the colour, the focus and the pattern are all hopefully evoking some kind of response. You can dictate where the audience is going to look. You can change from scene to scene.[22]

In *The Dramatic Imagination*, American designer Robert Edmond Jones wrote much on the power of light and shadow in the theatre. He wrote that the subject which is to be lighted is the drama itself. We light the actors and the setting, it is true, but we illuminate the drama. We reveal the drama. We use light as we use words, to elucidate ideas and emotions.[23]

Lighting designer Nick Schlieper (fig. 33) further expands on this point when describing the 'dramaturgical function' of lighting in performance, using light and shadow to 'underscore' an apparently solid world:

> I think you [as a lighting designer] have an enormous influence on the emotional climate on stage. The word 'atmosphere' is always bandied around a lot when talking about lighting. It goes way beyond those obvious things of dark and bright, gloomy or not gloomy. You can underscore so much and sometimes you do the very reverse — you juxtapose — an emotional climate, an emotional atmosphere. And it needn't be one that is obvious at all on the surface to an audience. Indeed, it is better when it is not.[24]

◄ Figure 33 **Marat/Sade**
by Peter Weiss, translated by Geoffrey Skelton
State Theatre Company of South Australia
1990
venue: Playhouse, Adelaide Festival Centre
director: Simon Phillips
set designer: Shaun Gurton
costume designer: Bronwyn Jones
lighting designer: Nick Schlieper
photographer: David Wilson

Schlieper's use of open-white light heightened the clinical, almost surgical, nature of the mental institution. Gurton referred to it as 'refrigerator-white light', illuminating but not supporting life, in a cold and unfiltered world.

[S. Gurton, interview with author, 23 August 1993]

▲ Plate 24 **The Glass Mermaid**

by Tobsha Learner

Playbox

1994

venue: Beckett Theatre, CUB Malthouse, Melbourne

director: Aubrey Mellor, with Nonan Padilla

set and costume designer: Jacqueline Everitt

lighting designer: Rachel Burke

photographer: Jeff Busby

in photo: Dino Marnika (lying down) in performance

Solution

Lighting's intangible quality is what makes it such a powerful force in performance. It can operate effectively with or without a designed set, creating and changing the space in seconds.

The way in which Graeme Murphy works demands that the design becomes a part of the choreographic process, moving towards a final solution in the rehearsal room. He believes that the design of his dance always 'has a theatricality to it. It becomes part of every step that I do, every piece of choreography. As I am creating a step, I am thinking of whereabouts in the design context the piece takes place'.[25] He loves to work with lighting because of its fluidity and ability to play with the dancers' bodies. John Rayment (formerly resident lighting designer and production manager with the Sydney Dance Company) describes his lighting design as being a journey through the performance — it must perform with the dancers in order to be alive. On his role as a designer, Rayment describes himself as the choreographer's confidante:

> You become the person who advises on the dynamic, who advises on the performance of the design.[26]

Geoff Cobham places himself in a similar role as a lighting designer:

> You are in an enormous power position at the last moment there ... You are really involved in the final moments of creating the production.[27]

The audience groups began their journey to the island by ferry. There were three sites, which represented and incorporated different elements: water, fire and spirit. As the sun set the audience were guided to a large open area where pyramid sculptures emitted phosphorescent light, and the performers converged for the finale.

◄ Plate 25 **Utopia/Distopia**
devised by the company
Splinters performance group
1995
venue: Springbank Island, Lake Burley Griffin, Canberra
director: David Branson
composer: Matthew Fargher
set design: Ross Cameron with the company
photographer: Joseph Lafferty

► Plate 26 **Utopia/Distopia**
Splinters performance group
1995
see pl. 25
photographer: Joseph Lafferty

'We're also having projections on sails ... They're visual images on a grid that rotates. They'll relate to the three worlds ... and also to the temple space to which everyone is making their way. It's more like a technical homebase than a temple. If we look at the island as a circuit board, it's the motherboard. There'll be a natural symmetry in what we bring to this natural place but at the same time we're asking how does the human being with all of its [sic] various functions fit into this mechanical world.'
[D. Branson & P. Troy, 'Subtle spectacle', *RealTime 9*, Oct./Nov. 1995, p. 31]

Imagination

Lighting in this manner can become the key element in determining the success of a design. Although its role is often not thrown into relief until the technical rehearsals, it is the lighting that controls the atmosphere and emotional pitch of the design in performance.

In non-theatre venues, lighting can become the major scenic device, simply because of its ability to focus audience attention over a large area. Fire, fireworks, and hand-held lanterns (as used in the large-scale performance work of Canberra-based group Splinters) can also be utilised in the design, bringing ritualistic elements to a performance, as well as creating moving light sources. In the Splinters production *Utopia/Distopia* (pls 25, 26), lighting, special effects and moving machinery helped to create spectacular outdoor visions. Co-artistic directors David Branson and Patrick Troy insist that all individual design elements work co-operatively to create the whole, and encouraged artists from different disciplines such as puppetry, sculpture and electronics to become involved, crediting many people as leading the work in new design directions.[28]

Vision

'There are no arbitrary rules. There is only a goal and a promise.'[29] Edmond Jones effectively summed up the role of the lighting designer as being similar to that of a poet in his book, *The Dramatic Imagination*. Fifty years on, his written belief in the power of theatre lighting 'as an art, at once visionary and exact' continues to inspire not only designers of light, but designers of all performance mediums:

> The creative approach to the problem of stage lighting — the art, in other words, of knowing where to put light on stage and where to take it away — is not a matter of textbooks or precepts. There are no arbitrary rules. There is only a goal and a promise. We have the mechanism with which to create this ideal, exalted, dramatic light in the theatre. Whether we can do so or not is a matter of temperament as well as of technique. The secret lies in our perception of light in the theatre as something alive.
>
> Does this mean that we are to carry images of poetry and vision and high passion in our minds while we are shouting out orders to electricians on ladders in light rehearsals?
>
> Yes. This is what it means.[30]

'I think that there are two areas that I work in [as a lighting designer] ... One is an area of rich dense colour, non-naturalistic, or should we say slightly hyper-realistic lighting; a sort of "stretched naturalism" is perhaps

the description of it. Light that is in a world where all colour values are slightly richer than you will get them in real life and all the elements are slightly stretched ... The other area that I work in is a brutalist open-white harsh world where a light is a light is a light. A light is not a shaft of light coming through a door, or moonlight or sunlight or anything like that; it is just a theatre light, lighting an actor in an interesting and particular way.'

[N. Levings, interview with author, 1 March 1995]

1   D. Potra, interview with author, 22 November 1993.

2   W. Passmore, interview with author, 15 March 1995.

3   M. Cosic, 'Stage by stage', *Good Weekend*, *Sydney Morning Herald*, 12 August 1995, pp. 30–5.

4   R. Kemp, interview with author, 14 November 1993.

5   B. Kosky, interview with author, 5 April 1994.

6   P. Cochrane, 'Kosky pulls off a boo coup', *Sydney Morning Herald*, 17 August 1995, p. 17.

7   *Exile Trilogy* is *The Dybbuk*, *Es Brent* and *Levad*.

8   J. Bell, interview with author, 13 March 1995.

9   The Australian Opera and the Victorian State Opera amalgamated in late 1996, becoming Opera Australia. The main administrative base is now in Sydney.

10 Oxenbould employed NIDA design graduates Russell Cohen and Peter England to design his production of *Madame Butterfly* for Opera Australia in 1997. They were given studio space, development time and complete support by the company during the two-year time frame. The production design was considered an overwhelming success by audiences, and further enhanced OA's reputation as an innovative and risk-taking production house.

11 C. Martin, interview with author, 4 April 1995.

12 L. Hume, interview with author, 19 March 1995.

13 International Organisation of Scenographers, Theatre Architects and Technicians (OISTAT).

14 M. Moore, 'Performance for non-theatre spaces', in *Australian Theatre Design*, ed. Kim Spinks, Australian Production and Design Association, Sydney, 1992, pp. 141–6.

15 ibid., p. 146.

16 D. Potra, interview with author, 22 November 1993.

17 A. Lovejoy, interview with author, 24 March 1995.

18 A. Lovejoy, letter to author, 26 March 1996.

19 Brian Thomson and Roger Kirk won the 1996 Tony Award for production design for their collaboration on the Australian production of *The King and I* which opened on Broadway.

20 See Frank's fuller description of her work with Circus Oz in chapter 7.

21 L. Frank, interview with author, 20 March 1995.

22 R. Burke, interview with author, 15 March 1995.

23 Robert Edmond Jones, *The Dramatic Imagination*, Theatre Arts Books, New York, 1941, p. 118.

24 N. Schlieper, interview with author, 12 March 1995.

25 G. Murphy, interview with author, 30 March 1995.

26 J. Rayment, interview with author, 14 March 1995.

27 G. Cobham, interview with author, 9 March 1995.

28 D. Branson and P. Troy talk about their approach to performance in 'Subtle spectacle', *RealTime 9*, Oct./Nov. 1995, p. 31.

29 Jones, op. cit., pp. 127–8.

30 ibid.

ZELDA
ANNA VOLSKA

hat?

fine 3/4 length "pushed up" sleeves jacket - full style

sleeveless top

high waisted side buttoned 3/4 trousers - side pockets

bare legs

pl. 28a

CHARLES
DAVID CLENDINNING

cap

wool sports jacket
pen in breast pocket
lapel pin

"old school tie" type tie

belt

wool loose trousers
good quality &
old favourites

tweeds
dk green
olive
beige
pale blue

"LAST WEEKEND"
Queensland Theatre Co. 1989

Design:
EDIE KURZER

pl. 28b

NEW

When Ivana became the spokesperson for Roederer Cristal, one society snoot quipped, "I guess that means we'll all be switching to Krug."

NOTE: BEAUTY SPOT.

COSTUME MOOD

WIG.

JOCASTA:
IVANA TRUMP
OUT OF BLANCHE DUBO

OEDIPUS REX
FEB '93   R.O.

LYRIC OPERA
OF QUEENSLAND 59

pl. 29

TIGHT FITTING SHOWER CAP

GLASSES (SEE DETAIL)

OLD SCHOOL TIE UNDER FILTHY & TORN SINGLET.

ALL OVER:
IODINE YELLOW STAINS TO ARMS & LEGS, CHEST & NECK.

BUNSEN BURNER RUBBER TUBING TO HOLD UP SHORTS.

LATEX SURGICAL GLOVES.

I.V. DRIP BOTTLE & MEDICAL TUBES.

BLACK GARTERS & SOCKS

EYEBALL

SHOES

CHORUS.
MEN OF THEBES
MALCOLM FRASER IN MEMPHIS

OEDIPUS REX   LYRIC OPERA

fig. 34

Design down under:
the Australian theatre climate

I think it is really important [to consider] what we are trying to communicate to an Australian audience. in terms of our own identities. What is our relationship to the way we perceive the world in which we live. and what we are trying to offer to the people who are also perceiving it and experiencing it?

TESS SCHOFIELD [1]

What influence does 'being Australian' have on performance design? Is it necessary or of any value to look for what may define it? The factors that may influence Australian performance are merged within Aboriginal, colonial and migrant history; the types of venues and use of space, the language, music and context of new performance work; and, inevitably, the politics and sponsorship of arts funding bodies. As the majority of theatre artists currently creating work in Australia are now Australian-trained and employed, it is arguable that the choice of work produced, quality of materials used, colours chosen and emotional landscapes portrayed in performance are all indigenous to the Australian experience in some shape or form.

◄ Plates 28a and 28b **Lost Weekend**
by John Romeril
Royal Queensland Theatre Company
1989
venue: Cremorne Theatre, Brisbane
director: John Bell
set and costume designer: Edie Kurzer
photographer: Peter Holderness
Kurzer's costume renderings representing Zelda (Anna Volska) and Charles (David Clendimming).

◄ Plate 29 **Oedipus Rex**
by Igor Stravinsky
Lyric Opera of Queensland, in association with the Brisbane Biennial
1993
venue: Lyric Theatre, Brisbane
director: Barrie Kosky
set and costume designer: Peter Corrigan
lighting designer: David Whitford
photographer: Peter Corrigan
Corrigan's humorous costume collage illustrated a contemporary image of Jocasta.

◄ Figure 34 **Oedipus Rex**
Lyric Opera of Queensland, in association with the Brisbane Biennial
1993
see pl. 29
lighting designer: David Whitford
photographer: Andrew Campbell
Corrigan's costume concept for the Men of Thebes — 'Malcolm Fraser in Memphis'.

▲ Figure 35 **Away**
by Michael Gow
Playbox
1986
venue: The Studio, Victorian Arts Centre, Melbourne
director: Neil Armfield
set and costume designer: Stephen Curtis
lighting designer: Donna Broadbridge
photographer: Peter Holderness
Curtis's rendering of the fairies, in an assortment of Australian beach wear with wings.

▶ Figure 36 **Four Lady Bowlers in a Golden Holden**
by John McKellar
Sydney Theatre Company
1982
venue: Kinselas Cabaret, Sydney
director: Richard Wherrett
choreographer: Robina Beard
set designer: Brian Thomson
costume designer: Terry Ryan
lighting designer: Grant Fraser
photographer: Brett Hilder
in photo: (left to right) Linda Nagle, Tony Taylor, Sue Walker, Maggie Dence, John Derum and Bob Hornery

The set was simply a supermarket stacking of assorted boxes and bottles and powders and things, forming a bright and tacky wall of 'product' behind the sketches. The central panel occasionally revolved, revealing a Hammond organ being played by its diligent mistress.

Mirror images: historical definition

Australians have seen themselves represented in a variety of ways on stage during the twentieth century. The prevailing nineteenth-century images of Australians as bushrangers and convicts gave way to swaggies, cane cutters and working-class battlers in the years following the Great Depression and two world wars. Though the commercial theatres were importing American musicals, and many of the opera and ballet repertoires were based on European productions, the theatre writing of the post-war years tended to create Australian-based living room or backyard dramas. Designers created naturalistic settings within proscenium arches, giving their attention to details such as doors that closed, windows that opened and pianos that were tuned. Audiences saw their lives reflected on stage, with contemporary fashion and furnishings to complete the picture. Despite other developing theatre theories and modes of

Nominated for Best Design by the 1988 Green Room Awards, Sproul's design paralleled the play's themes — the masculine exploration of the Australian landscape

▲ Plate 30 **Black Rabbit**
by Ray Mooney
Playbox
1988
venue: CUB Malthouse, Melbourne
director: Peter Oysten
set and costume designer: Kathryn Sproul
lighting designer: John Beckett
photographer: Jeff Busby
in photo: Kylie Belling and David Bradbury

and its indigenous people. Sproul created three curved silhouettes from the rocks, using as her metaphor a feminine-shaped earth. A cave in the centre of the formation had a stylised map of Australia as an opening, mirroring the violent rape of the land and of the central female character played by Kylie Belling.

D'Arcy translated outback Australia through the mind of the central figure, Monk O'Neill, whose mad ranting in continued isolation is the driving force of the performance. The audience became silent voyeurs, encircling his dried-up world and watching him wither in an arid landscape of his own making.

▾ Plate 31 **A Stretch of the Imagination**
by John Romeril
Hoopla!
1984
venue: The Studio, Victorian Arts Centre
director: Lois Ellis
set and costume designer: Eamon D'Arcy
lighting designer: Derek Nicholson
photographer: Derek Nicholson
in photo: Stephen Kearney as Monk O'Neill

presentation, (including Constructivism and Brechtian styles of performance) being explored by various smaller companies to great effect, they tended to remain on the fringes of mainstream popular theatre. Though naturalism was important as an identifying cultural factor for Australian theatre audiences to relate to, it gradually became somewhat passé on stage as the growing Australian film and television industry began to document more and more of contemporary life on screen. Theatre artists reclaimed 'theatricality' in their modes of presentation. Much live theatre from the 1960s onwards moved out of the theatres and into found spaces — protest theatre, street theatre, pub theatre and the ubiquitous studio theatres of most university drama departments.

The combination of a new generation of playwrights and directors in the 1960s and 1970s, and the appropriation of disused buildings as theatre spaces by new companies, led to a bolder, rougher approach to staging. The 'in-ya-face' performance style of the Australian Performing Group (APG) at the Pram Factory encouraged its playwrights to write for a space without defined boundaries between audience and performers. Similarly in Sydney, the style of theatre being developed by the Nimrod Theatre Company kept the performers (and the design) in close proximity to the audience. Its tiny three-sided stage area (now the Stables Theatre) required designers to find simple design solutions on minimal budgets. Then the 'New Wave'[2] of theatre writing presented 'Aussies' as larrikins, louts and lousy lovers. The essence of 'ockerism' was distilled in the popular performance forms of comic humour and slang, experienced in the ready rapport of mateship and the emotional distance between genders. Dusty work boots and green council 'Stubbies',[3] sweat-stained singlets, terry-towelling hats and beer bellies became a staple costume for many of the male characters of the time.

By the 'Second Wave' of Australian theatre writing in the early 1980s contemporary writers were no longer basing their plays in the outback or larrikins' living rooms. Performers again left the world of vaudeville and moved back into the angst-ridden world of the rising middle classes. Many designers responded by increasing the presence of design on stage (see fig. 12). The look became stylish and sophisticated. As playwrights' concerns moved into an international arena, discussing politics, war, psychology and power, designers no longer referenced locales within specific Australian contexts. Archetypal landscapes became lost in the surreal mindscapes of characters.

Many politicians and arts officials have espoused the benefits of 'multiculturalism' in all areas of the Australian arts since the 1980s and early 1990s. Since then the divisions of language, experience and cultural traditions between performance forms have become blurred in many areas. The creative effects of this have been reflected in the funding policies of the Australia Council for the Arts, and the subsequent arts funding proposals from performers and performance companies. The expanding boundaries of Australian performance can be seen in the new plays being written, the actors being cast and the spaces being used (fig. 37). Annual and biennial arts festivals import and export performance events around the globe. Electronic media enables artists and directors to experience what is occurring around the world as it happens. Cultural definitions have become less distinct, though perhaps more complex.

▲ Figure 37 **Waterborne**

devised by the company, with dramaturgy by John Bayliss

Entr'acte

1993

venue: Australian National Maritime Museum on the western shore of Darling Harbour

director: Elisabeth Burke

composer and musical director: Robert Lloyd

set and costume designer: Pierre Thibaudeau

lighting designer: Pascale Baxter

photographer: Jennie Carter (ANMM)

in photo: The performers (David Branson, Peter Garran, Sawung Jabo, Bruce Keller, Katia Molino, Deborah Pollard, Anne-Marie Sinclair, Ta Duy Binh, Simon Terrill, Pierre Thibaudeau and Indra Utama) leaving by boat at the end of the performance

Common stages and cultural definitions

The definition of one thing is often only seen relative to the definition of another. Australians have a long history of comparing themselves and their actions to others. In an interview with arts writer Jo Litson, well-known performance designer Brian Thomson (pl. 32) expressed his opinion of what differentiates Australian design from British:

The various performance areas of this site-specific show required different performance solutions: 'there [were] two contrasting performance areas: the materially dense interior of the museum itself, and the expansive exterior dominated by the backdrop of Sydney Harbour. The creative response to the interior [was] to explore the role of people and objects in an institution such as a museum, and to play with the acoustic power and potential of the building itself. With the exterior, Entr'acte explored a combination of choreography, percussion, and responses to the visual and aural possibilities of the site itself'.

[programme notes — 1993]

'When the Australian Opera finally produced Richard Meales' opera Voss ... Thomson was confronted, as so many artists had been before, by the dilemma of having to convey the vastness of the land within the constricting parameters of the proscenium. Thomson and Sharman avoided the temptation to attempt to resolve this paradox. Instead the epic journey undertaken by Voss took place within an immense colonial mansion. This allowed the journey of the woman Laura to happen simultaneously. The set was truly a landscape of the mind.'

[notes by Shaun Gurton, part of 'Australian scenography since 1945', a paper presented to the Asian Scenography Conference, Tokyo, 1993]

▲ Plate 32 **Voss**
based on a novel by Patrick White; adaptation by Richard Meales
Australian Opera
1986
venue: Drama Theatre, Sydney Opera House
director: Jim Sharman
set designer: Brian Thomson
costume designer: Luciana Arrighi
lighting designer: Nigel Levings
photographer: Branco Gaica

Brian Thomson has said that the difference between British design and what is really good about Australian design is the simplicity. It is all around us in our culture. As an example, he used the Sydney Harbour Bridge and London Bridge. We are such a new, young culture (the white western culture that is, not the Aboriginal obviously), but we have got beautiful things; like that simple yet glorious Harbour Bridge which is completely different in style to London Bridge, steeped in its years of tradition. The British do tend to like things ornate; they will add on to things and decorate. Brian cited something like *Les Misérables* and I said 'I don't agree. The designer had a plain revolve and the barricades were strong'. Brian replied [that] 'if he had designed the barricades, there would have been nothing on them'. They would have just been the architectural shape — the structure. What the British designer had done was get that strong structure, but then covered it with all sorts of things. I think that at its best, that is what differentiates Australian design in a way. Our designers are not scared to pare it right back; right back to something very, very simple.[4]

On a more personal level, Yale-trained designer Andrew Carter (pl. 33) believes his Australian identity strongly influences his design approach:

> The reason I do not live in New York now is because I could not be an artist in another country. All my roots and everything I feel strongly about are linked to the landscape, or to being an Australian and being born here … It's not so much a case of me putting Australian symbols on stage, but the fact that I am coming from this particular lifestyle and background; a sense of living in cities that fringe this incredible huge continent. Being an Australian and being an artist used to be a real problem. We used to have to go overseas to get European 'endorsement'. Now knowing that we have such isolation is proving to be a really good factor in our work. Maybe it makes us a bit more original? Where I come from may affect what my work looks like in the end. I might design European architecture, but it is my image of how European architecture sits on the stage; my Western Australian sense and understanding. There are also mythical implications of living in an insular society and our isolation enhances our imagination. We are a bit more innocent — as much as we are becoming more cosmopolitan.[5]

Murphy's concept required Carter to create some sense of the vast expanse of the Australian continent, ranging from desert to rainforest to ocean to sky. Here the dancers form constellations across the night sky, under the Southern Cross.

The 'innocence' mentioned by Carter links to the notion that Australia's performing arts are not bound by traditional theatre conventions, other than those left by European and American legacies. Post-colonial performance consciously uses cross-cultural aspects of Australian society as a major source of expression. This cultural 'borrowing' has encouraged a certain freedom of expression and a tendency to transfer ideas and images from every part of the world. It may be that we will stop looking for what makes us indelibly Australian, since the outline is constantly changing. While attempting to sum up the elusive 'Australian' quality, costume designer Anna French described Australia as a 'melting pot' for ideas:

◄ Plate 33 **Vast**
National Bicentennial Dance
1988
venue: Opera Theatre, Sydney Opera House and national tour
choreographer: Graeme Murphy
composer: Barry Conyngham
set designer: Andrew Carter
costume designer: Jennifer Irwin
lighting designer: Kenneth Rayner
photographer: Branco Gaica

'*Lajamanu Kurra Karna Yani* was formed through human relationships between people of two cultures. Our common connection was an understanding of dance and design, and the need to tell a story.'

(notes — Tim Newth, February 1996)

▲ Plate 34 **Lajamanu Kurra Karna Yani**
devised by Tim Newth and the Lajamanu Community
1992
venue: Browns Mart Theatre Centre, Darwin
director: Tim Newth
choreographers: David McMicken, Sarah Calver and the Lajamanu Community
designers: Tim Newth, Faridah Whyte and Freddy Jangala Patrick in collaboration with the Lajamanu Community
photographer: David McMicken

▼ Plate 35 **Sistergirl**
by Sally Morgan
Black Swan Theatre Company in association with Melbourne Theatre Company
1994
venue: Russell Street Theatre, Melbourne
director: Andrew Ross
set and costume designer: Steve Nolan
lighting designer: Duncan Ord
photo: MTC archives

To create the rich mindscapes of the central characters, Nolan and Ord successfully amalgamated the cold clean edges of a hospital ward with the vibrant colours and shapes found in many of Sally Morgan's own paintings by employing a combination of projection and lighting techniques. (This was the last production to be staged by the MTC in the historic Russell Street Theatre.)

► Plate 36 **Waiting For Godot**
by Samuel Beckett
Black Swan Theatre Company
1993
venue: Subiaco Theatre Centre, Perth
director: Lucian Savron
set designer: Robert Juniper
costume designer: Steve Nolan
lighting designer: Duncan Ord
photographer: David Dare-Parker
in photo: (left to right) Kelton Pell as
Lucky and Geoff Kelso as Pozzo

We are more prepared to try different things and throw things together … Sometimes there is a larrikin quality, a less precious way of going about things. The English theatre has such a strong history, and so when designers depart from it they seem spectacularly inventive because they depart from their heritage by building on from it. I think in Australia there is less of our own heritage, more an amalgamation of what other people have brought.[6]

Though there are now many well-known Aboriginal performers, choreographers and writers working professionally in Australia, it is only since the late 1970s that non-Aboriginal Australians have publicly begun to qualify, appreciate and research the centuries of traditional art and performance within Aboriginal culture (pl. 34).

Although Black Swan Theatre (pls 35, 36 and 37) consciously promotes the work of Aboriginal playwrights and actors in Western Australia, it still uses European conventions as a means of linking actors with the audience. Space is an important factor in many Black Swan productions, and the direction and design often incorporate audience participation and promenade in non-theatre spaces. In a production acclaimed as the 'first Aboriginal musical', *Bran Nu Dae* (Black Swan, 1990), designer Steve Nolan and painter Robert Juniper used their knowledge of the Western Australian township of Broome and its surrounding landscape to give the production a naturalistic, 'laid-back' look, incorporating local symbols while emphasising the strong 'country and western' influences in Jimmy Chi's musical writing style. Juniper and Nolan have since combined their design skills many times (pl. 36), creating strong expressive environments that capture the hot dry landscapes and the characters that live in them.

'I wanted well-defined costumes that stood out from the landscape (in a similar way to the small human images that Bob Juniper uses in his paintings), but at the same time they were to be part of the landscape also. My scheme for this was to use black for definition, and shades of beige as a base.'

(notes — Steve Nolan, February 1996)

Kurzer created a vast and filmic set within the boundaries of an enormous warehouse. The audience were removed from the usual safety of 'a theatre seat' and placed on hard benches within the landscape. As land-rovers veered through the space, red dirt was sprayed in gusts over the audience and smoke from small fires filled the air. Though theatre reviewer Pamela Payne found problems with the set's marginalisation of some of the performances, she agreed that there was 'power in the image thus created': 'Visually the performance area is arresting: we walk to our seats past the scruffy hills, the sacred pool and the spinifex fires, through the thick red Wala Wala dirt. Ranged along the wall on our left are three cement slabs — anonymous white settlement rooms. And beyond them the steel-strutted lock-up'.

(P. Payne, 'Black, white and shades of grey', *Sydney Morning Herald*, 20 March 1994, p. 24)

▲ Plate 37 **Dead Heart**
by Nicholas Parsons
Black Swan Theatre Company, in association with Company B
1994
venue: Eveleigh Railway Yards, Sydney
director: Neil Armfield
set and costume designer: Edie Kurzer
lighting designer: Mark Howett
photographer: Frances Andrijich
in photo: Steve Bisley, Stanley Djunawong Mirindo, Kevin Smith and Peter Frances

Costume designer Melody Cooper was far more assertive: 'I thought Edie Kurzer's design for *Dead Heart* was incredibly significant. I can't think of any other production in the last two decades that has made as much impact'. Since this production the Eveleigh Railway Yards [now Sydney Technology Park] have been utilised many times for theatre performances, encouraging designers to stretch out and recreate the large warehouse space.

(M. Cooper, interview with author, 23 March 1995)

Contemporary dance companies such as the Aboriginal and Islander Dance Theatre (AIDT) and Bangarra Dance Theatre pioneered the amalgamation of Aboriginal traditional dance forms with the contemporary. Bangarra Dance Theatre, under the artistic direction of Stephen Page, has earned international acclaim for choreography and design. Much of its design strength lies in the simplicity of the environments used — landscaped but dormant, waiting for the dancers' bodies to become the main source of light, colour and movement (pl. 38). Like Graeme Murphy of the Sydney Dance Company, Page utilises lighting as a major design tool in his performance-making.

The amalgamation of cross-cultural influences can be seen in the growing number of theatre companies that cater for and cast from specific language and ethnic groups, such as Doppio Teatro in Adelaide and AIDT in Sydney. Added to this has been the eclectic mixture of performance forms within companies such as Ante Matter (pl. 6), Bizircus (figs 38, 39), Circus Oz (figs 27, 28), DeSoxy, Legs on the Wall (pl. 22, fig. 32) and Stalker Stilt Theatre (to name but a few of the hybrid companies to be funded), which have combined circus, cabaret, acrobatics, corporeal theatre and dance. Since most of the work created by these companies is self-devised or commissioned, contemporary Australian concerns are always very high in performance. Larger mainstream theatre companies are more likely to schedule works by known American and European writers than unknown (and even known) Australian writers. A couple of notable exceptions to this have been Playbox in Melbourne, Griffin in Sydney and Red Shed in Adelaide, as well as the funded 'new works' development arms of companies such as Opera Australia, the Australian Ballet, State Theatre Company of South Australia, Sydney Theatre Company and Melbourne Theatre Company.

▲ Plate 38 **Ochres**

developed by the company, in close association with Djakapurra Munyarryun

Bangarra Dance Theatre

1995 — (1996–97 — national tour)

venue: Enmore Theatre, Sydney

choreographers: Stephen Page and Bernadette Walong

music: David Page and Djakapurra Munyarryun

set designer: Stephen Page, with Spinning Eye and Luke Keon

costume designer: Jennifer Irwin

lighting designer: Jo Mercurio

photographer: Gerald Jenkins

'Ochres play an essential part in traditional life. Working with cultural consultant and dancer Djakapurra Munyarryun has provided us with valuable insight into the presentation of traditional paint-up and preparation. As a substance ochre has intrigued us. Its significance and myriad purposes, both spiritual and physical, have been the driving force behind this collaboration. The portrayal of each colour is by no means a literal interpretation, but the awareness of its spiritual significance has challenged our contemporary expressions: Yellow — women's business; Black — men's business; Red — sacred ceremony/ritual, youth, obsession, poison, pain; White — spiritual.'

[programme notes — Stephen Page]

◀ Figure 38 **Cyber Circus**

Bizircus

1994

venue: The Old Passenger Terminal, Fremantle

director: Russell Cheek

set and costume designer: Lou Westbury

lighting designer: Adam Richards

photographer: Matthew Dwyer

in photo: Brendan Colman (left) is soothed by the strummings of Ross Vegas

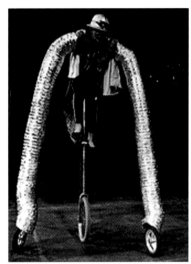

◀ Figure 39 **Cyber Circus**

Bizircus

1994

see fig. 38

photographer: Matthew Dwyer

in photo: 'The Unicycle' — Alex Glasgow

Due to the very physical nature of circus performance, Bizircus designs always display innovation and resourcefulness in their use of materials. Sets and props are often integral to the performers' costumes. For touring and space minimalisation most constructed elements must collapse, be recyclable or have the ability to be reconstructed at another venue.

Considering his performance company Entr'acte to have been on the 'fringe', designer-director Pierre Thibaudeau (pls 23, 42, fig. 37) is passionate about the impact that similar companies have had on the mainstream of performing arts:

[The] fringe is in fact the nourishment for a lot of ideas for the mainstream companies and everybody knows that. The thing is that they do not acknowledge that fact; they manage to use things up or to transpose ideas. They have influences like we all have influences; we all see things — we're all capable of absorbing and transforming. But what is obvious is that the fringes (or what we could call ourselves — the 'marginalised companies') are in fact the people who come up with ideas. We are the people who come up with ideas, with development and with questioning. Those things surface eventually to the mainstream and are being used.

Many of the performance forms developed within Australia's neighbouring Asian cultures are now being utilised by performers and artists who are exploring their relevance to contemporary Australia. Jennie Tate (pls 39, 40, fig. 32) is a designer who, like Thibaudeau, has spent time in Japan, observing, researching and participating in Japanese performance processes. She has returned many times to Japan, originally studying traditional Japanese puppetry techniques and more recently the use of ritual costume. The influence of the Japanese culture on her ways of thinking has translated successfully into many of her designs:

Whilst in Japan I became very interested and excited by the amount of contemporary performance happening in conjunction with a dynamic traditional culture. The Japanese have not lost the age-old connections with their social rituals. Folk performance occurs everywhere. On a daily basis the gods need to be thanked and asked for more. A lot of our Australian cultural traditions are connected with the land and yet so much of our modern lives is disconnected from these things. We do not celebrate our natural connections. I have been back to Japan five times. I take their culture very seriously and yet it has allowed me to become intoxicated by my own freedoms, space and lack of rules here in Australia. This comparison satisfies me on many levels. I hate the idea of cultural appropriation but there is a simplicity in my work that fits in with the Japanese aesthetic. I do not look for Japanese solutions, nor impose their particular aesthetics on a production, but I have been profoundly influenced by their ways of thinking.

Eiko Ishioka is the production designer for the Parco Company in Japan and is perhaps the greatest costume designer in the world. I try to complement an actor's body language with their costume like she does, but this [skill] is a state of mind, not an imposed style.[7]

◄ Plate 39 **The Head of Mary**
by Chikao Tanaka
Playbox, in association with the Melbourne
International Festival of the Arts
1995
venue: Beckett Theatre, CUB Malthouse,
Melbourne

director: Aubrey Mellor
set and lighting designer: John Beckett
costume designer: Jennie Tate
photographer: Jeff Busby
in photo: Helen Buday

To mark the fiftieth anniversary of the dropping of the atom bomb in Nagasaki, Chikao Tanaka's *The Head of Mary* and John Romeril's *The Floating World* were performed in Australia and Japan as cultural exchange projects between Japan's Black Tent Theatre Company and Australia's Playbox Theatre Company. Both plays explored the effects of the Second World War, each company performing and translating the other nation's work and recognising common themes within their own culture.

► Plate 40 **The Head of Mary**
Playbox, in association with the
Melbourne International Festival of
the Arts
1995
see pl. 39
photographer: Jeff Busby

► Plate 41 **The Head of Mary**
Playbox, in association with the
Melbourne International Festival of
the Arts
1995
see pl. 39
photographer: Jeff Busby

'The Playbox production managed to avoid the stereotypes associated with *The Head of Mary*, such as A-Bomb survivors dressed in rags. We wanted to indicate that the characters were attempting to piece together their lives: so the businessman's clothes comprised a patchwork of different suits — a 1960s single-breasted suit, a 1940s double-breasted suit, etc.'

(J. Tate interviewed by P. Cochrane, 'The Tate gallery',

Sydney Morning Herald, 23 April 1997, p. 12)

Reflecting these influences in theatre productions such as *The Head of Mary* (pls 39, 40 and 41) or *White Paper Flowers* (pl. 68), the designers (John Beckett and Jennie Tate, and Katherine Sproul respectively) consciously manipulated Asian imagery and stylistic devices in order to highlight the works' political themes. The audiences were pushed towards Japanese and Chinese performance conventions, filtered through an Australian direction and aesthetic.

In *The Return* (pl. 42) performer Ta Duy Binh and designer Thibaudeau used Ta Duy's experience of leaving Vietnam as a refugee 'boat person' to form the design's emotive base — kinetic images of boats and water projected overhead and surrounding the actor.

Similarly, Company Skylark combined Japanese puppetry with the traditional Punch and Judy shows of the United Kingdom in its production of *Inside Dry Water* (pl. 43) with designer Richard Jeziorny. Director Peter J. Wilson and writer Beatrix Christian created a story that joined the images found in Arthur Boyd's 'Bride in the Bush' paintings with Aboriginal bush spirits and barren desertscapes. One actor performed with creatures and objects that were animated by visible puppeteers on a journey through the bush in search of her father, and ultimately herself. The techniques drew on Japanese-style puppeteering while the stage imagery remained rooted in Australian mythology.

▲ Plate 42 **The Return**
devised by Ta Duy Binh, in association with the company
Entr'acte
1994
venue: Belvoir Street Theatre (2nd Asian Theatre Festival), Sydney
director: Elisabeth Burke
composer: Ngoc Huong Tuan
set designer: Pierre Thibaudeau
costume designers: Pierre Thibaudeau and Ta Duy Binh
lighting designer: Pascale Baxter
photo: Entr'acte archives
in photo: Ta Duy Binh in performance

The dominant feature of Thibaudeau's set was a translucent screen in the shape of an 'S', the shape of Vietnam, suspended above the performance space.

'Pierre Thibaudeau's setting is simple: a screen that could be a sail in mid-air, or a map suspended in space; a bowl of water, a pole like a mast — or a staff; and a blotch of red that flows down a back-wall like a distorted human shadow of blood.'

[Angela Bennie, 'Pearl opens Asian season', *Sydney Morning Herald*, 9 September 1994, p. 19]

Inspired by Arthur Boyd's 'Bride in the Bush' paintings, Skylark created a fantastical world, in which one actor and a large cast of puppets journeyed through the Australian landscape in search of their pasts.

'The starting point was a rough treatment of an idea about Boyd's images. We then went into the creative development stage where we built a number of the images and workshopped those ideas ... One of the examples was when we built a skeleton character because at one stage in the play the lead actor confronts her own mortality by meeting a death character [and doing a dance of death]. In the early stages we came up with somebody wearing a three-dimensional death costume attached to their legs, but I [thought it looked corny], so a

◄ Plate 43 **Inside Dry Water**
by Beatrix Christian
Skylark Puppet Theatre
1995 — national tour
director: Peter J. Wilson
designer: Richard Jeziorny
lighting designer: Phillip Lethlean
photographer: George Mackintosh
in photo: The Bride (John Hunt) and the
Groom (Bob Parsons) in Skylark's 1996
production

marionette was made [which didn't work either]. Then the puppet maker made a skull, and the whole set was draped in cloth. The cloth represented the desert and was used in about four or five different ways throughout the play ... "Try this," I said to the operator. "Grab the skeleton, bring it up from behind [the central disc], take the fabric behind and just lift it up." He came out, stood on the headboard and started to create this incredible monster creature out of all the fabric and the skull ... and all of a sudden, something I hadn't even expected occurred. It was absolutely perfect for what we were trying to achieve.'

[P. J. Wilson, interview with author, 20 March 1995]

Definitive interpretation: breaking through barriers

The traditional distinctions between opera, dance, and drama are lessening as performance practitioners embrace 'multimedia' forms of expression. Hybrid artforms and multimedia are a part of the modern performance vernacular. This has enabled designers to work with and in a variety of mediums to create the performance environment. Classic works are interpreted for their contemporary relevance and are often placed within recognisably Australian settings. It is these productions that often attract the most critical interest and audiences, since many will have previously experienced and interpreted the work in other ways.

During his time as artistic director of Playbox however, Aubrey Mellor has encountered the problems for audiences when classic European texts are updated, and links this to the relatively small number of audiences and productions cultivated in Australia:

> We have a big problem in Australia because we have so few events for people who are interested in theatre to go to … Modern European classics have hardly even begun to be a part of our repertoire here yet. Shakespeare still dominates and so we have been bolder with Shakespeare than with any other playwright … If we were to do a Jacobean play the period comes back at us. What we try to do is tell the audience a little bit about the period, because we know they are ignorant about it.

▲ Plate 44 **A Midsummer Night's Dream**
by Benjamin Britten
Australian Opera
1993
venue: Opera Theatre, Sydney Opera House
director: Baz Luhrmann
set and costume designers: Catherine
Martin and Bill Marron

lighting designer: Nigel Levings
photo: OA archives
in photo: Christopher Josey as Oberon,
King of the Faeries, with Puck
(Tyler Coppin) and the child Oberon
stole from Tytania

'By placing the opera into the exotic British Raj era, Luhrmann explained: "We've striven to restore the magic. *A Midsummer Night's Dream* is a simple, or better still, a naive tale, and we have striven to keep that naivete in our telling of it. But there are very dark layers in it — great fears and terrors." As part of their research into this era, Luhrmann, Martin and Marron went to Jaiphur. They travelled a few hundred metres from their Western style hotel to an outdoor theatre in the jungle. The theatre itself was festooned with fairy lights and little hangings of gold and red spangled paper: "as we went through the jungle to reach it, there was the weird screeching of peacocks in our ears. The very exoticism of it seemed to be a return to childhood mysteries".'

[Baz Luhrmann interviewed by A. Clarke, 'The magical world of *A Midsummer Night's Dream*', *Australian Opera News*, no. 24, June 1993, pp. 2-3]

For example, if there is a production of *Hamlet*, it may be the only production of *Hamlet* on in that town for maybe ten years. There will be a whole audience who has never seen the play before. Whereas if you are in England you could see ten *Hamlets* within a radius of 50 miles at any one time. I think we are caught between wanting to do something new and wanting to hang on to certain things that are to do with the integrity of the original play and the traditions associated with that play. This is probably why design (and the productions) are not very brave in Australia to any great degree. It makes us all slightly inhibited. Design directions are less bold in Australia than in other countries.

If you see a [classic Australian] play like *Summer of the Seventeenth Doll* you will see it so many times in its original, naturalistic setting — a terrace house. Then somebody like Jean-Pierre Mignon [former artistic director of ANThill Theatre] comes along and does a production where he sits the actors on top of columns [see Foreword, fig. iii]. By throwing away naturalism he brought out the Greek tragedy aspects in the work. Ray Lawler the playwright got terribly excited about that, even though the play is a real Arthur Miller-type play. It made us see it afresh. [In the same way] you can do anything you like with *Hamlet*. You cannot damage it. The more known it is the more we look for a new approach.[8]

When defining the process that she, Baz Luhrmann and other collaborators use when approaching a new production, Martin (pls 44, 45, 46 and 47) uses the word 'storytellers'. She simplifies the analysis of a script or libretto by asking the simple questions: What is this story about? How clear is it? Will the audience understand who everyone is in the play on a very basic level? Whether they are producing a classic opera such as *La Bohème* (pl. 16, fig. 23) or a film of *Romeo and Juliet* or a new play (and later film) such as *Strictly Ballroom* the Luhrmann and Martin philosophy is that they

> try and tell a story in the most simple sense. My first approach to anything, whether it's Chekhov or Williamson, is to read the play and to try and work out for myself what the story is. It would be very interesting to talk to David Williamson about how he views it all or how he envisaged the original play, but any work is the starting point, and then the collaboration of other people surround it. It is going to be something different every time.[9]

When asked to choreograph *The Nutcracker* (pls 48, 49, fig. 40) for the Australian Ballet's thirtieth anniversary, Graeme Murphy agreed on the proviso that it could become something more relevant for Australian audiences. Thus he and his designer Kristian Fredrikson added an entirely new beginning to the ballet that placed its context firmly within Australia. They created the 'memoryscape' of Clara, formerly a great ballerina of the

▶ Plate 45 **A Midsummer Night's Dream**
Australian Opera
1993
see pl. 44
photo: OA archives
in photo: Tyler Coppin as the blue-skinned Puck

▶ Plate 46 **A Midsummer Night's Dream**
Australian Opera
1993
see pl. 44
photo: OA archives
Martin's costume drawings of the Faeries — Puck, Oberon and Tytania.

▶ Plate 47 **A Midsummer Night's Dream**
Australian Opera
1993
see pl. 44
photo: OA archives
Martin's set model.

► Figure 40 **The Nutcracker**

Australian Ballet

1992

see pl. 48

photographer: Peter Holderness

One of Fredrikson's designs for Clara, played by Miranda Coney.

Ballets Russes who emigrated to Australia. The storyline followed Clara through the Imperial Palace of Tsar Nicholas, the premiere of *The Nutcracker* at the Maryinsky Theatre, through a myriad of exotic locations toured by the Ballets Russes, into the grey harbour of Melbourne and ended where it began, in a steamy Bondi Beach apartment on Christmas eve. It is here that Clara, her memory and life fading, unites her friends one last time and spins dreams from her memories. Said Fredrikson on the intricate remaking of Clara's fairytale life:

► Figures 41a and 41b **The Nutcracker**

Australian Ballet

1992

see pl. 48

photographer: Peter Holderness

fig. 41a: This costume was modelled closely on outfits worn by members of the Imperial Ballet. Similarly, the opulent costumes of Diaghilev's Ballets Russes were inspired by the clothes of that company's wealthy patrons.

fig. 41b: In the battle scene, Rats wearing Russian greatcoats fought Bolshevik soldiers.

The minute we said that she was coming to Australia, it developed the whole story … We worked through the synopsis, developed a detailed dramatic structure, and found that, without knowing it, we were guiding ourselves through the history of the Australian Ballet. There was a logic that almost took us by surprise.[10]

It was a brilliantly conceived work, but one that brought Murphy and Fredrikson as much criticism as acclaim from audiences used to the traditional sugar-sweet interpretations of the piece.

‘The Waltz of the Flowers’ unravels from the stories and memories of Clara's Russian emigré friends. As they share Christmas in her modest Bondi apartment, Clara recalls the Tsar's ball to which she, as prima ballerina, was invited.

▲ Plate 48 **The Nutcracker**
by Peter Tchaikovsky
Australian Ballet
1992
venue: Opera Theatre, Sydney Opera House
director: Graeme Murphy
set and costume designer: Kristian Fredrikson
lighting designer: John Drummond Montgomery
photographer: Don McMurdo
in photo: Artists of the Australian Ballet perform 'The Waltz of the Flowers'

► Plate 49 **The Nutcracker**
Australian Ballet
1992
see pl. 48
photographer: Don McMurdo
in photo: *Pas de deux* with Adam Marchant and Vicki Attard

Text with pictures

Since the majority of theatre design[11] is in response to a given text, Australian theatre writing has had a huge influence on the ways in which designers have chosen to portray character and environment on stage. Certain styles of writing demand certain design responses and solutions. As an example, the well-made play of the late nineteenth century created the need for box sets and poetic naturalism in design, as well as acting. Contemporary theatre writers (and directors) are very aware of the possibilities offered by staging and special effects and will often consult with designers or technicians while writing and rehearsing.

Image can be as powerful as text in the creation of meaning if audiences remain fluent in 'reading' and understanding visual metaphors. Audiences react to different visual stimuli depending on the cultural icons and symbols apparent within the work. Just as Shakespeare wrote for a bare platform stage within The Globe, allowing himself the freedom to traverse seas and fight bloody battles on stage, much of the work that has been

▼ Figure 42 **Away**
by Michael Gow
Sydney Theatre Company
1987
venue: Drama Theatre, Sydney Opera House
director: Richard Wherrett
set and costume designer: Robert Kemp
lighting designer: Nick Schlieper
photographer: Sandy Edwards
in photo: (left to right) Robert Alexander, Steve Vidler and Anna Volska on 'the beach'

Kemp redesigned the successful Stables show for transfer to the Opera House's Drama Theatre. With a much greater stage area on which to work, Kemp said that 'it was a matter of getting the actors closer to the audience while making them appear like small dots against the infinity of the universe'.

(Bob Evans, 'Designs on life and art', *Sydney Morning Herald*, 29 April 1987, p. 20)

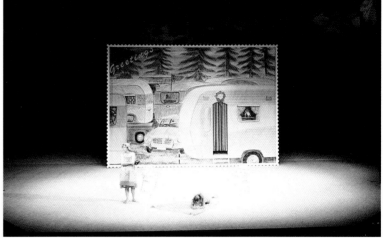

Carpenter's compact 'holiday snapshot' settings served as a memorable foil to the vastness of the surrounding Australian beachscape while providing strongly descriptive focal points for the individual families on holiday.

written by contemporary playwrights requires up to thirty locations or more within the one play. The scenic conventions needed to keep the action flowing in these episodic dramas has freed set and costume designers from realism and increased the importance of lighting as a major design medium. Writers such as Stephen Sewell, Louis Nowra, David Williamson, Hannie Rayson, Tobsha Learner and Noëlle Janaczewska have all incorporated the fluidity of Shakespearean staging into their work. It is a style that allows for action to flow from one scene, one room, one time to another. It goes back to the traditions of simple staging and removes the need for box sets or elaborate scenery. It sets up a challenge that designers can respond to enthusiastically.

In one classic example, *Away* by writer–director Michael Gow (pls 50, 51, figs 34, 42), the action moves from school halls to living rooms to holiday houses to lonely beaches. The most resonant image is that of the beach and its sense of vast space. Internal scenes can be simply indicated by props and strong lighting. The adults can become childlike 'fairies' with gaudy tinsel wings and 'magical tempest' lighting. The style of writing offers many design options. In Kim Carpenter's design for the 1987 STCSA production of *Away* (pl. 51), huge postcards became the linking device between scenes, stylising the interior backgrounds into cartoon environments. They framed the action and pushed the audience focus downstage. When the final postcard was removed in the final act, the long beach running across the back of the stage and the blue skyscape of clouds filled the space and were breathtaking in their expanse.

Shaun Gurton talked of being 'both excited and scared' by the possibilities presented by Australian writing, particularly when taking visual ideas into the written landscapes of those such as Louis Nowra, David Malouf and Stephen Sewell:

▲ Plate 52 **The Blind Giant is Dancing**

by Stephen Sewell

Lighthouse Theatre Company

1983

venue: Playhouse, Adelaide Festival
Centre

director: Neil Armfield

set and costume designer: Stephen
Curtis

lighting designer: Nigel Levings

photographer: David Wilson

I love using water and earth and dirt and mud. Being English-born, I've always been fascinated by how one can take this strange landscape and put it on stage … I love it when playwrights write 'a full dinner table setting in the snowfields', and it then changes to 'a world that's turned upside down'. It is much more interesting than someone saying, 'We'll need three chairs here'.[12]

Judith Cobb had a similar response to the work of American playwright Sam Shepard when she designed *A Lie of the Mind* (MTC, 1987) for Simon Phillips. She saw parallels between the Australian and American landscape in a spatial sense:

I love Sam Shepard's writing. It's raw, and poetic. It is harsh and poignant. You can really relate to it, being an Australian in the middle of a large hot country. It's not unlike being in the middle of America. The MTC production of *A Lie of the Mind* at the Russell Street Theatre had real trees on stage; twenty-seven of them with twisted white trunks and no leaves, naturalistic furniture sitting in really dusty sand (like desert sand) and a large full-in-the-sky moon. It echoed the visual poetry of the language … I love to pare things back and simplify everything so you end up with *essential* elements on stage. I'm not keen on lots of decoration or set dressing. I can understand that it is important for some texts but I do relish paring the design back and having simple, strong imagery. The design determines the way an actor is perceived. Visual contradictions can be evoked so that interest is created and the audience is stimulated.[13]

▶ Plate 53 **The Rivers of China**

by Alma de Groen

Sydney Theatre Company

1987

venue: Wharf 1, Sydney Theatre Company

director: Peter Kingston

set designer: Eamon D'Arcy

costume designer: Anne-Maree Dalziel

lighting designer: Mark Shelton

photographer: Hugh Hamilton

'Eamon D'Arcy's set is a welcome pleasure — imaginative in its imagery and suggestion of the almost infinite space through which a mind such as Mansfield's might travel; it functions as an abstract expression of her person.'

[Angela Bennie, 'Feminist odyssey a journey to nowhere', *Australian*, 11 September 1987, p. 9]

'Eamon and I had been discussing the play during my writing of [*The Rivers of China*] and even before I began ... It was Eamon who said that one of the things he wanted to do was to put a mind on stage.'

[Alma de Groen in an interview with Tom Bannerman, 27 August 1991, sourced from T. Bannerman, Image and scenographic considerations in Alma de Groen's *The Rivers of China*, unpublished essay, Department of Theatre Studies, University of New South Wales, Sydney, 1991]

▶ Plate 54 **To Traverse Water**

IHOS Opera

1992 — national tour

director and composer: Constantine Koukias

production director: Werner Ihlenfeld

choreographer: Christos Linou

set designer: Ann Wulff

costume designer: Caz Pellow-Jones

lighting designer: Jan Wawrzynczuk and Hugh McSpedden

photographer: Ann Wulff

The opera depicted a Greek woman's journey to her new homeland Australia, exploring an immigrant's cultural displacement. The audience walked from one side of the space to another, following her experiences and changing their original seating perspective. Visual metaphors for the journey involved flooding the warehouse venue as well as installing a dream-like corps de ballet of boats floating above the audience's heads during the water sequences.

'Part one ends with Despina's highly stylised journey, hand-in-hand with Galani, across an immense space. This great unknown is suggested superbly, psychodelically [sic], by patterns of light moulding movement and space, by masses of water that begin to flow over the floor, and by the 'ballet of boats' hanging high up, diagonally from the rafters. The lights go from blue to gold and to green and purple, now with long shadows and smoke effects, now luminous and radiant.'

[M. Shevtsova, Greek–Australian odysseys in a multi-cultural world, unpublished essay, University of Sydney, Sydney, 1995, p. 4]

Landscape, light and space: Australian design(ers) defined

Clear skies and flat horizons have affected the way in which Australians have traditionally perceived their position, both geographically and on stage. The Australian landscape has been the inspiration for countless writers, painters, filmmakers and photographers, as well as imprinting itself into the cultural consciousness of a people. Although it has been romanticised, bastardised and criticised on different occasions, the notion of an Australian landscape remains a strong image. Design responds to this. There is a strong sense of the horizontal plane, and the visual relationship of people to the vast Australian environment. This does not mean a constant portrayal of stereotyped 'outbacks' of hot sand and red earth. The contemporary theatre is generally dominated by more urban concerns. It does however indicate the use of landscape as a departure point for the personal mindscapes of characters.

Since a unique element of the Australian landscape is the quality of light and the ways in which that affects the ways colour, shadow and tone are perceived, the lighting design can often define an Australian style. The quality of light is unique and, as John Rayment (pl. 55) believes, is a huge inspiration in his work:

> The Australian landscape and the quality of light that we have here — it's marvellous. It is brilliant. It is what sets us apart. The more I go overseas the more people remark on my bold use and intensity of colour. And that seems quite endemic to the Australian designers in general. If there was an influence that you cannot quantify, it is that you spend your life in Australia, and what we think of light.[14]

If there is a common defining factor in Australian performance design it is hotly debated by the designers themselves. The following quotes were in response to the question, 'Is it possible (or necessary) to define an Australian design style and, if so, what influences it?', and come directly from conversations with designers across Australia.

Most designers were reluctant to define 'Australian' design. Not one felt that there was an overall style that represented Australian theatre, since the resources that are drawn on are so diverse. From the bulk of responses, however, the one common theme was an exploration of landscape, light and space.

▼ Figure 43 **To Traverse Water**
IHOS Opera
1992 – national tour
see pl. 54
photographer: Ann Wulff

'Part two opens with familiar all-Australian icons that clamour for immediate recognition … There is a Hills Hoist, a backyard lawn, a barbecue, a white outdoor table and chairs, a concrete footpath that the married Despina hoses down, and a lawn-mower, start-up rope, smoke and all.'

(M. Shevtsova)

▲ Plate 55 **Harold in Italy**
by Justin Flemming
music by Berlioz and Max Lambert
Sydney Theatre Company in association
with One Extra Dance Company
1989
venue: Drama Theatre, Sydney Opera
House
directors: Richard Wherrett and Kay Tai
Chan
set designer: Brian Thomson
costume designer: Terry Ryan
lighting designer: John Rayment
projections designer: Peter Holderness
photographer: Don McMurdo

This piece was inspired by Berlioz's score *Harold in Italy* (which in turn had been inspired by Byron's poem *Childe Harold's Pilgrimage*), and used both actors and dancers to create the mythical story of a half-woman/half-horse. Using a revolving glass pyramid with projected images reflected on all facets, Wherrett and Thomson found a sculpturally inspired way to form an intangible world of forests and moving skies. The two front panels of the pyramid could lift up and out to form a flat reflective glass wall and, by descending, trap the beast-woman within a glass cage.

▶ Plate 56 **Shepherd on the Rocks**

by Patrick White

State Theatre Company of South Australia

1987

venue: Playhouse, Adelaide Festival Centre

director: Neil Armfield

set designer: Brian Thomson

costume designer: Julie Lynch

lighting designer: John Comeadow

photographer: David Wilson

Is there an Australian style? Most designers around the world would say that they approach each piece on its own merit and don't necessarily impose a national style on to that work. Therefore anything that comes across as being particular to one country is really for other people (and maybe even critics and scholars a decade later) to objectively assign to a body of work. I think in Australia we would like to think that we can apply a certain boldness and risk-taking — in not just the design but in other areas of production as well. But boldness and risk-taking is not exclusive to Australia either. I think because we are geographically so far away from Europe and America it is harder to broaden our frame of reference regularly with visits and first-hand exposure to other performance work. The tyranny of distance can often create an individual style that is not influenced by other works.[15]

John Hoenig (production manager and lighting designer)

There is something broad and panoramic about a lot of Australian work. In both cases there is the sense of isolation — whether it is to deal with living in an urban environment or a natural one. A sense of isolation is always there, and conflict.[16]

Wendy Osmond (set, costume and exhibition designer)

Perhaps our relationship or indeed our lack of relationship with the landscape we inhabit is one of the reasons why we are so often drawn to the epic, the elemental, the classic core. This may help to explain our constant need to reassess and interpret the classics.[17]

Jennie Tate (set and costume designer)

The way we work in Australia is that we tend to tailor everything towards the common goal. This leads to a lot of compromises, and in purely visual terms sometimes a very watered down design that you look at. The area that interests me is how you get that degree of boldness and still seek to serve the whole process rather than just making a fantastic-looking picture and letting everybody swim and flounder within it. No-one I've ever come across in Europe has a clear picture of an Australian style, or probably has not had any exposure to it. Those that have, perceive it (and I think not without justification) as basically English in form, look and feel. I hasten to add that I think it is an advantage. I think there are some things that Australian actors do markedly well. There is a particular style of very truthful naturalism that Australian actors slip into very quickly and do extremely well. They are not nearly so disposed towards stylised or formalised theatre in general, and I think that aligns them with English theatre. It may be a difference of degree rather than approach. I don't see enormous differences between Australia and England.[18]

Nick Schlieper

(set and lighting designer)

'My work derives inspiration from the visual arts, in particular the paintings of the Belgian surrealist artist Paul Delvaux. Because these paintings are in a sense landscapes of the soul where anything seems possible, a *mis-en-scène* is able to be built (inspired by the paintings) in which both an image and its timelessness are emphasised. The intention here is to stimulate a relationship between the performance and the audience which allows for a greater interplay between the active and passive possibilities of both.'

(notes — Jenny Kemp, 1996)

▼ Plate 57 **The Black Sequin Dress**
devised by Jenny Kemp
Playbox
1996
venue: Beckett Theatre, Melbourne
director: Jenny Kemp
set and costume designer: Jacqueline Everitt
lighting designer: Ben Cobham
photographer: Jeff Busby
in photo: (left to right) Natasha Herbert, Mary Sitarenos, Margaret Mills (lying down), Greg Stone and Ian Scott

'The setting is a nightclub with a shiny floor. Into this space run two tunnels. The upstage tunnel has a railway track which runs straight across the nightclub floor ... The back wall of the nightclub consists of a large white wall which can become a wall of light, or can be projected onto ... Stage right, about half-way upstage, is a rectangle of earth where a woman lies down to sleep.'

(programme notes — Jenny Kemp)

◄ Plate 58 **The Flying Dutchman**
by Richard Wagner
Victoria State Opera
1986–87
venue: State Theatre, Victorian Arts
Centre
director: Elke Neidhardt
set and costume designer: Shaun Gurton
lighting designer: Nick Schlieper
photographer: Jeff Busby
in photo: Marilyn Richardson climbs up
towards a projection of the Flying
Dutchman (Malcolm Donnelly)

Design is international. People who are excellent at what they do are far and few between and their work will travel.[19]

Michael Scott-Mitchell (set, costume and event designer)

I don't think there is anything specifically different between my way of designing and that of Australian designers. There are always differences between the people who do it. I always think it is like sex; you don't know how anyone else is doing it, you only know how you do it yourself.[20]

Rory Dempster (lighting designer)

I get really pissed off in this country. I think there is a great sense of Australian design here and fabulous colour, but having seen a number of productions of *The Man From Mukinupin* by Dorothy Hewett I've never seen a row of hills at the back that looks essentially Australian yet. Dorothy Hewett is a great poet and dramatic writer of her own culture and her own landscape. It's written in the words and you can feel it. I don't think many designers know their own outback. I think we tend to do a lot of overseas work, musicals and overseas plays and we very rarely get to do an Australian play. Everyone's very good at doing a caricatured gum tree. But a piece of cut-out scenery is not Dorothy Hewett.[21]

Ian Robinson (set, costume and event designer)

▼ Plate 59 **Meander**
by Sibelius
Australian Ballet
1984
venue: State Theatre, Victorian Arts Centre
and Opera Theatre, Sydney Opera House
choreographer: Graeme Murphy
set and costume designer: Roger Kirk
lighting designer: William Akers
photographer: Branco Gaica

I think that one of the things I am critical of generally about Australian designers is that they have fallen a long way behind painters in the ways they see the landscape. I have seen a number of Australian productions set in landscapes that actually look as if they're set in an American Western. It is unfortunate that so many people in the Australian theatre have been (and still are) unfamiliar with the Australian environment and don't see it directly. Their reference points are in fact very often the cinema or other theatre design, and they are very concerned about fashion. I think fashion is a very oppressive and repressive thing. I think it wouldn't hurt for Australians to be brave enough not to worry about whether their productions look as if they're going to stand up as 'fashionable' in London or New York. It is just reinforcing the assumption that those places are the artistic capitals of the world, assuming there is an artistic capital in the world.[22]

Andrew Ross (artistic director of Black Swan Theatre Company)

I certainly believe there is an Australian light and that is what excites me. That is what brings a lump to my throat. The feeling of being able to reproduce it. I have toured a lot through the desert and the Australian outback enjoying the light. Trying to recreate that on stage is as all painters have tried to do with Australian light. It is a fascinating thing and there is nothing else like it in the world. The clarity of it, the crispness, the way that colours come up so cleanly. I can see it in my brain but to put it in words is very difficult. The land is so big that you do always have that feeling of shadow and the length of everything — which is one of the reasons I like to work with a lot of sidelight. To me the beautiful times of the day are dawn and dusk, with that length of the shadows. The clarity of everything at those times, it is just a moment when it all clicks in. Everything seems to become very simple and clear and very sharp-edged, which is what sidelighting tends to do.[23]

Geoff Cobham (lighting designer and production manager)

▶ Plate 60 **The Hope**

by Heather Nimmo

Playbox, in association with the West Australian Theatre Company

1987

venue: The Studio, Victorian Arts Centre

director: Andrew Ross

set designer: Robert Juniper

costume designer: Steve Nolan

lighting designer: Duncan Ord

photographer: Robert Walker

in photo: Juniper's original set painting

Juniper's painting for the floor and backcloth drew inspiration from the Western Australian landscape. The finished canvas stretched over the entire stage floor and continued up to the fly lines.

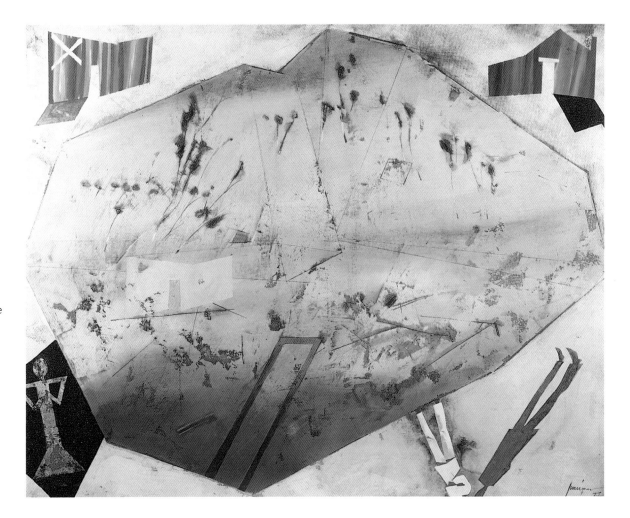

The things I find appealing are the edges of the new world; the trailer park edges, the frayed edges, the dreary suburban edges, the edges with fantastic tension, lacklustre and bad taste. The badly put together edges. I find that particularly potent as a source for theatre. They cannot be fully reconstituted on stage. They simply become a palette that you put together in different ways. You can do Shakespeare, Molière, Shepard or Lawler with these ingredients. It is, however, rather hard doing Williamson in this model.[24]

Peter Corrigan (set and costume designer and architect)

If something is relative to the Australian environment (whether it is an Australian script or not) it definitely alters which way you go with your colour palette. Something that I find is really strong in Australian characters is that there is a quality — like the environment has weathered them as people — which somehow comes through in the costume design, hand in hand with the quality of the character. You might get a character, for instance, that wears glasses and carries an umbrella on sunny days. So they are not going to be very affected or weathered by the environment. But the fact that they have to cover themselves up to protect themselves from the sun affects your costume design. Someone else might just have a Bonds T-shirt that is faded by the sun, with an incredible tan like your average Australian workman on the streets. So often your characters are affected by the environment of Australia.[25]

Amanda Lovejoy (costume designer and naturopath)

I've designed an enormous amount of new Australian work and I think that there is often a component in Australian works that gives them a slightly daggy, humane quality. Louis Nowra's plays on the surface are quite slick and stylish, but underneath there is always a component that is awkward, slightly clumsy or not slick. It is that ingredient that I think is particularly Australian, and particularly interesting in theatre. I think it is on that level that we connect with the human being in the audience. It is relatively easy to create spectacle and say, 'Wow, that looks great!' when the spectacle is pulled off brilliantly but, personally, I think that is what film does particularly well. I would always be trying to find something other than [spectacle] in theatre.[26]

Stephen Curtis (set and costume designer and former head of design at the Australian Film and Television School)

◄ Figure 44 **Dinkum Assorted**
by Linda Aronson
Sydney Theatre Company
1988
venue: Drama Theatre, Sydney Opera House
director: John Bell
set and costume designer: Stephen Curtis
lighting designer: Nigel Levings
photographer: Peter Holderness
in photo: Curtis' costume renderings for Florrie (Althea McGrath) and Little Beat (Maree D'Arcy)

▲ Figure 45 **Mr Melancholy**

by Matt Cameron

Griffin Theatre Company

1995

venue: The Stables, Sydney

director: Ros Horin

set and costume designer: Michael Wilkinson

photographer: Robert McFarlane

in photo: Andrew Gilbert with arms outstretched; Odile le Clezio and Jenny Vuletic behind

I have no interest whatsoever in doing the outback, the desert or the bush. It is dross — a load of romantic nonsense — the stuff of Sydney. When you use sand to represent the desert it is the death of imagination. Sand sets are an old joke, and a comprehensive yawn ... Stick a red gel in a lantern and get on with it ... Allow the audience to imagine it more and save your money.[27]

Peter Corrigan (set and costume designer and architect)

A visual theme of the original Belvoir Street production was the eternal state of night and the effects of an omnipresent moon. As madcap scenes raced from regal to vaudeville, the lighting chased them, mirroring the spontaneous nature of the performers, all 'seemingly' under the influence of the moon.

◄ Plate 61 **Popular Mechanicals**
by Keith Robinson, William Shakespeare and Tony Taylor
Belvoir Street Theatre
1991
venue: Belvoir Street Theatre, Sydney
director: Geoffrey Rush
set and costume designer: Stephen Curtis
lighting designer: Mark Howett with Liz Allen
photographer: Marco Bok

▼ Figure 46 **Popular Mechanicals**
Belvoir Street Theatre
1991
see pl. 61
photographer: Marco Bok

'The fictional world of the *Popular Mechanicals* is a hybrid one. They stand with one leg in the twentieth century and the other in the seventeenth, where ruffs nestle against polyester skivvies, gold phones stand near cowpats, childhood jokes share the same scenes as iambic pentameter. In a yellow world of madness, there is gunge and gloss, like the bit of floor between your stove and your fridge.'

[MTC programme notes – Geoffrey Rush, 1992]

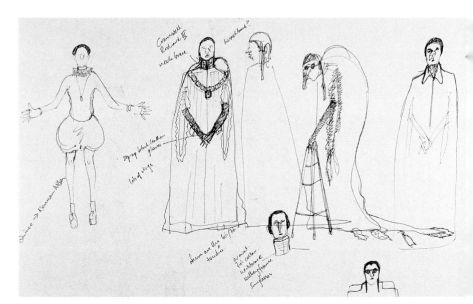

When discussing his design work, Curtis used *Popular Mechanicals* as an example of what he strives to do: 'A lot of very strongly visual design work for theatre remains "design", and the actor must fit into it or remain as an appendage. Their relationship is as a "theatrical being", rather than a human being. I have always been interested in adding an ingredient to which an audience could respond very personally — a very tacky or homely element. [In] *Popular Mechanicals* ... we set up a sense of quite homely squalor so that there was a mixture of things as you would find in an actors' rehearsal room ... I often think theatre (and particularly theatre in the past) sets itself up as being an artificial world. The more that style is pushed as being the most important thing,

▲ Plate 62 **Popular Mechanicals**
Belvoir Street Theatre
1992
see pl. 61
photographer: Marco Bok
in photo: Keith Robinson, Paul Blackwell, Kerry Walker and Gillian Hyde

the more pretentious and meaningless it becomes. A show may look great but unless the audience is able to feel on a really basic level that they are part of that world (just as the actors are part of it), then for me it always misses out. The work that I remember most fondly is where the theatrical world and the human world have been combined very strongly'.

[S. Curtis, interview with author, 15 November 1993]

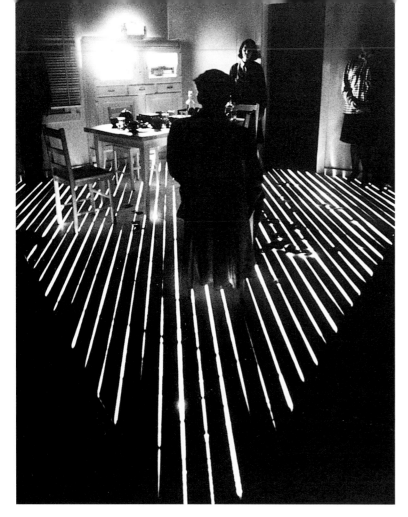

Simplicity and suggestion

Summing up the way in which Australian design is being utilised and constructed on contemporary stages, Judith Hoddinott (fig. 47) spoke for many of the designers interviewed when she described her own approach to performance design:

> I think stylisation can say a lot more about what is the content of the play and the hidden text rather than following the stage directions quite literally; rather than creating the minutiae — the wallpaper, the skirting boards — and getting bogged down in detail. It is a larger stroke than that, and like a painting it creates a big sweep across the stage canvas ... Don't have a prop on stage unless it's used. I find when I go and see other people's design work the most rewarding thing is how they can use the same chair or table in different ways. I really don't enjoy seeing a million tricks done on stage. I find it exhausting when the audience's focus is changed and grabbed from what's really important. Theatre is about the action, what the play is really about, not just that the toaster's popping or the kettle's boiling. Sometimes that detail is important, but I personally don't find it interesting.[28]

Hoddinott's quote reflects Thomson's quote at the beginning of the chapter. Design has become less illustrative of fact and more suggestive of meaning. This is understandable when considering that the majority of funded companies are existing on inadequate budgets for their planned production seasons, and designers are frequently employed to come up with solutions for staging problems with a minimum of money and time. This is not specific to Australia but representative of performance and performance design internationally. Other contributing factors are that mainstream audiences are more willing to participate as spectators in non-naturalistic and non-theatre environments than a generation before, and their increased visual literacy has been promoted by the televisual and electronic mediums. Simplicity, stylisation, interpretation and practicality would seem to be at the heart of contemporary design in Australia.

▲ Figure 47 **The Secret House**
by Noel Hedda
Griffin Theatre Company
1987
venue: The Stables, Sydney
director: Michael Gow
set and costume designer: Judith Hoddinott
lighting designer: Liz Allen
photo: Griffin archives
in photo: David Franklin, Bob Hornery, Pat Thomas and Susan Leith on Hoddinott's set as a light passes like an X-ray through their world

1   T. Schofield, interview with author, 22 November 1993.

2   The 'new wave' of playwriting included the work of Alex Buzo, Jack Hibberd, Michael Boddy, Dorothy Hewett, John Romeril and the early works of David Williamson. Patrick White could also be included here, although his work is not usually associated with this group nor the APG. The 'second wave' encompassed the early work of Stephen Sewell, Louis Nowra and Alma de Groen among others.

3   'Stubbies' is the slang term for the hard-wearing drill shorts favoured by Australian workmen.

4   J. Litson, interview with author, 15 March 1995.

5   A. Carter, interview with author, 19 August 1993.

6   A. French, interview with author, 13 April 1995.

7   J. Tate, interview with author, 23 November 1993.

8   A. Mellor, interview with author, 14 March 1995.

9   C. Martin, interview with author, 4 April 1995.

10 K. Fredrikson, interview with author, 18 November 1993.

11 The term 'theatre design' is used here to define text-based theatre design, not non-text, dance or opera-based design. The term 'performance design' is used when all forms are being discussed.

12 S. Gurton, interview with author, 23 August 1993.

13 J. Cobb, interview with author, 24 August 1993.

14 J. Rayment, interview with author, 14 March 1995.

15 J. Hoenig, interview with author, 5 March 1995.

16 W. Osmond, interview with author, 22 March 1995.

17 Notes delivered by Jennie Tate as part of 'Australian Scenography since 1945', a paper presented to the Asia: Scenography Conference, Tokyo, 1993.

18 N. Schlieper, interview with author, 12 March 1995.

19 M. Scott-Mitchell, interview with author, 20 November 1993.

20 R. Dempster, interview with author, 10 March 1995.

21 I. Robinson, interview with author, 17 November 1993.

22 A. Ross, interview with author, 10 March 1995.

23 G. Cobham, interview with author, 9 March 1995.

24 P. Corrigan, interview with author, 23 March 1995.

25 A. Lovejoy, interview with author, 24 March 1995.

26 S. Curtis, interview with author, 15 November 1993.

27 P. Corrigan, interview with author, 23 March 1995.

28 J. Hoddinott, interview with author, 15 November 1993.

Set on the rooftop of an outback jail during a flash flood, the tense relationship between Aboriginal and white Australians was played out on a tiny stage. The production received critical acclaim for its examination of deaths in custody, and for its simple yet evocative setting. Hoenig incorporated into his lighting rig the effect of a helicopter descending onto the stage (pre-*Miss Saigon*), with great success.

 Figure 48 **Black River**
music by Andrew Schultz, libretto by Julie-Anne Schultz
Sydney Metropolitan Opera
1987
venues: Parade Theatre, NIDA, Sydney and the Victorian Arts Centre, Melbourne
director: John Wregg
choreographer: Pierre Thibaudeau
set and costume designer: Derrick Cox
costume co-ordination: Tim Kobin
lighting designer: John Hoenig
photographer: John Clutterbuck
in photo: Maroochy Baramba spotlit by helicopters

The nature of collaboration

Collaborating with other people artistically seems almost impossible for a lot of artists. They don't want to share their concept or give away any ideas until it is all finalised by themselves. In a performance piece I'm quite happy to be a collaborator. You have to be, as a designer. If you can't become a part of that, then all you do is make your own visual statement and you are not much fun to work with. When you impose yourself, your personality and your view, the production becomes about an artist doing their own thing and everything must fall into line with it, as opposed to all of us using our expertise to enhance the final product. Such is the nature of collaboration.

ANDREW CARTER[1]

◀ Plate 63 **Two Feet**

Meryl Tankard and the Australian Dance Theatre

1994 — national tour

see fig. 50

photographer: Regis Lansac

in photo: Meryl Tankard as Olga Spessivtzeva

▼ Figure 49 **Kikimora**

devised by Meryl Tankard

Meryl Tankard and the Australian Dance Theatre

1993

venue: Space Theatre, Adelaide Festival Centre

choreographer: Meryl Tankard

set and lighting design: Regis Lansac

costume design: Meryl Tankard and Gaelle Mellis

photographer: Regis Lansac

in photo: Meryl Tankard as a Kikimora, a malevolent Japanese female spirit

Design communion

The roots of theatre are in ritual and ceremony. The act of sharing a story, describing a history and defining a belief is an act of communion. Not only is there a relationship established with the persons present watching, but also a combined effort behind the scenes and beyond the theatre walls that has made the interpretation or creation unique in its presentation.

Collaboration is the oil that keeps the wheels in motion on and off our stages. It can be explosive, argumentative, diverse and difficult. It can go on for years between individuals; each collaboration mining greater and deeper depths of understanding and trust. Alternatively, many performance partnerships change from project to project, giving choreographers, directors, actors and designers the chance to work with a diverse range of performing arts practitioners.

The language of text, music, bodies in performance, a director's thoughts, a designer's sketches and models are all dialects of the performance language that the audience hopes to understand. To find a creative collaborator who 'speaks' the same performance language as oneself is rare and precious. Those partnerships can open up new worlds of movement and meaning, pushing the boundaries of performance further. In Australia there have been some extraordinary partnerships between artists in the last two decades. These can be seen in the range of productions that are still remembered and talked about by audiences long after the performance has closed. Some names are immediately linked; names such as Luhrmann and Martin, Murphy, Rayment and Fredrikson, Armfield, Levings, Schofield and Thomson, Kosky and Corrigan, Hodgman, Lewis and Tripp, Phillips and Gurton. Others are not so obvious, nor promoted so well. Smaller companies and smaller budgets do not excite the public eye as often, nor as loudly. Their long-time collaborations are not so talked about or noticed by those unfamiliar with the industry. Lighting designers are less visible than set and costume designers in reviews. Directors and choreographers change direction and, with that, their designers. The performance world is a small one in Australia. Stay in it for long enough and one will probably work with everyone at some stage. Collaborative skills are important. The common thoughts that tie the following impressions together therefore are that satisfying, successful productions are most often about the relationships established behind the scenes, and whether the collaboration has been synergic, not whether the individual elements of a design were noticed, or a portfolio expanded.

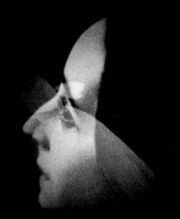

'In Tankard's 1988 solo work *Two Feet* (the story of Russian ballerina Olga Spessivtzeva), Lansac's projections function mainly as evocative backdrops. Spessivtzeva seems to disappear and reappear in and out of imperceptible breaks in a brick wall. On the whole however, the projections serve to illustrate the narrative — such as with enlargements of the instructions for the Shrimp Dance the young dancer is learning, and of the photographs of the triumphant or despairing Spessivtzeva.'

(Ann Hutcheson, 'The photographic art of Regis Lansac', *Dance Australia*, Aug./Sept. 1991, p. 25)

▲ Figure 50 **Two Feet**
Meryl Tankard and the Australian Dance Theatre
1994
venue: The Playhouse, Adelaide Festival Centre and Her Majesty's Theatre, Sydney
director: Meryl Tankard
set designer: Eamon D'Arcy
costume designer: Dianne Bridson
lighting designer: Toby Harding
projections and visuals design: Regis Lansac
photographer: Regis Lansac

'The towering cliffs of silk act as an illimitable context for the action and are

constantly alive, moving with their own respiration and reflecting the ripples of

water or the shadows of sailors, guards and watching shepherd. The suspended

▲ Plate 64 **Tristan und Isolde**

by Richard Wagner

Australian Opera

1990

venue: Concert Hall, Sydney Opera House

director: Neil Armfield

▼ Plate 65 **Tristan und Isolde**

Australian Opera

1990

see pl. 64

photo: OA archives

in photo: Marilyn Richardson as Isolde
and William Johns as Tristan

'Under Armfield's direction the starting
point for Brian Thomson and myself is
the creation of a work space which
acknowledges the stage architecture.
A playground complete with essential
devices is made, and within this
metaphorical space, a dream space is
created to convey the emotional scale
of the piece.'

[notes by Jennie Tate, part of 'Australian
Scenography since 1945', a paper
presented to the Asian Scenography
Conference, Tokyo, 1993]

More than any other recent production, *Tristan und Isolde* was reviewed (and criticised) on its set. The mount-

ing expectations of Australia's second production of *Tristan und Isolde* in over fifty years were reported in

every major paper on the east coast. The running debate of the limitations of the Concert Hall as a venue for

major operatic works seemed to have been silenced when Thomson's design was reviewed. Thomson had been

inspired by the thought of suspending the singers in a state of clouds, enveloping them in a totally

uncompromising and isolated world. Armfield agreed, interested in the possibilities of mixing glass, water and

silk (as suggested by Thomson's use of a glass sheet in the stage model) to capture the constantly shifting

spirit of the opera. He said, 'We had to provide a medium in which sound and light would be extraordinary'. This suited lighting designer Dempster's intuition 'that the world of the opera should be a world unto itself, which he would light entirely from within the stage'.

(J. Litson, 'Sumptuous and sensual', *Australian*, 4 February 1990, p. 10)

'The play is about repression, about people not fulfilling themselves, or fulfilling themselves at other people's expense. So there is a great advantage in setting it in the period in which it was written, the very end of the nineteenth century. The restriction of the clothes is a very strong metaphor in its own right. But when I looked through photographs I kept seeing all these marvellous pictures of the 1860s — big crinolines with wonderful dropped shoulders. We have ended up creating a period, manipulating form and detail to create something that is a real expression of the play ... You are looking at images and clothes that reflect psychological states.'

[Jennie Tate interviewed by Pamela Payne, 'Offences of perspective', *Bulletin*, 30 April 1991, pp. 108-9]

Working within the ensemble

In the world of performance design a successful collaboration is seen in the final stages of its creation: the first act of an opera, the rise of a curtain, the slow cross-fade from warm to cool and the tonal palette of a chorus's costumes against the texture of the sets. How well these elements work together depends on how integral designers are to the entire production process.

Australia has very few theatre companies that keep the same designers and actors on from season to season. The European-style ensemble theatre model has been resurrected many times but has seldom lasted longer than a few years. The companies that continue the longest are usually government-subsidised companies that retain an administrative core, hiring creative artists individually for each new production. This is best illustrated by the state theatre companies, and national opera and ballet companies, who can announce a season of work every year. Directors and designers come together for one or two of those shows and then move on. Although some names will gain popularity and begin to appear regularly, others will move on to the next company, the next show, the next collaboration.

One designer who has been a driving force in the way in which Australian audiences see theatre is Brian Thomson. His first professional collaborations were with Jim Sharman in the early 1970s. Their partnership resulted in now famous productions such as the *Rocky Horror Picture Show*, *Jesus Christ Superstar* and *Death in Venice*. Since working with Sharman, Thomson's portfolio of work now spans three decades of collaboration with most of Australia's top directors, including Richard Wherrett, Gale Edwards and Neil Armfield. He continues to work for both large and small-scale theatre productions, as well as for opera, dance and

▼ Plate 67 **The Government Inspector**
by Nikolai Gogol
Sydney Theatre Company
1991
venue: Drama Theatre, Sydney Opera House
director: Neil Armfield
set designer: Stephen Curtis
costume designer: Tess Schofield
lighting designer: Mark Shelton
photographer: Stephen Curtis

Curtis pushed beyond the limiting dimensions of the Drama Theatre's low proscenium by counterpointing it with a heavy ceiling piece, the sheer weight of which looked poised to crush the inhabitants as the play unravelled.

'The Government Inspector was a huge room that disappeared in false perspective; the floor, the ceiling and the walls all meeting at a point at the far end — the doors that the Inspector finally arrived at. It was a massive and very startling space to walk into because the full expanse of the Drama Theatre was used. The walls were lined with the clutter of Russian bribery; there were carpet rolls and furniture and things that would have been accrued by a corrupt official (who was the man whose house we were in). It was that component that provided the visual texture for the actors to make a home of that room rather than it being just a set that they were obliged to inhabit. It meant that you got a really interesting dynamic. It meant that the performers could be both subtle and at home there. For example Geoffrey Rush just put his arm on the table and slightly misjudged it (you know that old gag where the elbow goes off the table?), which in the context of the room he happened to be in, it looked like the kind of thing that anyone does when they're in a slightly awkward social situation and then feel like a real goof having done it. [The set] enabled nice little homely bits of action like that, but also enabled hugely theatrical performances.'

[S. Curtis, interview with author, 15 November 1993]

'For a start it was a comedy so it needed to have a certain tone about it that was not totally self-conscious. It did not need to be realistic. It could afford to have a lightness to it but there were certain things that it had to feel. It had to feel Russian, and in feeling Russian we endeavoured to find Australian parallels — that heavy world of bureaucratic bungle and the incompetent politician, and the kind of scraggy corruptness that you find in suburban electorates. For me they were things like, in simplistic terms, people with dribble on their coats and bifocal glasses (you know the national health specs) — some mass Australian symbols that related to that Russian world. It was [set in] period as well but it felt quite Australian, I think. The environment was full of things like standard lamps with frilly lampshades and piles of fabric in corners, things that the mayor had stashed away. So the mayor's house served as a micro-world for Russia and Russian politics.'

[T. Schofield, interview with author, 22 November 1993]

▼ Figure 51 **The Government Inspector**
Sydney Theatre Company
1991
see pl. 67
photographer: Robert McFarlane
in photo: Frank Whitten

film, depending on his interest and time commitments. In the mid- to late 1980s Thomson worked extensively in commercial theatre again, due to a renewed interest in producing musicals locally by producers such as Cameron Macintosh and the Gordon/Frost Organisation. His designs for *The King and I* (along with Roger Kirk's costumes) won much praise, as well as the illustrious Tony Award for Best Design in 1996, when the Australian production opened on Broadway (pls 97, 98 and 99). In theatre and opera, Thomson and Armfield have often collaborated with Jennie Tate (as costume designer), as can be remembered in ground-breaking productions such as *Tristan und Isolde* (pls 64, 65), *Ghosts* (fig. 22) and *The Master Builder* (pl. 66). Brian Thomson recalls his early work with Jim Sharman:

> Sharman and I changed the face of Australian theatre in the early 1980s. Looking back it was quite astonishing. I don't think it's ever been fully understood but there was a time when we could take on the world. It swept away the old-fashioned, stilted ways of theatre. There was a new language to be invented and I think we did it ... I did that for the first decade of my career, when I worked with Jim Sharman. We did heaps and heaps of things together back in the 1970s. I think it was slightly detrimental to me because it meant that people would always associate the ideas and the work as being a collaboration. I just wanted my part of it to be understood to be my part, not to be something that was necessarily coming from somebody else ... Being associated with one director, people thought, 'Well, they have a collaboration and I wouldn't ask Brian to do something because he always works with Jim'. I really needed to break away from that and, as a result, I think since 1981, I've made sure that ... I'm linked to a lot of directors, but not necessarily to one in particular.[2]

The restrictions of consistently working in close collaboration with only one or two other artists was mentioned by several designers as being detrimental to their careers. Frustrated by the industry's tendency to 'box' them in as a particular kind of designer, many designers believe that they are perceived as being only as good as their last show. It is also commonly felt that directors and theatre companies will choose their designers from a very limited knowledge of what they can do. Kim Carpenter (pls 79, 80) believes that:

> Directors can fall into the trap of typecasting designers and not really seeing their range, their full potential. Or the other can apply, where they hit on one designer and that designer keeps on being used all the time, because it's convenient, when they're not necessarily the right casting for all the number of pieces they've been asked to do ... Society does pigeonhole everything, even in the arts.[3]

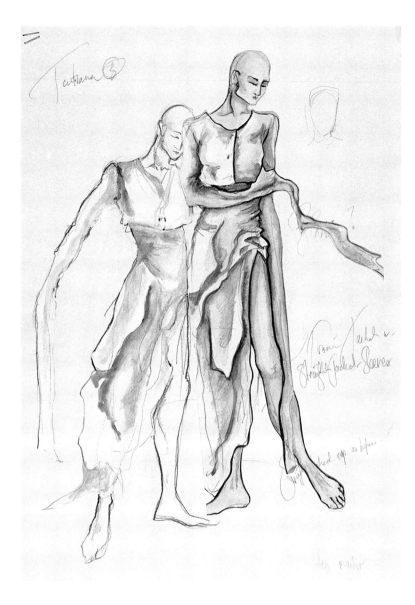

▲ Figure 52 **Diary of a Madman**
by Nikolai Gogol; adapted by David
Holman
Belvoir Street Theatre
1989
venue: Belvoir Street Theatre, Sydney
director: Neil Armfield
set designer: Catherine Martin
costume designer: Tess Schofield
lighting designer: Mark Shelton
photographer: Peter Holderness
Schofield's costume for the mad
Proproshin — the seemingly flowing
sleeves were stiffened into a straitjacket-
like vestment.

Another well-known designer who has worked both in ensemble and freelance situations is Stephen Curtis. Curtis went straight from the design course at the National Institute of Dramatic Art (NIDA) to Adelaide in 1977 and began to work for Jim Sharman's newly established ensemble-based Lighthouse Company. He spent several years working with the company as a resident designer and established working relationships with directors and actors with whom he still regularly collaborates today. He recalled what it was like being a part of an ensemble company:

> It's a very expensive operation. It is a limitation on directors to have a small pool of actors to cast from. It's like having a limited palette, you have to make the most of what that palette offers, which means that you exploit the capabilities of every individual component. So, in the case of the Lighthouse Company, there was a company of eight actors and I was one of the resident designers. There were three resident directors: there was Jim and Neil [Armfield] and Louis Nowra … Over that period of time every actor's, every director's and every designer's strengths and weaknesses were identified. When you're forced into a situation where you're going to be working with those people for two years, you really do have to overcome those limitations. So it was a great experience as quite a young designer to be constantly pushed to challenge my own sense of design, and also to challenge my directors and their casts.[4]

Curtis also talked of his early collaborations with Neil Armfield in Adelaide as being very productive. Together they worked on finding different ways of pushing and heightening the theatricality of a play without losing touch with the basic human elements on stage. The visual theatrical language that formed between them appeared on stage, supporting the strong acting, direction and performance environment. As with Thomson and Sharman, however, there was a point where they decided to increase their work with other people to avoid being pigeonholed as a pair. Though Curtis frequently designs both set and costumes, he often collaborates with one of Armfield's favourite costume designers, Tess Schofield, as can be seen in *The Government Inspector* (pl. 67, figs 51, 52).

Kathryn Sproul (pl. 68) worked as a designer with many of the local South Australian companies and directors, and was resident designer for several years with the Magpie Theatre Company for young people, based at the STCSA in Adelaide. She associates creative ensemble work with the establishment of strong trust and communication between designers, directors and performers:

'I said to Neil, "I've got two ideas. Maybe it should be a tasteful Russian cream ...

really peely old cream or, alternatively, maybe a Van Gogh idea — like the cafe,

because all those colours are actually Victorian". Finally we thought, Yes, it does

suit the madman and with Geoffrey Rush's character much better to use Van

Gogh's colours. One of the ideas of using the roof [piece] was that everything was

up-lit (like it was in Victorian times), and you can have a dingy, more oppressive

sense of the night because you don't have that nice overhead light that obliterates

shadows, where everything is thrown up on the wall. I was very strong [in my

opinion] that you should have a real sense that it's a period piece and that his

madness is [due to] the strictures of the period in which he was living.'

[C. Martin, interview with author,
4 April 1995]

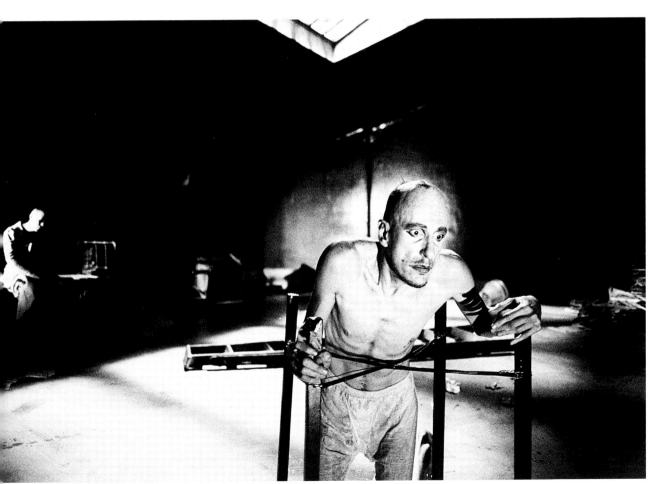

◄ Figure 53 **Diary of a Madman**
Belvoir Street Theatre
1989
see fig. 52
photographer: Robert McFarlane
in photo: Geoffrey Rush as Proproshin
'Martin's set is one of the best box-sets
ever devised. It is a stunning, ominous,
spare loft with scarlet walls, an electric
green sloping ceiling and leaking
plumbing and is evocatively, perfectly lit
by Mark Shelton.'
[P. Goers, 'Diary jewel in the crown',
Adelaide Advertiser, 16 March 1992, p. 13]

We will be working together as a team for eighteen months; an ensemble of five actors, the director, stage management and myself [as designer]. We get to be a very close-knit team; we know each other and our strengths and weaknesses. Consequently, the theatrical form is pushed forward ... I think one of the sad things about Australia's theatre climate is that we don't have ongoing ensembles in the style of European theatre. People come into an environment and begin a relationship with a group of people and then move on. It is maybe a few years before they come back together again. We are looking for a sense of trust in which we can feel free to experiment, and in that sense the ensembles, which quite often exist with theatre for young people, do allow risks to be taken.[5]

▲ Plate 68 **White Paper Flowers**
by Mary Hickson

Magpie Theatre Company

1991

venue: Playhouse, Adelaide Festival Centre

director: Angela Chaplin

choreography: Xiao-Xiong Zhang

set and costume designer: Kathryn Sproul

photographer: Lisa Tomasetti

in photo: (left to right) Richard Margetson, Ian Boyce, Nick Hope, Claire Jones, Kate Roberts

'This play explored the events, personal and historical, leading up to the massacre at Tiananmen Square seen through the eyes of two young students ...

The climax of the piece was the massacre which was told through monologue amidst chaotic movement sequences and projection of news footage ... In doing this we created an impression of the scale of the event counterbalanced with the personal moments. This production was performed in repertory with STCSA's *Spring Awakening*, which I also designed. The minimum turn-around time for the set was 45 minutes. In light of this, my designs had to incorporate central elements that could support both Beijing 1989, and Germany 1898. I designed a permanent raked stage area with trap doors and stair wells whereby specific elements could be flown in or emerge from the traps. *White Paper Flowers* also used enclosing walls that tracked into place.'

[notes — Katherine Sproul, 1995]

Some of Australia's nationally and state-subsidised companies, such as Opera Australia and the Victorian State Ballet, have actively encouraged young designers to join them, and to learn the added complexities of collaborating with directors, choreographers and conductors up to five years ahead of their opening nights. The Melbourne Theatre Company (MTC) had, until recently, kept its tradition of using a designer-in-residence to work closely with the current artistic directors, workshops and technicians on the majority of its productions. An overall house standard was established, with guest designers fitting into the existing structure. Kristian Fredrikson, Hugh Colman, Judith Cobb, Richard Roberts, Dale Ferguson and Tony Tripp have all been resident with the MTC. Although this has worked very well for some designers, others have not benefited from the rigidity of the process and have moved on to other kinds of companies. Hugh Colman spoke about the reasons why working full-time within a company structure is at times not so successful:

I suppose the reality is that [theatre companies] don't have resident designers and in a funny way I think that's probably a good thing. It is difficult to go on being stimulated all the time. I think the best thing about being a freelance designer is that most of the time you go from one job to the next and everything about it changes. If you are resident in a theatre company the only thing that would change would be the director and the piece that you're working on. Your relationships probably remain pretty much the same. Certainly your relationship with the management doesn't change and I don't think that's a recipe for stimulation as far as the designer goes. There was a whole theory back in the 1960s and 1970s that you had to develop a design style or a house style ... and what happened a lot of the time is that theatre got very boring.[6]

Colman did go on to say, however, that his collaborative work with the director Colin George at the State Theatre Company of South Australia (previously the Lighthouse Company) was beneficial to his development as a designer:

I had a very good time with Colin George, largely because it was the range of work that I was suddenly being asked to design. It was fantastic to work on really big projects. A lot of Shakespeare, and *Peer Gynt*-pieces that you might wait a lifetime to do. Colin was a remarkable man to work with. He'd taken the company that he wanted, he built up the company that he wanted and he liked my design work, so I suppose we had a very good collaboration from that point of view. But I would say chiefly it was just that he gave me the opportunity to work on a fantastic range of plays. It was very exciting.[7]

When Shaun Gurton was an associate director and resident designer of the STCSA he underlined the need for the designer and director to share the same visual language:

◄ Plate 69 **Aïda**
by Giuseppe Verdi
Australian Opera
1995
venue: Opera Theatre, Sydney Opera House
director: John Wregg
set and costume designer: Kenneth Rowell
photo: OA archives
in photo: The chorus of Opera Australia during performance

◄ Plate 70 **Carmen**
by Georges Bizet
Victoria State Opera
1994
venue: State Theatre, Victorian Arts Centre
director: Keith Warner (original production) and Ross A. Perry
choreographer: Ross A. Perry
set and costume designer: Kristian Fredrikson
lighting designer: Donn Byrnes
photographer: Jeff Busby
in photo: The chorus of Victoria State Opera during performance

▶ Plate 71 **Turandot**
by Giacomo Puccini
Victoria State Opera
1987
venue: Playhouse, Victorian Arts Centre
director: Richard Wherrett
set designer: Brian Thomson
costume designer: Terry Ryan
lighting designer: Nigel Levings
photographer: Greg Noakes
in photo: The chorus of the Victoria State
Opera during performance

Wherrett described his production of *Turandot* as having 'an element of nightmare', using elements of dark

fantasy and fairytale to make sense of the events and characters within the opera. The opening scenes place

the story within the imaginings of a lonely 'Black shirt' soldier who dreams of Turandot, and how she might

learn to love him. He described the steps as 'a stairway to Heaven', and used their inherent chiaroscuro to

heighten the dark hierarchy of Turandot's night world.

'The concept led me to keeping the chorus on stage

all night in red bloodied robes ... they were masked ... faceless ...

an angry mob.'

[R. Wherrett, interview with author, 16 February 1998]

◀ Plate 72 **Turandot**
Victoria State Opera
1987
photographer: Greg Noakes
in photo: Gregory Dempsey as Emperor
Altoum

Simon Phillips and I had been working in Melbourne ... I am always interested in finding new collaborations; people to work with who are exciting, and Simon had a tremendous amount of energy. When he got the job [as artistic director of the STCSA] he said: 'Why don't you come over so that we can continue in some of the ways that we wanted to work, as an associate ... Come as a designer so that we get a strong visual link' ... I'm very keen to spend a lot of time in the rehearsal room with the actors and the director so that all of that [design side] isn't like a separate world. The collaboration needs to be spread right across [the entire process].[8]

Geoff Cobham worked for many years with Kim Carpenter's Theatre of Image as a lighting designer and production manager (pls 79, 80), and speaks very highly of their collaborative relationship:

I have been working with Kim Carpenter for about twelve years. He now involves me from the very beginning — from when he gets the script or develops the idea, right through to the end result in the theatre — obviously taking my suggestions. He certainly involves me and I feel [my work] fits in much better with the productions now. To be trusted is one of the few delights of a lighting designer because people are very suspicious that you might ruin their production by putting green light over everything.

Once you get to a position where you are trusted by the director, it is fantastic because then you can experiment. When you are not trusted you tend to play safe.[9]

'The performance was in-the-round and the newly restored Albert Hall was the perfect setting for Marguerite Duras' haunting work. These four pages of sketches (only two shown here) look at the options for stage lighting and look at the behaviour of reflections on a highly polished wooden floor, the glare factors for the audience and the actors' lighting angles.'

(notes — David Longmuir,

12 January 1996)

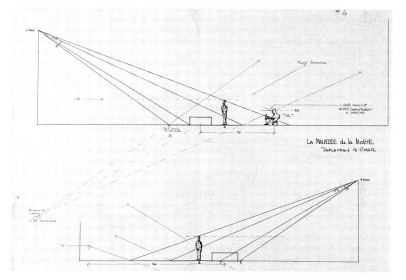

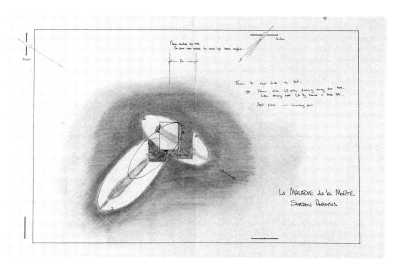

▶ Plate 73 **Paquita**

by Ludwig Minkus

Australian Ballet

1988

venue: Victorian Arts Centre

choreographers: Marius Petipa and
Evgeny Valukin

set and costume designer: Hugh Colman

lighting designer: William Akers

photographer: Peter Holderness

in photo: Christine Walsh and Linda Ridgway

▶ Plate 74 **Alice in Wonderland**

based on the story by C. S. Lewis

West Australian Ballet

1984

venue: His Majesty's Theatre, Perth

director: Barry Moreland

set designer: Charles Blackman

costume designer: Anna French

lighting designer: Kenneth Rayner

photo: WAB archives

in photo: The Lobster Quadrille by the
corps de ballet

In their interviews, both Cobham and Nigel Levings mentioned that lighting designers do tend to freelance between companies and productions far more than any other form of designer. To start with, they can put their entire design onto a computer disk and insert it into any computerised lighting board in the country. Secondly, it is very difficult to present a lighting design in model or sample form. Even though a lighting designer may be able to draw conceptual drawings (figs 54a, 54b) or create three-dimensional images with computer graphics to illustrate their ideas, many design ideas can only be tested once the performers are in the space alongside the set and costumes. Therefore they tend to come in at a much later stage of the collaborative process and have a labour-intensive collaboration with the director during the final production week. Because of this (and the need to earn a living) they can do more shows in one year than all their directors and designers put together. There is no chance, however, to develop the ensemble ideals or to spend a long time refining the imagery.

One exception was Graeme Murphy incorporating John Rayment's ideas early on into the rehearsal process, enabling the Sydney Dance Company dancers to explore fully the possibilities created by light. This experimentation in turn fed the lighting design and enriched the finished product on stage:

I like a set that has simplicity but also has versatility. In dance the worst thing you can do is have a new set for each scene ... I like the dancers to change the atmosphere ... Lighting to me is the sister to choreography. I think that when you are playing with subtle changes of atmosphere ... all you are doing is changing the focus of an audience's attention and the psychological feeling that an audience receives by changing the colour.

When you have a resident lighting designer like John Rayment who can come in and whack some lights on the floor and give you an idea it is a huge advantage. I use it in the same way that I use Jennifer Irwin [Irwin has worked many times with Murphy as his costume designer] to come in and throw a piece of fabric round, look at what the dancers are doing, and say, 'They can't wear this because of this or that'. I hate the [possibility] of losing flexibility because of the planning that you have to do so far in advance. That [planning] is a reality but you can minimise it by having people who are good around you when you need them.[10]

Interestingly, John Rayment believes that the most successful work between him and Murphy has come from the fact that they trust one another's working processes enough not to discuss it at length. Rayment feels that his skills come to the fore during the final rehearsal week, once everything is in the theatre, and it is then that the most creative collaboration can occur:

[The collaborative dialogue between us is] particularly well expressed with Graeme and the work that he does ... The designs that I am most happy about — the ones that I think have been the greatest success — are the ones, ironically, where there's been the least amount of discussion prior to the production week. It all comes together ... I think [the reasons why creative] teams form and continue to work together is because it has far more to do with the personalities at play than it has to do with their individual design skills. When you get to a certain level in the industry it is assumed or accepted that you have design skills and you have a professional basis on which legitimately to call yourself a professional designer. It is then about a number of people all responding to the central stimuli created. It is not just a blank sheet of paper, it is a black void. There is nothing. And then off we go ... It would be very interesting to track the creative sequence as to how far ago we talked about a particular work, but only in the loosest terms. We never ever sit down and have a design meeting per se, particularly about lighting.[11]

▼ Plate 75 **Aurora**
based on Tchaikovsky's *The Sleeping Beauty*
Meryl Tankard and the Australian Dance Theatre
1994
venue: Playhouse, Adelaide Festival Centre
director: Meryl Tankard
production design: Meryl Tankard, Regis Lansac and Dean Hills
lighting designer: Toby Harding
photographer: Regis Lansac
in photo: Act 1, scene 3, 'Fairies and Friends' dance. The dancers included: Tuula Ruppola, Michelle Ryan, Ingrid Weisfelt, Shaun Parker, Vincent Crowley, Grayson Millwood, Steev Zane and Gavin Webber

In this collaboration with Welch, both designers chose to use methods and materials not usually seen in classical ballet. Leyonhjelm used many industrial fabrics, including vulcanised rubber, and pleating sourced from air-conditioning units. Anderson worked with metallic piping and kinetic projections. Anderson described his use of computer-generated images in this production: 'The [projection] screen itself changed size. There were two tracking cloths so that the screen could actually change its proportions. So that you might be looking at a very low, long image at the bottom, about two metres high, and then a full screen. Then you might have a screen which was only a slit — three metres wide but on stage-left going all the way up. I used it in this way because I wanted just seconds of imagery so you have to work out what the images are, but by the time [you have] finished, a new image is already starting'.

[B. Anderson, interview with author, 3 May 1995]

▼ Figure 55 **Divergence**
Australian Ballet
1994
venue: State Theatre, Victorian Arts Centre
choreographer: Stanton Welch
set designer: Ben Anderson
costume designer: Vanessa Leyonhjelm
lighting designer: William Akers
photographer: James McFarlane
in photo: Vicki Attard in a publicity shot, modelling one of Leyonhjelm's costumes

Lines of communication

I think the most important thing for anybody in our position is to be able to communicate, either with your drawing skills or with a model (or whatever you are using) so that you can talk to a director through those. They can see immediately what you are on about. It then goes all the way — from the person who is going to make the costumes and the jewellery to the lighting people — even, to a certain extent, sound ... theatre, finally, is communication.[12]

Graham Maclean (set and costume designer)

Trust is the foundation stone of creative communication. For most directors and choreographers, working with a designer for the first time can be a slow process of developing effective communication and trust in each other's work. Regardless of who begins a project, it should belong to everyone by the end of the rehearsal period. The art of compromise and of trust is the collaborative glue that binds visions together.

◄ Plate 76 **Fun and Games with the Oresteia**
by Luke Devenish
Kickhouse Theatre Company
1991
venue: 28 Brunswick Street, Fitzroy, Melbourne
director: Julian Meyrick
set and costume designer: Louise McCarthy
lighting designer: Geoff Cobham
photographer: Andrew Samson
in photo: The cast during rehearsal

The need for a shared language of performance and imagery is vital to most designers and is mentioned frequently as being the point at which a creative partnership can be either made or destroyed. Robert Kemp felt a strong camaraderie and empathy with the visiting English director Jules Wright when they worked together on *The Revenger's Tragedy* for the Sydney Theatre Company. He described the framework of their communication as being 'incredibly creative and easy to work in. We just understood each other and I suppose it was a question of taste. Hating and loving similar things always helps'.[13]

Like Kemp, who regularly collaborates with the writer-director Michael Gow, Lou Westbury, the associate director and resident designer of Barking Gecko Theatre Company in Western Australia is in a position that many designers might envy:

My collaboration with Grahame Gavin (who is also my partner) is a fairly unique arrangement. I'm part of the developing process and that means building the input of the design right from the very early stages. This radically changes the outcome in that some of my designs have actually changed the script. The

▼ Plate 77 **The Marriage of Figaro**
by Wolfgang Amadeus Mozart
Victoria State Opera, in association
with the Melbourne Theatre
Company and ANThill Theatre
1991
venue: Playhouse, Victorian Arts
Centre
director: Barrie Kosky
set and costume designer: Stephen
Curtis
costume designer (MTC only): Angus
Strathie
lighting designer: Jamieson Lewis
photographer: Jeff Busby

The opening scene: a large clove of garlic, reputedly an aphrodisiac, sitting somewhat oddly within an elaborate frescoed box set.

This production was one half of an unusual collaboration between Melbourne Theatre Company, ANThill Theatre and the Victoria State Opera. Using the same venue and setting designed by Curtis, both companies mounted productions of *The Marriage of Figaro*, directed separately by Kosky and Jean-Pierre Mignon.

'We begin in the morning and end in the evening ... a marriage ceremony is being constantly threatened, postponed or interrupted. Private domains are scandalously invaded. A seemingly empty space is presented as a wedding gift but transformed into a patriarchal hunting ground frequented by an onanistic

adolescent, a vindictive doctor, a concupiscent aristocrat and his ecclesiastical side-kick. A woman's bedroom becomes a theatre of disguise and fetish ... the world becomes darker and darker.'

(programme notes — B. Kosky)

◄ Plate 78 **The Marriage of Figaro**

Victoria State Opera, in association with
the Melbourne Theatre Company and
ANThill Theatre

1991

see pl. 77

photographer: Jeff Busby

in photo: The chorus of the Victoria State
Opera in performance

writer would see how it could actually happen by seeing the designer's view of their world and therefore the designer's way of seeing a play performed.[14]

Similarly, Meryl Tankard and her husband Regis Lansac always collaborated on Australian Dance Theatre productions (pl. 63, figs 49, 50), creating a successful marriage between projected and choreographed images. Lansac's work as a photographer translates beautifully to the stage, and his use of focused and kinetic light sources enables the settings to move seamlessly with the dancers. Tankard involves him throughout the development process, incorporating many of his design ideas into her choreography.

Designer Louise McCarthy (pl. 76) has worked very closely with the director Julian Meyrick from Kickhouse Theatre Company in Melbourne. She collaborated with him on many projects and productions, keeping design as an intrinsic part of the working process, from the initial thoughts and commissioning of work, to the finished performance environment. She enjoyed the intense involvement because, as she says:

> In big companies you can have a whole heap of people contributing to the same piece of theatre but working separately, not communicating.[15]

In smaller companies, the opportunity to become involved in all aspects of production, to communicate creatively on all levels and develop shared notions of performance and design remains open to a wider group, simply because the delineation of role and function is not as defined. The lines between director, designer, writer, initiator and facilitator are not as clearly drawn.

Of course there can be problems within all partnerships. Miscommunication (on large and small scales) is a big factor. Kathryn Sproul has had the experience of communication going wrong, and its effect on the production design:

> The problem is that design as a language of communication isn't totally understood by other practitioners, so you're constantly trying to make sure that you are asking questions of them so that you know what they expect of you and what you are offering is understood by them. I've run into a number of situations with directors who are not visually aware and are not aware of the potency of visual statements and, consequently, don't think it's a problem if they change their minds and don't tell you ... If you asked an actor to change a core aspect of their character you would understand that would then affect how they viewed this character as a whole. I don't think that people understand that if you ask a designer to change a major element of a design that of course it will affect the balance of the whole, and the designer needs time to take that on board.[16]

◀ Plate 79 **The Happy Prince**

based on a story by Oscar Wilde; adapted by Kim Carpenter and Richard Tulloch

Theatre of Image, in association with the Sydney Theatre Company

1993

venue: Wharf Theatre, Sydney Theatre Company

director and production designer: Kim Carpenter

composer: Sarah de Jong

choreography: Julie-Anne Long

lighting designer: Geoff Cobham

photographer: Lorrie Graham

in photo: (left to right) Ronald Falk as the Happy Prince and Tom Weaver as the Swallow

Dictating design

There is always the possibility that the visual statement may overpower the textual or psychological meaning. Stephen Curtis points out that the changing phases (and fashions) in theatre development are also responsible for how the director's and a designer's input is perceived:

> There was a phase … where the most important person in the production seemed to be the designer, judging by what productions looked like on stage. Designers were getting away with absolute murder on stage; designs that were quite indulgent and only marginally appropriate for the production or the cast or the theatre or the director. I think there was a bit of a backlash from that. It goes through phases where the director is the most important person, or the actor is, or the designer or the writer. At the moment it's probably going back to the director, or to a collaborative approach where a group of people can shape what the production is. I think that will be a very good thing because that's when everyone is able to contribute positively so that the contributions are shaped and directed by a strong vision. It doesn't necessarily have to be the director's vision.[17]

As a director, Aubrey Mellor supports this idea. He is always welcoming of the designer's input as it can help him shape the overriding metaphor for a production:

> Sometimes certain plays will defeat me. These are the ones where the central metaphor is quite obscure and you think 'Whatever do we do here?'. I am so grateful when a designer can come up with an idea that unlocks it. I have always provoked them to go one better because I am a great believer that several heads are better than one. It is very hard to say which is which [i.e. whose idea is whose in the finished work]. Sometimes I will give them a total say, other times I'll encourage them to work very closely with the actors to evolve the clothes, and sometimes I won't be the least bit interested in the costumes. I'm very interested in the space that I am going to work in so I

Carpenter's re-telling of *The Happy Prince* used actors and puppets, moving scenery and picture-book graphics. Visual humour jostled visual pathos for attention. The audience grew accustomed to seeing an image of a sculpture become a three-dimensional sculpture, become a real man and back again. He played with scale, so that a tiny puppet left the stage and returned full-size. Both adults and children were entranced.

'This is a production that sweeps aside traditional notions of text as words for dialogue. Here the text is multi-faceted. It is visual, and includes music.'

[P. Payne, 'Puppet state wields surprises', *Sydney Morning Herald*, 4 January 1993, p. 7]

want to make sure that the space is going to work in a practical way for the sort of production that it is going to be. The spatial relationships are very important.[18]

John Bell concurs:

I like to work in close collaboration with a designer from the very beginning. I always bring something along. It might not be an actual stage picture but it will be a series of images ... I try to refrain from putting all that on the table because that might put the designer in a cage. I will tell the designer why I want to do the play, why I think it is important, what I want to achieve with it and then let the designer come back to me with some of their own ideas because that might give me a much better option than the one I had first thought of. If the designer fails to do that then I have my own fall-back positions which I have thought of in advance.

What I will say to the designer is 'I want to do this play in a totally contemporary Australian way and I want a particular actor—audience relationship and this is the kind of mood I imagine'. I say those things up front so that he or she knows the area we are working in but I try not to be too explicit at the beginning until I have talked to the designer and the actors: (a) so they all feel they have made a big contribution and been part of the organic process; and (b) because so many heads are better than one. People sit down in a circle and talk about the play and their impressions — you can get revelations of things you haven't thought of.[19]

Kim Carpenter (pls 79, 80) does dictate the design and direction of his productions. His is a unique position — artistic director of a theatre of

◄ Plate 80 **The Happy Prince**
Theatre of Image, in association with the Sydney Theatre Company
1993
see pl. 79
photographer: Lorrie Graham
in photo: Phillip Dodd as the Ugly Duchess and Christine Mahoney as the Seamstress

imagery and visual magic. He has worked as an art director, teacher, designer, director and writer on many other projects and sees these roles as having equal value:

I don't distinguish between the two — I see myself as a specialist. A lot of people would probably put that in the too-hard basket because we're still a white Anglo-Saxon theatre community that does plays with actors, a director, a designer and maybe a choreographer. That is still the basic format for making drama in this country, which we've inherited from England. Around that we are making other works that are really much more distinctively Australian and distinctively individual through all sorts of combinations. It's not just me, but there are lots of companies now that are breaking down the barriers. So I think that it's the designer or visual artist in me that is the basis of the direction that I choose to take. Our work will try and throw further light on other forms. All the arts are brothers — they're not separate, it's all the same language. Whether it's applied to painting or whether it's applied to theatre work it's a balancing act, in a sense, to orchestrate the whole ... You don't set out with a particular style completely because I think the work becomes its own style.[20]

1   A. Carter, interview with author, 19 August 1993.
2   B. Thomson, interview with author, 18 November 1993.
3   K. Carpenter, interview with author, 18 November 1993.
4   S. Curtis, interview with author, 15 November 1993.
5   K. Sproul, interview with author, 5 March 1995.
6   H. Colman, interview with author, 18 August 1993.
7   ibid.
8   S. Gurton, interview with author, 23 August 1993.
9   G. Cobham, interview with author, 9 March 1995.
10 G. Murphy, interview with author, 30 March 1995.
11 J. Rayment, interview with author, 14 March 1995.
12 G. Maclean, interview with author, 9 March 1995.
13 R. Kemp. interview with author, 14 November 1993.
14 L. Westbury, interview with author, 30 August 1993.
15 L. McCarthy, conversation with author, 19 March 1995.
16 Sproul, op. cit.
17 Curtis, op. cit.
18 A. Mellor, interview with author, 14 March 1995.
19 J. Bell, interview with author, 13 March 1995.
20 Carpenter, op. cit.

▼ Figures 56 and 57 **Four Little Girls**

by Pablo Picasso; adapted by Ariette
Taylor

Handspan Theatre

1988 — national tour

director: Ariette Taylor

production designer: Ken Evans

lighting designer: Phillip Lethlean

photos: Handspan archives

in photo: Danita Hanson, one of the four
little girls

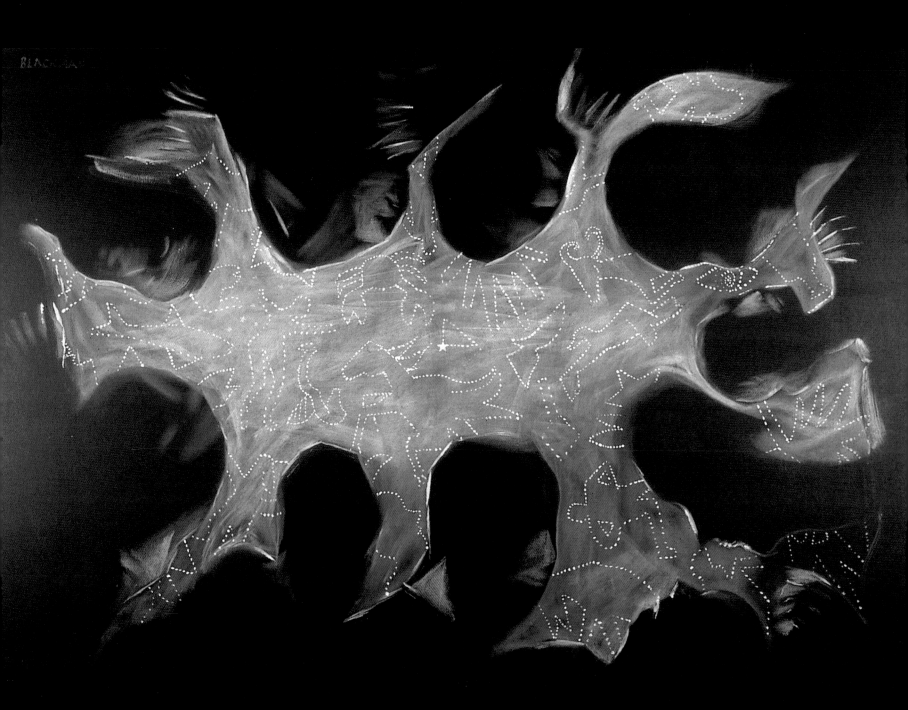

The design process

What is challenging is to be able to cut one's suit to fit the cloth.

STEPHEN CURTIS[1]

You ask about the colours? What are the colours that Shakespeare has indicated for us? Do not first look at Nature. but look in the play of the poet.

EDWARD GORDON CRAIG[2]

◄ Plate 81 **VISIONS** — The Celestial Mirror

West Australian Ballet

1988

venue: His Majesty's Theatre, Perth

choreographer: Barry Moreland

set designer: Charles Blackman

costume designer: Anna French

lighting designer: Kenneth Rayner

photo: WAB archives

Blackman's set rendering of the backcloth.

▲ Plate 82 **VISIONS** — The Celestial Mirror

West Australian Ballet

1988

see pl. 81

photo: WAB archives

in photo: Artists of the West Australian Ballet
in performance

Beginning the design process

The design process is a matter of beginning at one point and travelling to the end. It incorporates ways of seeing with ways of doing. It involves the marrying of practical considerations to creative skills, and an understanding of world histories — of war and travel, race and fear, of changing and repeating patterns in fashion and politics. The designer in all areas of performance must ask: What is the space? Who is the target audience? What is the budget? Why are we doing this performance? What does the director want?

Whether a designer is creating the lighting for a show in an outside arena, assembling costumes for a classical ballet or designing a production that can tour throughout country Victoria, the problem-solving process is the same. The solutions distinguish good design from bad or none at all. Although it is true that no two designers are the same, the practical process involved in the making of a performance is a fairly standardised model for developing an idea and creating it in three dimensions by the given deadline. As in any creative field the process is partly based on theory, partly on practical skills and mostly on response to the factors affecting performance. The 'why, what and how' affect the decision making and determine the outcome.

Australian People's Theatre in association
with the Sydney Theatre Company

1993

venue: Wharf Level, Sydney Theatre
Company

director: John Howard

set and costume designer: Kym Barrett

photographer: Peter Holderness

▼ Figure 58 **The Loaded Ute**

Australian Peoples' Theatre in association
with the Sydney Theatre Company

1993

see pl. 83

photographer: Peter Holderness

Barrett's development of costume ideas.

We asked all designers interviewed how they would define their design
process and how they combine practical methodology, theory and instinct.
Their mixed responses have been incorporated into the following sections
which examine the influences affecting the design concept, the realisation
of ideas and the actual creation.

Design standards

In 1992 Arts Training Australia prepared a consultative document entitled
Analysing the Design Process,[3] which defined a set of competency standards
to be used when crediting the skills required by production designers. It
included film and television in its scope and was unspecific in its detail of
particular jobs relating to live performance, but it tried to cover the basic
approach to any design brief. It analysed the performance industry very
much in terms of what skills are required in order to carry out the process of
production design within a conventional performance framework.

▲ Plate 84 **The Country Wife**
by William Wycherley
Sydney Theatre Company
1987
venue: Drama Theatre, Sydney Opera
House
director: Neil Armfield
set and costume designer: Stephen
Curtis
lighting designer: Mark Shelton
photographer: Peter Holderness

► Plates 85a, 85b and 85c
The Country Wife
Sydney Theatre Company
1987
see pl. 84
photographer: Peter Holderness

According to the Arts Training document, production design can be split into seven units: development and assessment of the design brief; development of the design concept; finalising of design; documentation and presentation of design; physical realisation of design; installation of the design; and then evaluation. Although the Arts Training approach provides a solid base from which to analyse the step-by-step design process, it would seem at odds with the more inspired response that most designers say they employ. It does not allow for the additional areas that a designer may need to go into during the process, including involvement with the performance. Nor does it mention that once a design has been approved it can also change and grow from its initial realisation on paper. The processes described form the basis of what is taught at theatre schools, but they are the springboard to a broader curriculum. Designers very quickly learn the art of improvisation and how to think on their feet. The average design brief includes continued dealings with other designers, choreographers, writers, directors, dancers and actors. Good designers will be able to incorporate change into their otherwise 'finished' concept as the performance moves and mutates through rehearsal. Peter Cooke, NIDA's head of design, pointed out that:

> The design footprint on a production is very broad. One develops whole processes for working with people in very different areas. The inverse is not always true. To survive as a designer one needs to be enormously skilled, pragmatic, politic, managerial and creative; otherwise one does not get employed again.[4]

The course Cooke teaches emphasises design as a core aspect of the whole production process:

I almost never separate design from the collaborative process of 'doing theatre'. It is a group of people heading in a direction, and although their contribution may be enormously individual and to do with the arrangement of chairs in space, I expect them to have views on every single aspect of the production.[5]

In his evaluation of what is taught to design students at NIDA Cooke dwelt more on the need to encourage creative thinking and flexibility than on the physical design process. Experienced designers have the 'nuts and bolts' process working subconsciously while they continue to take on new ideas and react to unexpected stimuli. The conventional process that is suitable for one type of management, company or performance will not necessarily fit so smoothly into another situation.

For example, Stephen Curtis (pls 84, 85) used to consciously undermine the 'cut and dried' approach to design presentations by incorporating unplanned decisions into his design:

> I'm still trying to find an element of humanity in my designs — the common touch. That is something I believe in very strongly, to the extent that in the past I used to leave a component of the design unfinished in the model. Not unfinished in a way that anyone else would have been aware of it, but unfinished because it would demand an on-the-spot contribution from someone during the production period rather than being pre-planned. We must not forget that theatre is a 'human experience' rather than an 'entertainment' experience. I think theatre can be entertaining and look good, yet also be human and meaningful. The balance will always change but even so I think it is possible and it is my constant quest.[6]

Costume designer Anna French is an integral participant during the buying, construction and fitting of costumes, and is able to make on-the-spot changes as they are needed. She also stresses the human elements of the design:

> One of the really important skills (and it probably doesn't seem important in the overall scheme of things) is the ability to deal with people and be able to get the best out of the people that you're working with, to get them enthused about working on the production because the more enthused they are the better they work and the happier they are ... It's often analysing the way people work and what they actually need, of getting to know them so that you can help them through the areas that they feel unconfident about ... When they finally see the play they understand what the designer's been going on about.[7]

▲ Figure 59 **Katya Kabanova**
by Leos Janácek
Australian Opera
1995
venue: Opera Theatre, Sydney Opera House
director: Neil Armfield
set designer: Brian Thomson
costume designer: Jennie Tate
lighting designer: Nigel Levings
photographer: Peter Holderness
Tate's rendering of the costume for Katya Kabanova.

▲ Figure 60 **Katya Kabanova**
Australian Opera
1995
see fig. 59
photo: OA archives
in photo: Eilene Hannan as Katya Kabanova

LUCKY WIESZBOWSKI

Warren Coleman

▶ Plate 86 **The Quartet from Rigoletto**
by Nick Enright
Q Theatre in association with the Ensemble Theatre
venue: Q Theatre and the Ensemble Theatre, Sydney
director: George Ogilvie
set and costume designer: Wendy Osmond
lighting designer: Andrew Kinch
in photo: Osmond's costume collage for Lucky Wieszbowski, played by Warren Coleman

Part of Brian Thomson's design process is associated with finding and encouraging skilled crafts-people who can interpret his designs:

The people I work with are people that I've worked with in some cases for twenty years, who I can completely trust and if I say what I want, I know they will do it or they will give me a reference ... I always try and find out from the theatre company what their strengths are. I see their works from beforehand and think, 'Well, they've got hopeless scene painters but wonderful propsmakers' or 'They've got great set builders and all the painting is wonderful'. These things have got to be done by a certain time and you've got to be there. The thing that I refuse to do is not come up with what I've promised, and that to me is the most important thing. It's very easy to sit around and have a lot of terrific and smart ideas but it's another thing to bring them off. I would always hope in my work that I do bring off what I talk about. It is not easy and it requires a lot of work, a lot of inspiration and a lot of dedication to make it work. I think it is important that the ideas you have discussed with the director are on stage as fresh and strong as they were when you first talked about them — not watered down. A lot of things come in that will compromise it, but you still have to hang onto them, incredibly firmly. You are driving this thing through and as you do that you've got to get everybody that's with you 'on side', and that includes theatre companies and workshops.[8]

Thomson realises the importance of methodology in his work, particularly when working on several projects at once. He often employs people to carry his design work through different stages of development — usually the presentation and documentation of the design, such as rendering, model-making and drafting — leaving him free to attend rehearsals and continue his collaboration with directors. Although this may seem an ideal situation for the professional designer, not many designers in Australia are currently in the position of being able to employ others to work for them. A freelance designer usually realises the design singly and is involved in all stages of the scale model's development, the drawing up of the plans and the costume working drawings. The time commitment of designers is greatly affected by the fact that they are often working on several projects at once. The long hours demanded by performance schedules means that many designers run from one job to another, often missing out on the finer details during rehearsals.

Conceptual form

The text and music provide a blueprint for the emotional as well as the physical performance space. Although many directors and designers choose to ignore the specified settings within a script, preferring to move the text into new areas unfettered by previous directions, the development of a design stems from the writing. This places responsibility for the original staging concepts back with the writer who must use words rather than images.

The playwright Hilary Bell, when asked if she is aware of the staging when writing, made it clear that although she does not define the space (preferring to leave that to the imagination of whoever is designing), she does try to capture a sense of space that will permeate the play:

> I think it has got to be brought across psychologically and emotionally and, hopefully, any designer who is sensitive will pick that up and translate it visually. I would never specify those sorts of things ... [My play], *Wolf Lullaby*, is very theatrical and I am very conscious of the space. In my mind I have actually designed it already. The parameters of the space and the boundaries are very important to the play and they have informed the writing. As an example, I know that the ceiling has to be very low in one corner even though it has nothing to do with the play and it is never mentioned. But the sense of a corner and walls coming in is very important. I use it for my own means to create a claustrophobia which I would like visually ... In *Wolf Lullaby* I did actually specify a particular lighting technique. It's divided into fourteen scenes and I want each scene to decrease in the amount of light; it starts off almost blinding and the fourteenth scene is completely black. I have never imposed my design or lighting thoughts that much before.[9]

▼ Plate 87 **Three Writers' Project**
three plays by Hilary Bell, Pam Laversha and Luke Devenish
Kickhouse Theatre Company
1994
venue: unstaged
director: Julian Meyrick
set and costume designer: Louise McCarthy
photographer: Peter Holderness

McCarthy's original idea — costume cut-outs of archetypal characters given to each of the writers.

Some artistic directors have brought designers and writers together to encourage the spatialisation of the dramatic written space before the plays are finished. Aubrey Mellor described his input:

> I have been encouraging a series of designers to stimulate writers to think about the use of the space, and how to actually write stage directions that are exciting, that create some visual action. I don't think writers think visually enough. I think that is a whole education that the writer has got to be exposed to.[10]

Eamon D'Arcy collaborated with Adelaide playwrights (Playworks, 1998) using a model box to inspire performance texts. Using a similar basis for inspiring writers to work visually, Louise McCarthy initiated an interesting production process with Kickhouse Theatre Company called the *Three Writers' Project* in 1993. Instead of being inspired to design a space by the cues provided by a script, she drew several silhouettes of archetypal characters including The Woman, The Stranger, The Angel and The Man (pl. 87). In a series of workshops with three playwrights McCarthy and Kickhouse director Julian Meyrick encouraged the writers to draw inspiration from the designed characters. Hilary Bell was one of the playwrights involved and described the process thus:

> They were designed, drawn and given to us and they were faceless, so they weren't imbued with any particular personality or characteristic. And their dress was very simple and kind of timeless. It was meant to be an empty vessel into which we could pour whatever we wanted. Each of us were given five little cards with the characters' pictures on them and asked to come up with scenarios. It was very interesting in the first meeting because we all came up with extremely different ideas. We were given no guidelines. It could be about anything — any length, any style, it could be musical or could be wordless. When we met [the scenarios] were all set in different countries. My play was set in the 1850s, Pamela Laversha's was set in the 1970s and Luke Devenish's was set in the 1930s. They were in very different styles: Luke's was a romantic gipsy musical comedy, Pamela's was a thriller and mine was a tragic ethereal little mood piece. The project was on a tiny budget, and the plays were given a reading rather than a staged performance. It was an interesting method of combining a sense of design within the writing itself, not adding it at a later date, from a different vantage point.[11]

Practicalities

It is an interesting design process bringing words into three-dimensional being. Peter Cooke expects his design students to read plays with a richness of understanding that goes beyond the purely academic discussion: 'We look at it from the actors' point of view, the audiences' point of view and the designer's. We ask: 'Why are we choosing this play? What does it have to say, and what does it do?'.[12]

This type of analysis draws on a designer's knowledge of the subject, era and style of the play as much as it does from the content. Standards of reading and comprehension must be developed to the same standard as all the technical skills. An understanding and appreciation of contemporary social issues will feed into the final layering of images and structures. One passionate believer in the need for theatre to reflect contemporary issues is Kathryn Sproul:

Staged as part of the Adelaide Festival, this was the premiere production of a new Australian opera, which utilised state-of-the-art video projections and computer-generated sounds.

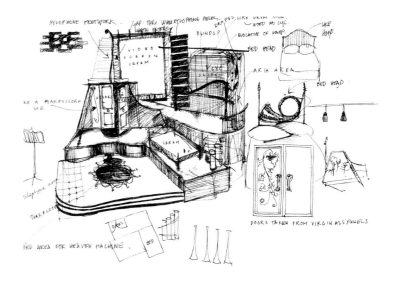

▲ Figure 61 **The Seduction Opera and The Heaven Machine**

Seduction Opera Company

1992

see pl. 88

Cobb's initial set rendering

◄ Plate 88 **The Seduction Opera and The Heaven Machine**

by Martin Friedl

Seduction Opera Company

1992

venue: Odeon Theatre, Adelaide

director: David Myles

set and costume designer: Judith Cobb

lighting designer: Ian Fidders

video design: Marshall White

photographer: Eric Algra

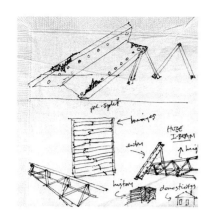

◄ Figure 62 **Bring The House Down**
by John Romeril
Arena Theatre Company
1992 — schools tour
venue: CUB Malthouse, Melbourne
director: Barbara Cizsewska
music: Irene Vela
set and costume designer: Trina Parker
lighting designer: Liz Pain
photo: Peter Holderness
A rough concept sketch drawn by Parker
on a restaurant serviette.

'I think sometimes I get an idea on an old serviette. I've designed plenty of shows where I haven't built a
model at all because I have worked in areas where there has never been any money or time to make a model.
And often it is unnecessary — if I sketch it and if I can get the right people to build it the way I want it to be,
so what? There can be a lot of undue emphasis on that kind of detail which is really only there to make the
real thing happen. I think that's why in a way I call myself a "theatre worker". I do call myself a "designer"
because that's the job I do but in a way I'm a lot happier with the term "theatre worker" because I'm part of
a group of people working in theatre, not a kind of isolated artist who lives in a garret producing fabulous
drawings.'

[Trina Parker, interview with author, 11 August 1993]

► Figure 63 **Bring The House Down**
Arena Theatre Company
1992 — schools tour
see fig. 62
photo: Trina Parker archives

The bare bones of theoretical understanding (in terms of the history of performance art) is necessary, and that is taught at most institutions. For an understanding of the theory, or a historical perspective of performance art, students look at the history of visual arts, they touch on literature and they touch on music. It is important to have an understanding of all the artforms and also to put them in terms of their social, historical and political contexts ... It is to be aware of what is going on around them [designers], to seek to be informed, to take on new challenges so that they don't become boxed into thinking: 'This is the performing arts and I am not aware of the life of a racing car driver or what it is to be a teacher in an outback community'. Yet the experiences of all these people are valid to your work and to your own life, so it's no good being insulated. It is only by understanding aspects of other people's life that your work has any validity for them. Otherwise why else would you ask them to come and see it?[13]

Judith Cobb (pl. 88, fig. 61) has also taught design and she pushes for the students to look beyond the narrow world of theatre for ideas:

I think that it is a little bit insular to be looking at other set designs and designers for inspiration. What you need to do is look to the fine arts, sculpture and painting, modern jewellery, architecture, interior design. Use those as primary sources for your design rather than other set designs.[14]

When discussing this with Trina Parker (head of design at the Victorian College of the Arts), she spoke about the need for the designer to read and question widely from all available sources:

One thing I say to the production students is to read the paper every day. You can't work in theatre unless you know what is going on. The most challenging theatre is theatre which is about what is going on. Read the reviews. Know what is happening. Read about the war in Bosnia. You might do a production about it one day. If you're not generally well educated, if you don't have opinions about issues, then how can you contribute to really interesting work?[15]

Parker (figs 62, 63) defined her approach to work as

solving problems all the time. Sifting through, ideas come — particularly when you're in the conceptual stage. I don't put pen to paper until quite late. I do it in my head. I see things quite clearly. I'll be shifting images or positions of things in my head so what I am doing is basically sorting through and rejecting, keeping this bit and rejecting that, just constantly churning. After that it's a question of sitting down at your desk, or measuring something or finding out something, and then it's just 'work, work, work'.[16]

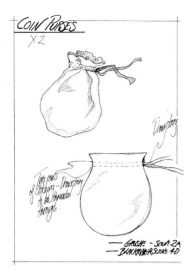

COIN PURSES
x2

Drawstring

Two rows of Stitching - Drawstring to be threaded through.

— GRUSHE - SCENE 2A
— BLACKMAILER SCENE 4D

FOOD BASKETS x3

White Sheeting
Stock Baskets to be oversstuffed
Black Straps bound round basket bundles.

i.e. these baskets have been packed in a hurry and should look, rather haphazard

PALACE SERVANTS - 1D

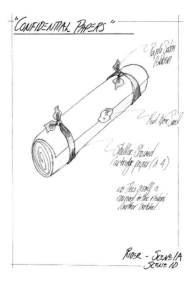

"CONFIDENTIAL PAPERS"

Purple Satin Ribbon

Red Wax Seal

Stellar Stained (cartridge paper (A 4).

i.e. This scroll is carried in the riders leather satchel.

RIDER - SCENE 1A
SCENE 1D

▲ Figures 64a, 64b and 64c
The Caucasian Chalk Circle
by Bertolt Brecht
Australian Theatre for Young People
1991
venue: The Performance Space, Sydney
director: Mark Gaal
set and costume designer: Tess Schofield
lighting designer: Nigel Levings
Schofield's prop drawings for the ATYP's
workshop performance.

Parker summed up her design process as being in three clear stages — research, selection and execution:

The *research* part is where you find out everything about it. It doesn't matter if it's now or any time. You do your research and that also involves talking to the director; filling yourself up with the stuff of the piece. Then the next bit is *selection*. That's the hard bit. I've got it in my head. What bits of that am I going to put in my set? Should I be putting in three chairs or five? *Execution* is the making of the model and doing the working drawings. I often do a rough model, so selection and execution might overlap. Essentially execution stems from the selection.[17]

A long-time designer for the New Theatre in Sydney, Tom Bannerman always asks logistical questions of the director in order to kick-start his process of problem-solving, particularly as he was often the head of construction:

Well, I guess the big question for me is what am I trying to say in the show? How am I going to use this theatre to support an idea? Several things may happen simultaneously. First thing I want to know is: What is the theatre space? I want to know the boring logistical things — how big the entrances are, how big are the openings, so you can get things on and off the stage. Do we have to have things go up and down stairs. Also I want to know, even before I read the script, any information from the director about her or his opinions about the show. I much prefer them to talk abstractly than specifically.[18]

Wendy Osmond (pl. 86) believes that:

The designer's role is inherently to supply the actors with what they need. I guess that is the bare bones of designing anyway. Do they need to sit down? Do they need a blank space? What props do they need? They always need something. Rather than thinking, 'All right. Here is a blank space, and I now have to decorate it', I think that a good way to start is from the actors out, rather than the outside in.[19]

Leaping from the page and into the dark

Osmond's approach — actors first — is illustrated by the work of Pierre Thibaudeau. His company, Entr'acte, did not work in repertory (a situation that implies designers present a finished design prior to the rehearsal process) and his designs maintained an ongoing evolution of ideas in direct response to the work of the performers within the rehearsal space:

Murphy and Fredrikson chose to re-present the classic fairy story of *Beauty and the Beast* as a modern representation of the beasts in our present world. Shown is a 'Syringe' dancer from the hard-core Rock world. The other two 'beasts' were from the Gothic and the Corporate worlds.

▼ Figure 65 **Beauty and the Beast**
adapted from the traditional story by Graeme Murphy
Sydney Dance Company
1993
venue: Metro Theatre, Sydney
choreographer: Graeme Murphy
musical director: Carl Vine
set and costume designer: Kristian Fredrikson
lighting designer: John Rayment
photographer: Peter Holderness
The 'Syringes' costume drawing.

Within Entr'acte everything has always been evolving from all directions from the start, around the subject. So if the company decides on a theme, we start looking for source material, research, reading, lots of discussions, and viewing videos. From early on I'm doing sketches while Elisabeth Burke (the director) will be doing her own research and development with a dramaturge. Each individual in the company does their own thinking so that when we come into the rehearsal room we start working around the theme and the individuals' ideas. Everything is explored, everybody has their chance to be heard and we try to explore those different themes and ideas. As this goes on I keep thinking of the possibilities for a set. I show my drawings to the others and get feedback. If that feedback is positive about one style, I go more directly into that area, or I may transform it completely and come back with something else. So in that sense the design remains an ongoing creation. The first sketches to the real thing might have gone through metamorphoses of about five to ten different things before it really ends up to be what it is, although it is still very simplistic … We don't have a story [because] we are not story-based, but we are much more influenced in a way — influenced by feelings and emotions and by trying to create meaning. The meaning is different for everybody who sits and watches, but we are trying to create work with a sense of purpose and meaning and evocation through spatial atmosphere and dramatic movement, style and the theme. We develop around the theme.[20]

Graeme Murphy believes very much in the explorative process of design that can occur during rehearsals, and builds his performances around thoughts rather than words:

You are taking the abstractions first, not the solid words — not using words as building blocks. You are taking thoughts [and] by the end of the day you have converted them, put them on a body, and you actually have something physical … I have worked with a number of painters, sculptors and architects. I find that I like what they bring. I often feel that my theatricality is pretty rich. My ability to actually envisage the space in which my dance works happen is fairly developed, and sometimes it is really nice to work with someone who is coming from a very different point.

I am working with Brian Thomson at the moment. He's certainly very 'there' in theatre. But he works very differently when he works with dance I find, because he doesn't have the restrictions. So much theatre [relies on] 'the bed must be there, the window must be there, and the door must be there' syndrome. It is nice to get away from that and a lot of directors are getting away from that concept [although] often there are real practical requirements …

Dancers tend to create the space around them and tend to create the atmosphere around them by what they are doing.[21]

Kathryn Sproul enjoys using both text and improvisation as the basis for the design process:

I have done fifty-fifty. Looking at both [methods], sometimes my most joyous experiences have been with a text and other times it has been without a text. I like the balance. I enjoy the structure of words, I enjoy the skill of good writers, and [it] is extremely stimulating for me to have them as a starting point. But it is different to then work on a collaboration where, for example, the design may be the starting point to the performance. That happened a number of times at Magpie Theatre Company. Or the writer has given me a one-line description of where the play starts and I have designed it from there. Hopefully the play evolves from the same direction that the design started out in. Then it becomes a question of collaborating and being in the rehearsal room; seeing and understanding what it is that is being created, and making sure that this translates thoroughly as the design is being realised by the carpenters and the wardrobe people in other spaces.[22]

Laurel Frank spoke of the challenge involved when taking a non-text picture-based cartoon script to performance:

I was working with Handspan Theatre on an object performance based on Mary Leunig's drawings [*Daze of our Lives*, Handspan Puppet Theatre, Melbourne, 1995]. Handspan do a very particular sort of theatre that is object based, not performance based. Our starting point was Leunig's drawings … We selected objects which we wanted to deal with, that … we thought would capture the mood of the drawing. With those animated objects we made little scenarios — little frames on stage. We found it didn't work to translate like that, to put the things on stage (no matter how well the objects were made or how clever) and it really had to go through another process to become a theatre piece. The objects had to develop their own logic and they had to have their own development [in order] to hang together. The design had to make a quantum leap beyond just merely illustrating or re-illustrating her work … We had to put the drama back into the objects and [give] them the expression that you might expect an actor to [have]. I think that sense of excitement and challenge really happens when as a designer you are involved from the beginning and you're actually helping to create the idea and shape it into a theatrical experience.[23]

The designer must now move from initial words and pictures to an actual setting, involving the creation of objects, costumes and lighting.

▲ Plates 89a and 89b **Pierrot and
Columbine**

by Terence Crawford

Theatre of Image, in association with the
Sydney Theatre Company

1995

venue: Wharf 2, Sydney Theatre Company

director and designer: Kim Carpenter

composer: Sarah de Jong

lighting designer: Geoff Cobham

photographer: Miki-Nobu Komatsu

Carpenter's original storyboard outlining
the action and design.

De-sign language

Part of the process of design is the ability to represent the ideas in some form that allows the other collaborators to use it in performance. All members of a production team including the performers need to understand very early on in the production process what shape the designs are forming. Negotiation of costs and practicality are discussed, as well as voicing of stylistic concerns. By using photographs, collaged images and fabrics, scale models and technical or working drawings, the set and costume designers have a variety of mediums which communicate ideas clearly.

Richard Roberts is a strong advocate of the model box as a three-dimensional way of exploring the stage space:

A skilful designer is somebody who can sketch quickly, whether that's on a page or sketched in three dimensions, and is someone who can communicate an idea quickly and effectively. I've always found (and it's probably a reflection of [the] inadequacies [of] my drawing skills) that my drawings can lie terribly. Rather

▼ Plate 90 **The Pearl Fishers**
by Georges Bizet
Australian Opera
1994
set and costume designer: Kenneth Rowell
photo: OA archives
Rowell's model for Act III.

than sit down and draw something on the page I've always tried to sketch in three dimensions from the word 'go' … I usually try to cut away decorative things as much as I can to try and find the core of a shape or a dimensional space … Of course I am interested in 'the picture' of what it looks like, but I'm more interested in its spatial qualities and that often means that I am not interested in decorative drawn surfaces at all.[24]

Shaun Gurton agrees with this. He trained as an actor and as a director before moving into design, and spoke of his process as being very 'hands on' and practical:

I don't draw very much and I hardly ever sketch. I'm not very good at drawing … I work all the time directly within the model box, and so the way I'm building up allows me tremendous flexibility.[25]

Tony Tripp, William Passmore and Dan Potra are designers for whom sketching and painting does work effectively. They use the two-dimensional freedom of quick sketching to explore aspects of the performance. Tripp (figs 79, 80) worked in many areas of art and design before committing himself to theatre. His experience as a painter and graphic artist shows up in his love of drawing, a common feature of his design presentations:

The drawing is the act of articulating an idea. The drawing is intended to persuade the director to go with it. It is the best time of all, doing the drawing. At that early stage it is a pure and untroubled thing — nothing to do with the practicalities of realisation. It is a piece of art to seduce.[26]

William Passmore (fig. 67) also uses his drawing skills to influence the direction that a production takes:

I usually visualise the whole thing … and because I draw the stuff I am the first one that gets the design up. I just draw the whole show as a comic book storyboard. It is usually movement by movement, and it could involve people and action, or it can involve atmosphere. From the storyboard the design is broken down into scenes, into locations or into sets and then we start to plot the various models that we need for them. We make white-card models first to establish the scale, and we make full-colour and textured models later, or only make bits of them. It all depends on how big the show is.[27]

Passmore (who comes from a graphic art background) criticises the modern tendency of theatre schools not to emphasise drawing. For him it is one of the most important tools of the performance designer:

▸ Plate 91a **Lulu**
by Alban Berg
Australian Opera
1994
venue: Opera Theatre, Sydney Opera House
director: Mark Gaal
set and costume designer: Angus Strathie
lighting designer: Nigel Levings
photo: OA archives
Strathie's model for Act II.

▸ Plate 91b **Carmen**
by Georges Bizet
Australian Opera
1987
director: John Copley
set designer: Robin Donn
costume designer: Vicki Feitscher
lighting designer: Nigel Levings
photo: OA archives
Model of Act IV.

▸ Plate 91c **Love's Labours Lost**
by William Shakespeare
Royal Queensland Theatre Company
1986
set designer: Andrew Carter
photo: Andrew Carter
Carter's preliminary set model.

▲ Figures 66a, 66b and 66c **Carmen**

by Georges Bizet

Australian Opera

1995

venue: Opera Theatre, Sydney Opera
House

director: Lindy Hume

set designer: Dan Potra

costume designer: Victoria Feitscher

lighting designer: Stephen Wickham

photographer: Peter Holderness

Feitscher's costume renderings for
Carmen and chorus women.

You need the drawing skills because in the bigger shows, with the bigger responsibilities that you have, people expect to see something. You can sit there in front of a director, a production manager or a producer and draw the stuff in front of them, because they want to see something there and then ... I, personally, do not see how you can be in the business unless you can draw. As a designer you need a big visual repertoire and certain skills.[28]

Michael Pearce (pls 93, 94, fig. 68), however, chooses not to draw his set designs (despite being an established painter) since it defeats the most important aspect of the design — use of space — preferring the sculptural freedom presented by the model box:

> I can elaborate on things but I just don't want to. If I had to describe my work, I would say it's very strong, often bold in use of colour and shape, and I'm really interested in using the space. I only ever work from models. I never ever do drawings although I am a very good drawer.[29]

Dan Potra trained as a fine artist from an early age in Romania before studying stage design. His black-and-white cartoon storyboards (fig. 69) quickly capture the movement of a performance in response to the music and script. His skills as a painter come through very strongly in the design presentation. He has an eye for texture and colour, as well as being influenced by the surrealist artists of Europe. He does not engage in painting pretty backdrops, however. Instead, the structure of the space and the texture of objects within it are painted and worked into the overall picture. He often plays with colour in space and utilises its emotive power on the audience's senses.

Similarly, Sue Field is a trained painter as well as a designer. Her designs often play with strong colours and textures within the three-dimensional performance space. Her work on Griffin Theatre Company's *Passion* (fig. 98) season of new works transformed the Stables Theatre into a canvas of hot colours and rich painted textures which formed the constant background to a changing array of plays. Her costume renderings are also heavily painted, often incorporating parts of the set as well. Her drawings for the Bell Shakespeare Company's production of *Richard III* (pls 13 and 14) are a good example of this.

▲ Plate 92 **Lend Me A Tenor**

by Ken Ludwig

Kevin James Promotions

1990

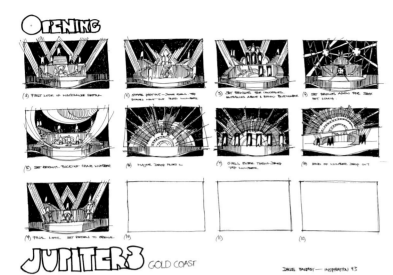

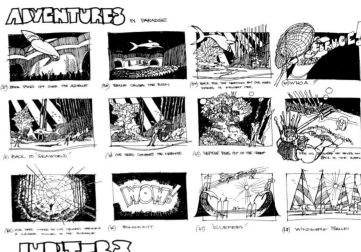

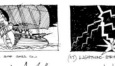

▲ Figure 67 **Odyssey**

devised by Richard Hannah and William Passmore

produced by Conrad Jupiters

1993

venue: International Showroom, Jupiter's Casino, Gold Coast

director: Richard Hannah

choreographer: Ross Coleman

set designer: William Passmore

costume designer: Costume Design Centre

lighting designer: Werner Henkel

Passmore's storyboard for the *Odyssey* spectacular helped to shape the direction of the show.

▲ Plate 93 **Sand Siren**

Australian Ballet

1992

venue: Opera Theatre, Sydney Opera
House

choreographer: Gideon Obarzanek

set and costume designer: Michael
Pearce

lighting designer: Roderick van Gelder

photographer: Robert Colvin

Pearce's costume renderings for Sian
Stokes and Stephen Heathcote.

Although lighting designers such as Rachel Burke (fig. 73) and David Longmuir (figs 54a and 54b) also sketch ideas and rough directions of light before working out the more technical aspects of the lighting rig, lighting designers can find it hard to describe the effect, for example, of a colour as it is bouncing off a cyclorama and creating a halo around an actor's head. They can describe it in terms of hue and intensity and position on stage, but the effect on the senses is intangible — it is felt, not seen. They deal in a purely visual medium that cannot be realised until the lanterns are rigged in the space. There is no lighting model box to demonstrate or fully evaluate ideas, as is used by set designers. Language and sketches are one-dimensional representations of the final effect. Nigel Levings (fig. 74) still finds that:

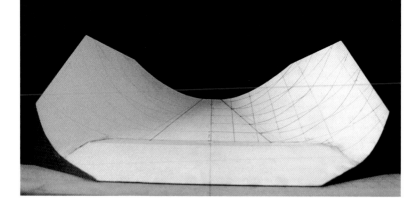

▶ Plates 94a, 94b and 94c **Sand Siren**
Australian Ballet
1992
venue: Opera Theatre, Sydney Opera
House
choreographer: Gideon Obarzanek
set and costume designer: Michael
Pearce
lighting designer: Roderick van Gelder
photographer: Michael Pearce

The progression from

concept and model, to

the workshop and paint-

room floor, to finished

performance, is always in

many stages. The original

small-scale model

remains an accurate

guide throughout for all

involved with the making.

All of lighting design is really difficult to talk about. I used to wonder why I felt so hampered compared with my set design colleagues in presenting design. You begin to realise that part of the problem is that it is the great artists of the world, like Patrick White, who have the skills to be able to portray light in words … in a really vivid way. Some of his descriptions of light are just so fantastic. [I find] it is very hard to explain the complexity of the lighting which you might have in your mind in words — three months before the rehearsal starts — to a director. The best way to do it is to get yourself in the position where the director knows that you will produce the works and you can show them on stage. Lighting designers don't have the equivalent of the white card models that set designers have. They cannot cut it out and push it around. You only do the 'model' when you actually get into the theatre.[30]

Nick Schlieper agrees with Levings and describes how he talks to a director and set designer about his ideas:

It is particularly difficult when you can't make a model to show somebody what it looks like. I do sometimes resort to sketching and make a series of storyboards for a play so that there's something tangible to look at but it's still a very different thing from seeing it there in three dimensions. [I can talk about it] in very vague, intangible, unspecific and therefore slightly dangerous ways — dangerous in terms of possible misunderstanding … When it all works there is a mutual filtration process — you all begin to arrive at the same conclusions. Though they might be quite specific and clear in practical terms, more often than not they have to do with the way you want it to feel, the general direction in which you want it to go and the general line you want to take on a play. In terms of the light, that has more to do with the emotional climate of what it should feel like rather than anything specific in visual terms. As the set designer starts to refine the more ephemeral things and is moving towards the set design, the lighting design in your brain starts to go along in the same direction. The rehearsal process itself then dictates what happens within those parameters.[31]

As part of his design process Levings makes extensive notes based on his reading of the script and works out his equipment needs from that:

I go through the text and I look for references in the text to light and light requirements. I try as much as possible to understand the structure of the text; things like the scene breakdowns, the moods, the time, the time frame of the play, if the thing happens in the time of day and the weather ... I spend a lot of time just looking at the set designer's model of the play and trying to understand the geography of it. I look at the architecture of the stage, the set and the shape of it, the entrances and the exits and how it fits together, trying to understand where the lights can be placed on the stage ... Then I make a list of all the things that I would like to be able to do. Sometimes they are mundane things — a blue sky, or a shaft of light through a window, or light behind a doorway ... Some of my notes will say things like 'a full facial cover and five area control' ... Sometimes I want a warm version and a cool version of that, and that doubles the amount of lights that I need ... It is a balancing process of trying to get the right range of equipment into the lighting rig. Then you add all the numbers up, fax it through to the producers, and they get back to you saying, 'You're 50 per cent over budget. Now is the time to do some cuts!'.[32]

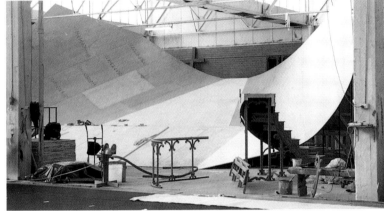

◄ Figures 68a, 68b and 68c **Sand Siren**
Australian Ballet
1992
see pls 94a, 94b and 94c
photographer: Michael Pearce
The set seen in various stages of construction and painting.

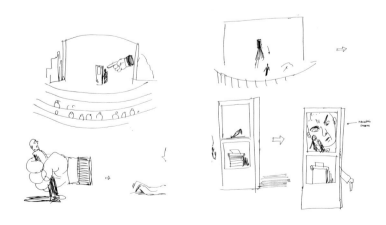

▲ Figure 69 **The Burrow**

composed by Michael Smetanin with libretto by Alison Croggon

Chamber Made Opera

1995

director: Douglas Horton

venue: National Theatre, St Kilda

set and costume designer: Dan Potra

lighting design: David Murray

Potra's original storyboard for *The Burrow*, an opera based on the life of Franz Kafka.

The language of lighting carries a technical jargon that is not easily understood by the layperson. Rachel Burke thinks that the absence of a rich visual language with which to describe and discuss light has a lot to do with the traditional methods of training lighting designers:

> I think because the training originally was very technically based lighting designers were not encouraged to develop a poetic language. You were not encouraged to think metaphorically or poetically. It was more like: 'Here's the set, here's the stage, here's the play; we just need this lit thanks'.[33]

Similarly, Efterpie Soropos encountered this problem when studying lighting at NIDA.[34] Soropos, along with many other lighting designers, is breaking away from the established patterns of lighting language and is developing other ways of talking about and designing light that do not depend solely on either a technical knowledge or an 'intuitive feeling', but incorporate both styles of communication. Computer imaging and three-dimensional lighting programmes have also helped designers in this area, allowing trial runs of lighting rigs to be seen on screen before being hung in place.

Two hand-drawn plan and elevation drawings of Scott-Mitchell's design, which were then given to the model makers, the production supervisors and construction workshops.

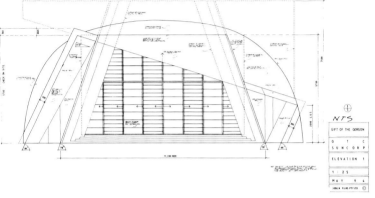

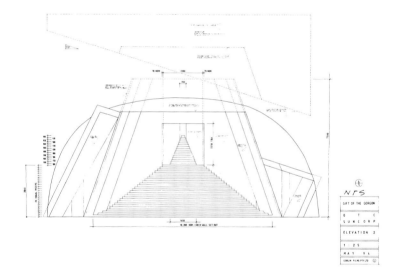

◄ Figures 70a and 70b **Gift of the Gorgon**
by Peter Schaffer
Royal Queensland Theatre Company
1996
venue: Suncorp Theatre, Queensland Performing Arts Centre, Brisbane
director: Richard Wherrett
set and costume designer: Michael Scott-Mitchell
lighting designer: David Whitford

(un)Conscious process

With what seems to be a fear of 'being definable' some designers have shied away from embracing methodology in case it undermines their position as 'inspired artists'. This is not true for all designers; in fact, there are some, such as Mary Moore and Lou Westbury, who consciously use a theoretical framework of ideas to inform their processes. Moore states that she is always aware of the gender of performance and the audience relationship to a stage space. This forces her to look at how she can affect our political and emotional understanding of a performance by playing

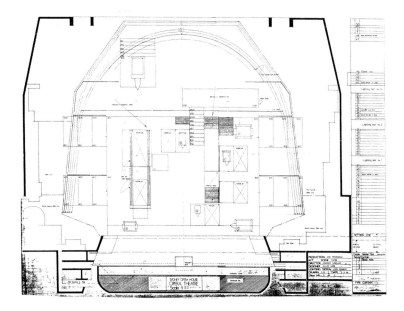

▲ Figure 71 **Das Rheingold**

by Richard Wagner

Australian Opera

1984

venue: Opera Theatre, Sydney Opera
House

director: Andrew Sinclair

set designer: Allan Lees

lighting designer: John Rayment

The ground plan for Scene iii.

with the spatial dimensions. Westbury considers much more than the interests and attention spans of children and youth when designing theatre for young people. As more and more working designers in Australia are coming out of institutions such as NIDA, VCA and WAAPA, a consciousness of process is increasing. The training institutions, by the very structure of their three-year and four-year studio-based teaching programmes, are imparting a definite methodology in design, forming a large part of designers' practice.

Designers are aware of their own processes but tend to use the language of visual artists when asked to describe their methods. Although it is possible to list the steps that a designer may take when designing for a production it is impossible to say whether any designer would consciously follow those steps. Performance design is constantly evolving and the relationship of the designer to the performance whole is one that changes from one collaboration to the next. Often the most organic of design processes is forced to adhere to an existing management's method in order to fit into the superstructure governing a production. Time lines, deadlines and budgets affect the process, as do the strength of collaboration with the director and the designer's response to the proposed performance.

► Figure 72 **The Ring**

adapted by David Bell based on Wagner's
Ring cycle

Queensland Performing Arts Trust

1990

venue: Cremorne Theatre, Queensland
Performing Arts Centre

director: David Bell

set and costume designer: Bill Haycock

Haycock's costume rendering for Albaich
(Russell Dylestra), the dwarf who steals
the gold.

1   S. Curtis, interview with author, 15 November 1993.

2   Edward Gordon Craig, *On the Art of the Theatre*, Mercury Books, London, 1962, p. 23.

3   Compiled by Linda Marson and Kym O'Neil, 'Analysing the design process: A consultative document', *Arts Training Australia*, Victoria, 1992. Another analysis of the formal design process can be found in 'Strategic Planning for Design Organisations', a report commissioned by the Australian Institute of Landscape Architects, the Australian Production Design Association and the Design Institute of Australia, with help from the Design Board of the Australia Council. It was compiled by Murray Brown, Frank Morgan and Jeremy Wright and published in November 1987.

4   P. Cooke, interview with author, 23 October 1995.

5   ibid.

6   Curtis, op. cit.

7   A. French. interview with author, 13 April 1995.

8   B. Thomson, interview with author, 18 November 1993.

9   H. Bell, interview with author, 23 March 1995.

10 A. Mellor, interview with author, 14 March 1995.

11 H. Bell, op. cit.

12 Cooke, op. cit.

13 K. Sproul, interview with author, 5 March 1995.

14 J. Cobb. interview with author, 24 August 1993.

15 T. Parker, interview with author, 11 August 1993.

16 ibid.

17 ibid.

18 T. Bannerman, interview with author, 2 March 1995.

19 W. Osmond, interview with author, 22 March 1995.

20 P. Thibaudeau, interview with author, 21 November 1993.

21 G. Murphy, interview with author, 30 March 1995.

22 Sproul, op. cit.

23 L. Frank, interview with author, 20 March 1995.

24 R. Roberts, interview with author, 23 November 1993.

25 S. Gurton, interview with author, 23 August 1993.

26 T. Tripp, interview with author, 14 August 1993.

27 W. Passmore, interview with author, 15 March 1995.

28 ibid.

29 M. Pearce, interview with author, 11 December 1993.

30 N. Levings, interview with author, 1 March 1995.

31 N. Schlieper, interview with author, 12 March 1995.

32 Levings, op. cit.

33 R. Burke, interview with author, 15 March 1995.

34 See Efterpie Soropos' interview in chapter 8.

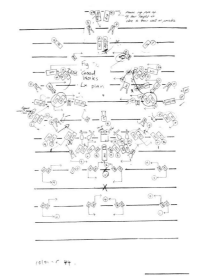

◄ Figure 73 **Good Works**

by Nick Enright

Playbox

1995

venue: Beckett Theatre, CUB Malthouse, Melbourne

director: Kim Durban

set and costume designer: Hugh Colman

lighting designer: Rachel Burke

Burke's hand-drawn lighting plan with notes.

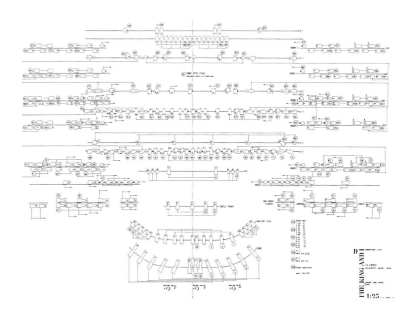

▲ Figure 74 **The King and I**

by Rogers and Hammerstein

The Gordon/Frost Organisation

1991 — national tour

director: Christopher Renshaw

set designer: Brian Thomson

costume designer: Roger Kirk

lighting designer: Nigel Levings

Levings' lighting plan for *The King and I*, drawn up using his own computer software program for lighting designers.

Becoming
a designer

When interviewing the designers in the research for this book, we were interested in how they had come to be working as performance designers in Australia. The responses were varied but familiar: a few older designers had fallen into professional design after working for smaller theatre companies and being noticed by the larger ones; most younger designers trained at NIDA before working freelance: some went on to form their own companies, or to move laterally across the industry into other roles. A selection of the interviews is presented here. illustrating the range of responses to the question: 'How did you become a designer?'.

William Akers

I was trained for the theatre for three-and-a-half years in a school where you were taught everything. You went there nine hours a day, six days a week. It was called the Rathbone Academy of Dramatic Art. As part of being 'top of the school' I got an audition with the John Alden Shakespeare Company. Every actor in Sydney wanted to be in it. In the Alden Company you did everything — you stage-managed, you did props. You certainly rehearsed every day of the week because it was a repertoire company. One also did a great deal of radio work at that time.

'My life has been diverse. I was taught to look at things, and the things I love most are skies and things of nature.

I watch skies ... The ability to know when a sky is alive and when it is not is something that I have learned.'

(W. Akers, interview with author, 8 March 1995)

From the Alden Company I went to Charles Matthews Company as an actor and became a stage manager there. From there I was employed by J. C. Williamsons on a semi-permanent basis so that my services were available to them as an actor–stage manager at any time they wanted me. When they bought you in those days (which they virtually did) they owned you. They could tell you to do anything. When they wanted me to go to Melbourne and become the assistant stage manager of the newly formed Borovansky Company I started the following Monday morning …

Luckily Mr Borovansky and I got on like a house on fire; I wound up being almost like his son. Every time there was a Borovansky Company (it wasn't a permanent company like the Australian Ballet later became) he would demand that I come back, but in the meantime I would go and do some acting or stage directing for Williamsons. I have been involved with ballet ever since then.

When Mr Borovansky was dying in hospital he said to me: 'Bill, I am dying five years too early for you. You'll have to light *Sleeping Beauty*'. But I had never lit anything in my life. They didn't have lighting designers then; they didn't know what they were. For example, Williamsons would bring musicals from overseas and they would also bring the stage directors and they would re-stage the musical for Australia. Williamsons would put up the lights and the head electrician would come in. Nevertheless, I did as I was told and did the lighting for the *Sleeping Beauty*. I was then referred to as the stage director …

I finally got to be called a lighting designer much later on when the new Australian Ballet left the Lebanon and we went to Covent Garden. The lighting was commented on and when Bobby Helpmann came back to Australia he said: 'You have to give Bill the international credit that he deserves. He's been lauded overseas!'. So the next time I went to the front of the theatre (which I don't do very often) and there on the billboards along with artistic director, musical director, etc. was 'Lighting Director — William Akers'. I nearly collapsed into the gutter. That was 1965. There was no other person in this country at that time who was called a lighting director-designer. There has seldom been anyone else who has been called a production director. I think the second one was Sue Nattrass, but that was twenty years later.[1]

▲ Plate 97 **The King and I**

by Rogers and Hammerstein

The Gordon/Frost Organisation

1991 — national tour

venue: premiered at Adelaide Festival
Centre

director: Christopher Renshaw

musical director: Peter Casey

choreography: Yuriko and Susan Kikuchi

set designer: Brian Thomson

costume designer: Roger Kirk

lighting designer: Nigel Levings

photographer: Branco Gaica

photo: GFO archives

in photo: Tony Marinyo as the King of
Siam (centre) in the Throne Room

► Plate 98 **The King and I**
The Gordon/Frost Organisation
1991 — national tour
see pl. 97
photographer: Branco Gaica
photo: GFO archives
in photo: Hayley Mills as Anna
(far right), addressing the Ladies
of the Court

▼ Plate 99 **The King and I**
The Gordon/Frost Organisation
1991 — national tour
see pl. 97
photographer: Branco Gaica
photo: GFO archives
in photo: Anna (Hayley Mills)
and the King (Tony Marinyo) in
the King's study

Kirk used original Thai gold-threaded silk sarongs on all the principals, and the King's gold-tinged costume in the opening scene was inspired by a famous painting in the palace in Bangkok. He incorporated authentic Thai masks and original colours from the 1950s production into the ballet sequences.

'It's no longer about Westerners ogling some strange society — it's about that society being intrigued by a Westerner and what she represents', explains Thomson. 'Many of the people who see the show have been to Asia and they know the difference between Indonesia and Thailand, India and China. This production is original and relates to the fact that in Australia we're very much a part of Asia — the days of being a part of Europe and London and America just don't exist anymore.'

[Thomson, quoted by Suzanne Olb, 'Designed for a king', *Stages*, Jan./Feb. 1992, p. 8]

Brian Thomson

I started [designing shows] here in Sydney and then I went away and did *Rocky Horror Picture Show* and *Jesus Christ Superstar* and things like that in England and America. To think now about going and working in the West End or Broadway does not interest me whatsoever because I feel that I've done it and done it in a way that was quite striking. *Rocky Horror* and the original *Superstar* are very important pieces in the fabric of [twentieth century] theatre. Those kind of things are part of me but it's part of a history that I don't necessarily want to repeat ...

I suppose if I hadn't started off by doing *Superstar* in the West End (which went for nine years) and then doing *Rocky Horror*, which went right around the world and is still going, my attitude would be different. Because I've done that I don't feel any need to [prove myself or take my work elsewhere] ...

Everything I've done has been accidental. I met Jim Sharman in a hamburger bar and we [worked together on] a couple of things here, then we did *Superstar*, then we went to London, so that was a fairly fast involvement with the business. In theatre I don't think anyone has ever had such a set-up, but if you were to set it up as you dream of doing it, I guess that's what you would do. I take this seriously but I don't suppose I'd ever really thought: 'This is my career'. I've thought: 'This is what I do and I've done it for twenty years and at the moment there's certainly no feeling that I'm bored by it or that I need more challenges'.[2]

▼ Plate 100 **South Pacific**

by Rogers and Hammerstein

The Gordon/Frost Organisation in association with the Adelaide Festival Theatre Trust

1993 — national tour

venue: premiered at the Adelaide Festival Centre

director: Christopher Renshaw

set designer: Brian Thomson

costume designer: Roger Kirk

lighting designer: Nigel Levings

photographer: Branco Gaica

▶ Plate 101 **Rockola**

by Tim Gooding

Nimrod

1978

venue: Nimrod Upstairs

director: Richard Wherrett

choreographer: Chrissie Koltai

set designer: Brian Thomson

costume designer: Sue Blane

lighting and sound design: Gordon Evans

photographer: Peter Holderness

in photo: (left to right) Kris McQuade (Angel Sugar), Tony Llewellyn-Jones (Pagliacci), Jackie Weaver (Velvet), and Robin Ramsay (Jet de Luxe)

Parker created a colonial environment made up of nineteenth-century furniture stacked high above the stage.

The performers utilised various chairs and trunks as part of their physical and symbolic journey through the opera.

▲ Plate 102 **Tresno**
by Jacqui Rutten
Chamber Made Opera
1995
venue: Beckett Theatre, CUB Malthouse, Melbourne
director: Douglas Horton
set and costume designer: Trina Parker
lighting designer: Margie Medlin
photographer: Trina Parker

▶ Figure 76 **Drumming up a Storm**
Southgate River Festival
1992
venue: South Bank, Melbourne
director: Bomber Perrier
composer: Graeme Leak
set and costume designer: Trina Parker
photographer: Trina Parker

Trina Parker

I went to East Sydney Tech[nical College] in the late 1960s to learn to be an interior designer and I did an interior design and architectural draughtpersons certificate — a combined course then. I started that when I was about nineteen; at the same time I had become involved in theatre. I joined the New Theatre, which was a very active semi-professional company. For five years every day I went to tech. and every night I went to the New Theatre. I did everything — I acted, stage-managed and prompted. I had no desire to work professionally in the theatre because there was no funding. The New Theatre was basically attended by communists and there was no money to support that kind of theatre. I didn't like the kind of work that they did in commercial theatre — commercial theatre then being a particular kind of English repertory piece or American musical.

I went overseas, like everyone did, after I finished and worked in architects' offices. When I came back in 1974 I stayed with a friend of mine in Melbourne who offered me a job as a designer and stage manager at the Arena Theatre, which was a fairly big company for young people. I became very involved in theatre for young people and I've worked in Melbourne theatre ever since — more on the edges and the fringe than in the mainstream, working for community theatre companies, individuals, circus and theatre. I was the artistic director of Handspan Theatre for four-and-a-half years so I've actually been a 'theatre worker' rather than just a designer. I've administrated and I've been in lots of different bodies — been on the Australia Council to assess grant applications and I've had a wider political interest in the world than sitting at home with a piece of paper.

I often laughed and said that I had never done a play with three acts or sets with doors in it ... I have always thought that I wasn't part of the establishment and now I think I am. [laughs] [3]

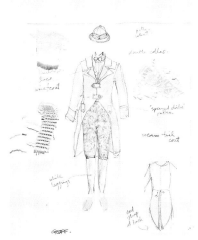

◄ Figures 77a, 77b and 77c **Tresno**
Chamber Made Opera
1995
see pl. 102
photographer: Robert Colvin
Parker's costume renderings for Deanne Flatley, Cazerine Barry and Geoff Dunstan.

▲ Plate 103 **Under Milkwood**

by Dylan Thomas

State Theatre Company of South
Australia

1993

venue: Playhouse, Adelaide Festival
Centre

director: Simon Phillips

set designer: Shaun Gurton

costume designer: Bronwyn Jones

lighting designer: Krystof Kysloski

photographer: David Wilson

in photo: The cast in performance

Shaun Gurton

It was actually all by chance. I grew up doing theatre at school. I did one
year of advertising art at a college when I was seventeen. Hated it. My
great love was acting and I wanted to be an actor and work in the theatre.
I found myself auditioning for the Melbourne Theatre Company [MTC] in
1967 as a young actor. This was in the days when the design schools were
just beginning. I stayed with the MTC until 1970 and then I went back to
England and I stayed there for a year trying to get work as an actor. I was
also writing a lot in my journal about the visual side of theatre and getting
more and more interested in experimental design rather than what was
then a very decorative style of theatre design.

When I came back from England I was very interested in directing and I
was part of a trainee-director scheme that the Australia Council ran in
those days. I directed at university and I directed the Orange Festival of
Arts for the Tasmanian Regional Players. I decided to apply to a few
companies to be a trainee-director and one of the companies that said yes
was to become the State Theatre Company in South Australia. The artistic
director then was a man called Peter Batey and he said: 'You can be a
trainee director but you'll have to do quite a bit of acting as well'. I did that
for about a year and then a great thing happened. George Ogilvie (when I
was a young director he was the major and the most admired director
working in Australia) decided to become the artistic director of the
company. I worked then as an actor but I was also a mask maker for the
company. It was like an apprenticeship and I was allowed to pursue some
thoughts that I'd had visually. One of the designers who was supposed to
do a play that season couldn't do it or wasn't well, and George said: 'Why
don't you do it? I'm directing it. It's a two-hander. It's a play set in a
background that you know about. Why don't you have a go at it?'. And I did.
Then I did two or three afterwards and some of them I acted in as well as
designing.

Finally I did the transition from doing the acting to doing the designing
in 1973. I learnt how to be a designer not through classes but actually
doing it on the job. Very fortunately there was a fantastic workshop where
the production manager and the construction manager allowed me to do
my apprenticeship. In a way I was a lot more adventurous because, as far
as I was concerned, there weren't any rules and I really wanted to do things
that were nearly impossible to do. And so in a way it was a much looser and
a much freer way of learning to do it. Hopefully some of that I still have,
except that as you get older you get a little more sensible.[4]

Tony Tripp

Well, I went to art school with the intention of becoming a commercial artist. That's what I seemed to think I was going to be when I began the course at the Newcastle Technical College. (I had left high school well before my final exams — a departure viewed by my family as terribly foolish.) As a result of the people I met there — the other students and lecturers — within a year I had changed my mind. I was going to be a painter, a true artist. I didn't confide this change of view to my parents (who were subsidising me) but that was my goal. However when I finished the course I found I had no choice but to work in commercial art. Simultaneously I began designing sets and costumes for amateur and student productions. I also performed (ineptly) in several plays. By now I seemed to be going in two directions at once. One was thinking that I might be a designer and the other was that fine art was going to be my destiny.

I moved to Sydney and began a job designing business stationery, which was incredibly boring but it was a living, and I was going to painting classes at night and going to the theatre regularly. I changed jobs, to design greeting cards for John Sands and proved a hopeless failure. My next venture was with an animated film company where I became a background artist, and also did some storyboards and some animation. During this time I was offered a play to design at NIDA and that felt like a real break-through. Perversely, I then returned to Newcastle to marry and needed to find a job quickly because we were expecting a child. I joined NBN (Channel 3, Newcastle) and they had me creating news sets and designs for quiz shows and variety. I did this for a couple of years until there was a live show cut-back and I switched to the graphics department, which I

▼ Figure 78 **The Importance of Being Earnest**

by Oscar Wilde

Melbourne Theatre Company

1990

venue: Comedy Theatre, Melbourne

director: Simon Phillips

set and costume designer: Tony Tripp

lighting designer: Jamieson Lewis

photo: MTC archives

in photo: (left to right) Richard Piper and Geoffrey Rush in the 'garden'

Tripp's inventive set was based on the famous *Yellow Book* illustrated by Aubrey Beardsley. The three acts were framed as different chapter illustrations in a large book. By turning the pages the Butler heralded scene changes. At the end of the show the book was closed to reveal a large open handbag.

► Figures 79a, 79b and 79c **The Tempest**

Melbourne Theatre Company

1990

see pl. 104

photographer: Robert Colvin

Tripp's costume drawings for the three goddesses, Iris, Juno and Ceres, who arrive to bless Miranda's wedding.

▼ Figure 80 **The Tempest**

Melbourne Theatre Company

1990

see pl. 104

photographer: Robert Colvin

Tripp's set rendering of Prospero's cave.

ran for about six years. All the while I was designing plays, in particular nine or ten productions for a small professional company set up at the Octagon Theatre on the campus of the University of Western Australia, Perth. I designed these long distance — excellent training in clarity of communication.

At the end of that period the ever-growing Tripp family departed for England. While in London I went to many plays and became excited by what I saw (in particular Peter Brook's *A Midsummer Night's Dream*, which I found to be life-changing), and came back to Australia with a determination to do it — to design for theatre. I didn't return to Newcastle but settled in Sydney and secured myself an agent. I was immediately offered the resident designer job at the Playhouse in Perth and worked there for three terrific years. I then came to the Melbourne Theatre Company on the invitation of John Sumner and here I have remained.

In a sense the reason I chose design was because I was stage-struck. I had some drawing skills and some artistic flair but I certainly was no actor. The logical way of combining those things was to become a designer. It was the logical coming together of a passion and a skill.[5]

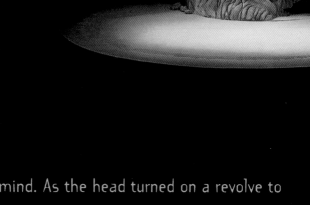

Tripp was inspired by the

ancient Mediterranean

world in his designs. The

large head, rising rock-like

from the floor, symbolised Prospero's mind. As the head turned on a revolve to

reveal a cave, the audience metaphorically entered his thoughts and was privy to

his innermost secrets.

▲ Plate 104 **The Tempest**
by William Shakespeare
Melbourne Theatre Company
1990
venue: Playhouse, Victorian Arts Centre
director: Gale Edwards
set and costume designer: Tony Tripp
lighting designer: Jamieson Lewis
photo: MTC archives

Cooper's set (painted by Anthony Bibacci), was done with three layers of painted texture and colour. This caused a lace-like pattern to show through the uppermost layer, giving the walls a subtle, bruised appearance.

▲ Figure 81 **The Cavalcaders**
by Billie Roche
Royal Queensland Theatre Company
1995
venue: Suncorp Theatre, Queensland
Performing Arts Centre
director: Maeliosa Stafford
set and costume designer: Melody
Cooper
lighting design: David Whitford
in photo: Kevin Hides (Terry) and
Errol O'Neill (Josie)

▶ Plate 105 **Desert Flambé**
devised by the Women in Theatre Project
1980
venue: Nimrod Downstairs, Sydney
director: Chrissie Koltai
set and costume designer: Melody
Cooper
lighting designer: Annie Heath
photographer: William Yang

Melody Cooper

I started [designing] in 1975 when Rex Cramphorn was my director in my final year at NIDA. It was the first time that Rex had found anybody who could understand what he was saying in terms of what he required of the design. After that every year I would go and do one or two shows with Rex at what was originally called the Theatre Workshop and what has eventually become the Centre for Performance Studies at Sydney University. We had fantastic resources made available to us. Although we did have performances that the public would flock to, that wasn't the *raison d'être* of the work [that we created]. It was to document the process so that the process [of performance-making] could be analysed, and a methodology of how theatre is produced, how an audience understands things, how a text is changed by different interpretations and different translations [could be developed]. We did a whole range of productions ...

When he died it was like the main mind with whom I had collaborated was gone. Rex was not an ego-driven person. We were all supported through the process by his immense intellect and his great feeling for all of us. I thought: 'There'll never be another director I want to work with, I'll never want to do theatre again'. I basically resigned. I retired from theatre after Rex died and moved to Darwin [although] I very quickly realised that I couldn't actually leave theatre behind. I became involved with the Darwin Theatre Company almost immediately upon arriving and gradually realised that there's something ... It's a disease, theatre. Once you get it, that's it. You've got it. It's something you will have forever.[6]

The imagery in this production was distinctly edible, with candy-floss clouds floating above ice-cream hills; at times the actors even licked the painted walls.

Laurel Frank

When Circus Oz began I was actually a performer. It goes back to my training. I worked at the Pram Factory in the 1970s for about eight years, and Circus Oz was an offshoot of the Australian Performing Group [that was operating collectively out of the Pram Factory]. It was the people involved with the Pram Factory who decided to use the circus form to develop a political theatre using a more guerrilla street theatre type of form but with circus skills ...

In those days everybody did everything. And I was someone with sewing and making skills so I tended to look after that side of it. It was not design in the usual sense, it was something that evolved out of the need to actually present the show. At first it was just jeans, shirts and T-shirts and no-one thought very much about presentation. The more we got into the circus side of it the more we started to exploit circus imagery, usually in a very twisted and ironic way. One snapshot springs to mind of someone in a camel costume and someone being the back half of the camel and someone being the front half, and completely overdressed, gorgeous, beautiful assistants sitting on the back of the camel. There is a wimpy looking strongman off to one side. It's taking the clichéd images of traditional theatre and sending them up, basically ...

It hasn't changed. I don't mean that I am still doing the same thing. But I have worked with so many different groups of people within Circus Oz and those ideas come up again and again. It's a challenge to find a new way to do it, or sometimes we just get out a 10-year-old costume and it's the perfect thing.[7]

◄ Plate 106 **Circus Oz**
1990–91 — national tour
venue: Circus Oz touring tent
director: Tim Coldwell
set and costume: Laurel Frank
photographer: Laurel Frank
The set within the tent.

▲ Plate 107 **Southgate River Festival**
Melbourne International Festival of the Arts
1992
venue: South Bank, Melbourne
director: Bomber Perrier
costume designer: Laurel Frank
photo: VIC Perrier archives
in photo: A roving musician in one of Frank's costumes. Each costume had screenprinted and handpainted detailing

▲ Figure 82 **The Trackers of Oxyrhynchus**
by Tony Harrison
Sydney Theatre Company
1992
venue: Wharf 1, Sydney Theatre Company
director: Mark Gaal
set designer: Michael Scott-Mitchell
costume designer: Tess Schofield
lighting designer: Nigel Levings
photographer: Robert McFarlane

'For *The Trackers of Oxyrhynchus*, the interior of the Wharf theatre has been decked out in rusty scaffolding. White electric cables and small lights are threaded round and about as though it was an excavation shaft leading to an archaeological dig. This is more than a gimmick of design: it heightens the sense of expedition, of journeying from the past to the present, of leaving everyday reality and entering an imaginary world where time, place and identity are all changeable ... Scott-Mitchell's set of red pebbles and packing crates, Schofield's tongue-in-cheek costumes and prodigious prosthetics and Peggy Carter's make-up as camouflage combine to create arresting visuals that serve serious art by some funny means.'

(B. Evans, *Sydney Morning Herald*, 23 January 1992)

Michael Scott-Mitchell

I launched into a Sydney University architecture degree and stayed there for just on two years of the first degree. During that time I became fairly unsettled because, although I was doing well in the course, architecture was not sitting comfortably with me. I felt that there was something a bit wrong with their whole priority structure. I was often criticised for designing things that were too sculptural and yet I see that as one of the key problems with contemporary architecture — that it isn't sculptural enough. I was then lucky enough to meet Robin Lovejoy.

Robin was one of the early driving forces in Australian theatre. He helped set up the Old Tote (which was the precursor of the Sydney Theatre Company) and he was also one of the early directors in Australian opera. He had actually started as an actor in the 1930s, moved into being a designer, then gradually became a director. He was working with the

◄ Figure 83 **The Trackers of Oxyrhynchus**

Sydney Theatre Company

1992

see fig. 82

photographer: Robert McFarlane

in photo: (left to right) Teo Gebert, David Field, Lydia Miller (behind), Paul Blackwell, Jeanette Cronin (behind) and Laurence Clifford as satyrs

Australian Opera at that point in time. We made an instant connection. I understood immediately where he was coming from and the language he was talking — it was to do with what makes up the performance space. There was a component about the way he expressed and manipulated space that immediately felt comfortable with the way I had been thinking. He became a great mentor to me and because he was just about to go to NIDA to take over both the design and the directing courses, I applied, stopped a couple of months short of the academic year at Sydney University, prepared myself for NIDA and got in ...

The design course was more immediate in form. You are straight into building shows (there is first-year slave labour in that place but at least you're getting your hands dirty and you're doing something!) and then the second year was like an intense studio year. By the third year you are up and running. I was very fortunate in having Robin there. He was definitely one of the driving forces pushing me along. We had great admiration for one another, though it was more to do with the fact that he challenged me. We were always arguing but it was terrific to actually have somebody call your bluff and get angry with you with that sort of volatility. He was critical in the true academic sense of the word. He would give me positive criticism for what I was doing and I would rebut it. There was a great dialogue going on in class. Judith Hoddinott, Robert Kemp, John Senczuk, Derrick Cox and myself were the group that finally graduated.[8]

► Figure 84 **The Trackers of Oxyrhynchus**

Sydney Theatre Company

1992

see fig. 82

photographer: Peter Holderness

Schofield's costume rendering for one of the prosthetically enhanced satyrs.

Lou Westbury

My first attraction to the theatre was the people, and I just loved them. I mean, I came from a street where most of the girls were pregnant by the age of fourteen. I was really searching for another way to be in the world, and I ended up in the fine art and design course at Deakin University (I think my father thought it was a nice hobby until I got married) and then through that course I met 'theatre' ... We would be experimenting with sculptures down by the river or something and the theatre students would say: 'Why don't you do some sculptures and we'll make some theatre around it' ... So we used to play with all of those ideas, though there were other people who just couldn't understand it. They thought we should just be playing with oil paints ...

Also at that time I got involved in contemporary dance. My big mentors at that time were James McCaughey (who was the artistic director at the Mill Community Theatre Company and also the head lecturer at the performing arts course at Deakin University) and there was Nannett Hassall, who is one of the leading contemporary dance choreographers in

Westbury's set very cleverly concealed a swimming pool within itself. The fold-up lid of the pool was hidden under the floor of the first scene, and when opened up,

gave the impression of an Olympic pool, complete with water. The design travelled to the Prague Quadrennial in 1993, and was the only representation of theatre for young people from Australia.

Australia and who was brought in to teach by James. James McCaughey's form of theatre is extremely physical ... The course he taught was called 'making the play' and that summed up his philosophy in terms of teaching theatre. He looked at what makes something theatrical and he wasn't *just* training actors to act, designers to design or writers to write; he also looked at what made something theatrical. Often he would turn to me and say: 'I want you to think about design and about how we'll stage it — is it going to be on a table? Are we going to use a round table rather than ramps or barrels?'. I started to do that, to think about such things, though I

▲ Plate 109 **Boss of the Pool**
Acting Out Theatre for Young Audiences
1993
see pl. 108
photo: Barking Gecko archives

had not at that point said I wanted to be a designer. I was just experimenting with everything ...

Then I went overseas in 1983 and studied at a summer school of contemporary dance because I was very attracted to movement and abstract concepts and contemporary dance. I was very much into exploring abstract concepts, exploring space and shapes. I went for a short time to India and I ended up in London. Then I applied to do the Amsterdam Summer School of Dance and I got in. I was a little bit worried because I was interested in *everything* — you know, 'general trades but no focus'. Then I decided to come back to Australia and I got a job with the Woolly Jumpers Theatre for Young People.

Working on the Woolly Jumpers programme were four of us. We were employed as actors but we had to do everything. We had to write the plays, select the programme, select the director and any other artist we felt we needed — a writer or a designer or even an administrator. I was the one who said: 'I'll do the design'. We all crossed over into other areas ... I still direct whenever I can and am collaborating on projects where I have an input into the writing and that whole building up of the concept of the performance.[9]

Michael Pearce

I think I always wanted to be a performer or a visual artist or both. I went to art school and then Flinders University and did drama, English and fine arts, and that's when I started doing some designing. I still also wanted to perform. Then when I came to work in the Melbourne Theatre Company as an assistant stage manager I saw a lot of frustration in performers. I thought there may be more challenge in designing and more worthwhile projects. Initially I did everything.

I was a performer with a group called Chrome, a three-male performing group which is still performing all around the world, but I left in 1988 to do my own work because I was being pulled in too many directions ... so I haven't performed for ten years. It started off with just two of us in art galleries, but then we brought in a musician. It was non-verbal based — it

Pearce created a literary space in which Woolf could

roam, yet remain confined. Designed for touring, the

uncluttered set encapsulated the mindscape of Woolf.

▶ Plate 110 **A Room of One's Own**
based on the novel by Virginia Woolf; adapted by Patrick Garland
Melbourne Theatre Company, in association with the State Theatre Company of South Australia
1994
venue: Russell Street, Melbourne and Belvoir Street Theatre, Sydney
director: Lois Ellis
set designer: Michael Pearce
costume designer: Alexandra Tynan
lighting designer: Jamie Revell-Hanson
photographer: Michael Pearce
in photo: Pamela Rabe as Virginia Woolf

◄ Figures 85a and 85b **Revelation and Fall**

as devised by the Australian Dance Theatre

Netherlands Dance Company

1986

choreographer: Glen Tetley

set and costume designer: Michael Pearce

lighting design: Jennifer Tipton

photographer: Sven Ulsa

in photos: 85a Simone Clifford (front) as the Muse fleeing across the set; 85b Simone Clifford and Gerald Tibbs

▼ Figure 86 **Revelation and Fall**

as devised by the Australian Dance Theatre for the 1984 Adelaide Festival

Netherlands Dance Company

1986

choreographer: Glen Tetley

set and costume designer: Michael Pearce

photographer: Peter Holderness

Pearce's working drawings for the Muse as drawn for the Netherlands Dance Company, based on his original design for the Australian Dance Theatre.

was movement and music based, and it moved out into street spaces — like a universal language. We appealed to people from a very wide cross-section, from theatre people and experienced people through to people who have never been inside a theatre in their lives.

I don't want to be designing all the time. It's very much necessary for me to do my own work but when I am actually on projects I am very good at intuitively stirring/disturbing people's visions. The good thing about dance [is] you are always working on a new work, so it's an unknown quantity. You're not working on an existing script. You never know what is going to happen. So the collaboration has to be really close and you can be the source of [stimulation] ... inspiration is too strong a word, or vice versa. So you really have to enter their way of thinking. [Luckily] I think I am very intuitive.[10]

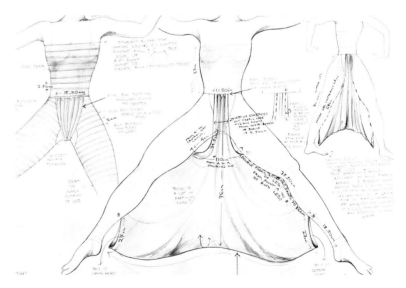

Efterpie Soropos

I knew that I would work in theatre from high school. My first theatre group was the Australian Theatre for Young People (ATYP) under the artistic directorship of Jane Westbrook. We had a grungy warehouse in Chippendale, Sydney, where one needed a torch to climb the stairs at night. I worked as a legal secretary during the day but eventually quit, went on the dole and spent all my money on drama workshops ...

Fate took me to NIDA and there I realised that design was where I wanted to be using my skills. I became interested in lights although my tutors were very discouraging. The way in which they viewed lighting did not fit in with the way they viewed me. It is not a sexist thing in particular. It was an attitude to the way I interpreted lighting. I am 'too organic and emotional' in my response to design. I refused to use 'boy banter' or adopt the uniform. This has made me very resilient in my career ...

I went to work at The Performance Space where the artistic director and administrator were very supportive of my desire to be a lighting designer. They allowed me a space in which to hone my skills. I then went to Canberra as a designer, from which time I have been recommended from group to group, show to show ... one's reputation grows from experience.

I have received grants to work on my own projects with computer-generated lights and dancers, based on the choreography of light and dance. The possibilities are very exciting for dance at the moment.[11]

This research project was funded wholly by the Australia Council, and Greater Union Technology provided the lighting equipment — interstellar beams, trackspots and the controlling system. 'The equipment has been used for many years in the club and entertainment industry. Their use is almost always to facilitate being bold, bright, loud and flashing, etc. I wanted to discover how subtle one could be with them, to find a rhythm and see if it could be synchronised with the human body.' The slides pictured illustrate one of the more successful pieces — Soropos used trackspots to create a cyclical pattern of lights finding the body; moving one after the other, up and down, pausing and fading in conjunction with the dancer's moving body. The piece began very slowly until both the lighting and dancer sped up their movement cycles, climaxing over ten minutes. It was a good example of the possibilities for using 'intelligent' lighting as an interactive medium in performance.

(notes — E. Soropos, 1995)

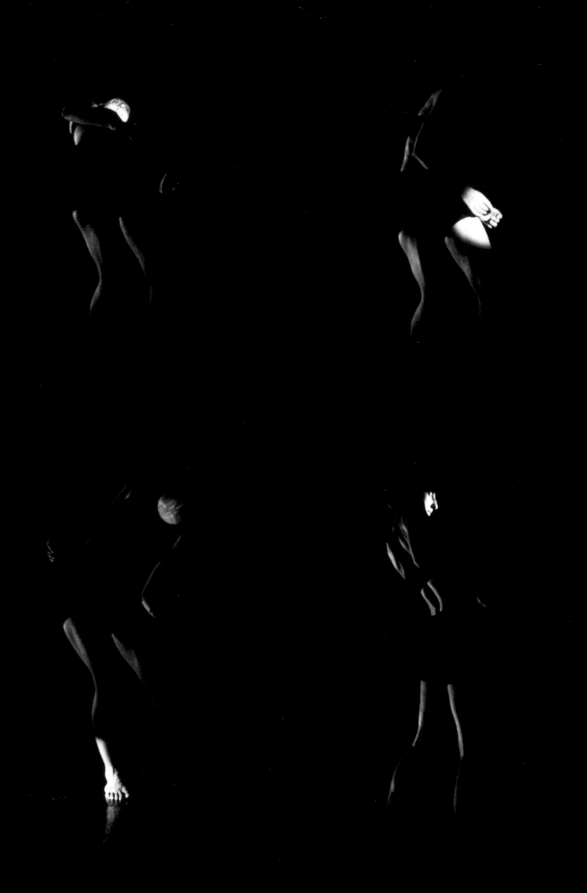

◄ Figures 87a, 87b, 87c and 87d **Research into the co-choreography of light and dance**

1994–95

Funded by the Australia Council for the Arts

venue: The Performance Space, Sydney

choreographers-dancers: Sue-Ellen Kohler, Kate Champion and Julie-Anne Long

lighting designer: Efterpie Soropos

lighting technician: Simon Wise

photographer: Sally Tsoutis

in photos: Sue-Ellen Kohler's body lit by computerised trackspots

Judith Cobb

I studied fashion design first. I don't think many students go from fashion to set design but I knew of no costume design courses. I didn't know about NIDA. I just went straight from high school to the Royal Melbourne Institute of Technology. It gave me the basics in design and I developed a design sensibility. It taught me about colour and form. It equipped me with a technical approach to making clothes which has stood me in good stead as a costume designer. Luckily when I finished that course I just happened to fall into a job as design assistant at the Melbourne Theatre Company. I trained there and I had to learn quickly how to draft sets. They had a small theatre called The Athenaeum Two which gave me a chance to do small set and costume designs and it was a good training ground. I eventually became a resident designer there. I was there for six years but then decided to leave and gain a broader experience, and since then I've been freelancing. I think freelancing has broadened my whole approach to

Drawing on the bold forms and colours of the Australian business boom in the 1980s, Cobb created a millionaire's mansion playground with hints of Brett Whiteley and other Australian painters in the setting — the symbols of excessive fortune acquired by avaricious entrepreneurs in the pre-recession days. Cobb described the differences between venues for this touring set: 'The original design was for the Merlyn Theatre

which does not have conventional "black box" theatre masking. The Merlyn has postmodern dark grey scaffolding gantries and the design was situated in the middle of this and related well to the theatre space. It was not confined by a "black box". There was a different dynamic at the Alexander Theatre with its conventional proscenium arch and black masking.'

(J. Cobb, interview with author, 24 August 1993)

design, working in lots of different theatres with different people and different approaches. I've been studying fine art and painting, which has opened up a lot of different ways of thinking about design …

I started theatre designing when I was twenty years old and was a bit overwhelmed at the whole process of getting things on stage and the way people seemed to approach design. Now I feel I can try out things … I like to experiment …

More recently I've become aware that there are hundreds and hundreds of ways to realise a creative idea, whether it be for a design or for a painting. All these methods are valid. I can approach design in [so many] different ways … I think what makes the live theatre special are those moments in theatre when the right actor at the right time says a fantastic piece of dialogue. It's the good thing about theatre. It is why it works; you have to 'be there' to appreciate it. I suppose that's why you keep doing it.[12]

Cobb created a space that mirrored the map of veins and blood cells in the body, physically illustrating the progress of the HIV virus through the body, a central theme of the play. It was the initial simplicity of Cobb's design that encouraged and enabled the actors to find different ways of moving within the space. Simple metal poles and floating transparencies defined the studio environment, providing a practical working area for the actors to explore the play.

▲ Plate 112 **Desire Lines**
by Michael Gurr
People Living With AIDS (VIC)
1993
director: Bruce Myles
set and costume designer: Judith Cobb
lighting design: Glenn Hughes
The director walking through the set during rehearsals.

◄ Plates 113a and 113b **Desire Lines**
People Living With AIDS (VIC)
1993
see pl. 112

Colin Mitchell

I didn't go to NIDA. I came up through amateur theatre in the country, basically. I started doing things when I was about fifteen with the amateur companies around a tiny little country town …

I'd always been a very good drawer or painter as a kid, and as I got into secondary education the teachers saw a talent and they encouraged me to explore it. A friend took me to an amateur theatre production at the age of about fourteen and it must have been dreadful when I think back to it, but I thought: 'This is what I want to be involved in. This is fabulous'. It was all colour and movement. I got involved in that company painting their sets and I ended up acting, choreographing, directing, designing and painting them. I even prompted. I did every job involved in a theatre. That's the way I've trained myself right from amateur theatre days onwards. There's no-one there to teach you because they are all butchers, farmers and doctors' wives …

It's taken me five times longer than if I'd gone to NIDA, mark my words. NIDA may not be the best school and it may not teach you everything, but it is an immediate short circuit into the industry as it stands. Everybody waits at the end of the year for that new designer to come out of NIDA, and they are immediately given a go somewhere and snapped up by an agent. When you start on the *Mikado* at fifteen, in a country town of 3000 people in Victoria, you've got a long way to go before people accept you as somebody who knows what they're doing.[13]

▼ Figure 88 **The Frogs**
based on the play by Aristophanes
Company B
1992
venue: Belvoir Street Theatre
director: Geoffrey Rush
set designer: Brian Thomson
costume designer: Colin Mitchell
lighting designer: Mark Howett
in photo: The chorus in performance

In this crazy updated version of *The Frogs*, Thomson and Mitchell came up with: 'a cross between an ancient Greek ruin and a contemporary Greek restaurant, with everything conceivably Greek thrown in along the way. The play involves a journey to Hell: "I suppose the idea of Hell in this is a Greek restaurant on a bad night!", laughs Thomson'.

(J. Litson, 'Theatre's master builder', *Australian Weekend Review*, 21 November 1992, p. 12)

Kim Carpenter

I am a conceptual designer. Initially, my talent was to draw and paint, and I was also exposed to the theatre at a young age. When I went to NIDA I did the technical production course, not the design course. In order to graduate you had to direct a one-act play and I chose a very visual piece of work, Artaud's *Spurt of Blood*. In a sense it was the forerunner to what I do now. Nobody acknowledged that this kind of 'visual' theatre existed. They did overseas, but in Australia (this was the end of 1969) nobody said, 'You can actually direct like this and make a piece of theatre.' I used to read about it in books, but it certainly wasn't happening here. So I worked as a designer and earned my living. At times, periods of frustration drove me away from design to painting, and I held art exhibitions as well.

When the opportunity arose to apply for the job as co-artistic director at Nimrod, I decided to put all my eggs in the one basket. Neil Armfield and I were appointed and, in association with John Bell, formed the artistic triumvirate at Nimrod. This gave me the opportunity to put my visions and images on stage so that they became *living* images, as opposed to being simply a visual component of a play.

When I applied for the job I stated that I wanted to direct from a visual point of view. Paul Isles was the general manager at that time and could see this was a strong direction, so was willing to give it a go. I designed a lot of conventional plays in my time there, but *Slice* (figs 14a and 14b) was the first production that I fully directed and designed. That began the cycle of what I do now. For the next ten years I still designed other people's productions — opera, theatre and dance — but I also directed, designed and devised my own works.

It culminated when I went overseas to work. I had a grant and worked with [the conceptual performance artist and sculptor] Robert Wilson in New York for a while. I started to feel that I should form my own company and in 1988 founded Theatre of Image. That is what it is — literally. It is telling theatre stories through images as opposed to text.[14]

Designed for touring, Carpenter's travelogue of snapshot images showed the changing landscape as seen by an optimistic Australian youth, sent from a small country town in Australia to London.

▲ Plate 115 **Carnival of the Animals**

by Kim Carpenter and Richard Tulloch

Theatre of Image, in association with the Sydney Theatre Company

1994

venue: Sea Level Space, Sydney Theatre Company

director and production designer: Kim Carpenter

choreography: Sue-Ellen Chester

music arranged by Raffaele Marcellino and Greg White

lighting designer: Geoff Cobham

photographer: Lorrie Graham

in photo: Darin Griffiths-Jones and Jessica Yeend as the Giraffe Twins

1 W. Akers, interview with author, 8 March 1995.

2 B. Thomson, interview with author, 18 November 1993. Since this interview, Thomson won a Tony award on Broadway for *The King and I*.

3 T. Parker, interview with author, 11 August 1993. Since this interview, Parker became Head of Design, VCA.

4 S. Gurton, interview with author, 23 August 1993.

5 T. Tripp, interview with author, 14 August 1993. Tripp retired from the MTC in 1999.

6 M. Cooper, interview with author, 23 March 1995. Since this interview, Cooper has been resident at QTC, and begun freelancing again.

7 L. Frank, interview with author, 20 March 1995.

8 M. Scott-Mitchell, interview with author, 20 November 1993. Scott-Mitchell designed much of the staging for the Sydney Olympics 2000 opening ceremony.

9 L. Westbury, interview with author, 30 August 1993. Westbury co-created Barking Gecko Theatre for Young People and continues to direct and design.

10 M. Pearce, interview with author, 11 December 1993.

11 E. Soropos, conversation with author, 23 November 1993.

12 J. Cobb, interview with author, 24 August 1993.

13 C. Mitchell, interview with author, 20 November 1993.

14 K. Carpenter, interview with author, 18 November 1993.

forms, where only the

puppet itself is the

expressor, Carpenter's

expression goes

beyond the marionette.

His is a combination of

genres. Mask, puppet,

object, mime, film and (slides), lighting, dance, sound and music

— all are synthesised to create the sensory event.'

(Tom Bannerman, Inanimate links in Kim Carpenter's theatre, unpublished essay,

Department of Theatre Studies, University of New South Wales, 1991, p. 4)

▲ Plate 116 **Rapunzel in Suburbia**
devised by Kim Carpenter; inspired by
the poetry of Dorothy Hewett
Kim Carpenter in association with the
Marionette Theatre of Australia
1983
venue: Marionette Theatre of Australia,
The Rocks, Sydney
director and production designer: Kim
Carpenter
photographer: Sandy Edwards
in photo: Jennifer Claire

◄ Plate 117 **Rapunzel in Suburbia**
Kim Carpenter in association with the
Marionette Theatre of Australia
1983
see pl. 116
photographer: Sandy Edwards
in photo: Christine Mahoney

Design training

To survive as a designer one needs to be enormously skilled, pragmatic, politic, managerial, creative, otherwise one doesn't get employed again. It defeats a lot of people. A lot of very talented people don't make it in the profession and a lot of mediocre people survive.

PETER COOKE[1]

The study of design within a performance context is not simply the learning of practical skills and technical knowledge. It is a means of understanding the broader issues current in the profession. The student designer learns the making of theatre — interpreting text and music psychologically as well as visually, and putting the ideas into the creation of models, drawings, plans, fabric samples and choice of colours.

Training history

Before the establishment of a 'theatre design' diploma designers came to the profession via a variety of paths. Some were already professional artists with an interest in theatre, others might have had an art or architectural training, while others became designers after serving apprenticeships in other facets of theatre production, such as stage management, set construction and costume making. Determination, luck and perseverance played a big part in a design career (as they still do) for it was considered something one 'fell' into, not aimed for. Aspiring young Australian designers had to travel overseas to study theatre arts, and generally they stayed there. One example of this was the designer Loudon Sainthill, who had a successful career in Europe between 1940 and the 1960s. The first recognised theatre designer to be employed within Australia was Anne Fraser, whose involvement with amateur design in Melbourne led her to work full-time as the designer with

the Union Theatre Repertory Company (UTRC). Her time as a resident designer for the UTRC, the Melbourne Theatre Company (MTC) and the Old Tote inspired many others to look at theatre design as a career. Kristian Fredrikson scored his first professional design job by leaving examples of his design work at the hotel room of the Sadler's Wells Ballet Company when it was touring New Zealand in 1967, and was encouraged to continue by Dame Peggy van Praagh. He went on to be one of the resident designers at the MTC (with Richard Prins) and has since worked for most of Australia's major theatre, dance and opera companies. Acknowledging this uncertain path, Kenneth Rowell (another very successful expatriate designer) wrote in his 1968 design handbook *Stage Design*:

> Many successful designers ... have had no formal art training. The conclusion must be that there is no specific way of becoming a stage designer; it is largely a matter of temperament of the individual and the idiom in which he intends to work that determines the means of entry into the theatre.[2]

From the 1950s onwards more Australian plays were being written and professional, subsidised theatre companies were established in all states, so the need to employ stage and costume designers who had an understanding of the Australian idiom also grew. Designers came through the ranks of the amateur and university theatre groups (which had a very strong and healthy following in all cities) or the art schools, getting their training through practical experience and involvement in all areas of production. Theatres on campus were exploring many new ideas, combining classics with contemporary work, modern art with philosophy and politics. The University of Melbourne was home to many new writers, directors and actors who were pushing the bounds of Australian theatre. The New Theatre and the Ensemble were nurturing both backyard realism and Brechtian styles of theatre, allowing designers to play with the space, creating minimal settings on shoestring budgets.

Designers worked closely with directors, writers and actors in the creation of an Australian theatre. Much of the playwriting was exploring naturalism, and designers found themselves recreating kitchens, parlours and outback verandahs, defining theatrically how audiences saw their 'Aussie' environment. The theatres were generally small converted spaces and the relationship of the audience to the space was often a major concern for designers. Wendy Dickson, Allan Lees, Yoshi Tosa, Ron Reid and a young Brian Thomson (among others) were soon working at the Old Tote during the 1960s and 1970s, visually interpreting European and American classics, with a sprinkling of Australian plays.

▲ Figure 90 **The Love of Three Oranges**
A National Institute of Dramatic Art design class project
1994
see pl. 118
photographer: Peter Holderness
A page from Thorn's sketchbook, showing the development of ideas.

Dean of Law

▲ Figure 91 **A Dream Play**
by August Strindberg
A Western Australian Academy of
Performing Arts student production
1993
director: Chris Edmunds
set designer: Kristen Anderson
costume designer: Carol Turney
lighting designer: Adrian Sterritt
Costume concept for the Dean of Law.

Large companies, such as the Australian Opera and the Australian Ballet, were still, in the main, importing their designers from overseas, claiming that there was no-one experienced enough here to take on such big-budget production designs. They would only use Australian or New Zealand artists if they already had international careers, such as Kenneth Rowell and Desmond Digby. On occasion, inspired by the artists used by touring companies from Russia or England, they would ask Australian visual artists such as Sir Sidney Nolan to paint the backdrops, giving their productions an 'Australian feel'. As an internationally recognised artist, Nolan was not considered an artistic risk by conservative managements.

Commercial theatre continued in the tradition of J. C. Williamson, who was still the biggest theatre management in the country. Williamsons either imported their glitzy designs with the shows, paid their scenic artists to copy the originals or simply re-used the costumes and settings from previous shows. The constant importation of overseas artists helped to foster the 'cultural cringe' mentality of aspiring directors, designers and actors. It was not until the establishment of vocational drama schools in Sydney and Melbourne, however, that the teaching of Australian theatre artists was undertaken on a formal basis.

Tertiary institutions

The teaching of performance design in Australia is still a very young field, the longest-running course being the one at NIDA (which was established as a school in 1958) in the grounds of the University of New South Wales. NIDA worked in conjunction with the Old Tote Theatre for many years, providing its graduates with the opportunity to work closely with a professional company. In 1962 technical production was taught, training students as stage managers, stage directors, carpenters, painters and lighting technicians. Since 1972 design has been included on the NIDA syllabus and forms an integral part of its training programmes. It was first set up under the guidance of an English designer, Arthur Dicks, who used the English theatre schools as his teaching model. As a relatively new course of tertiary study (being but thirty years old), the present-day course structures are still based on the original principles of design teaching, incorporating new technologies and ideas as they become applicable to industry demands.

Design at NIDA functions as an integral link between the streams of acting, directing, theatre craft, technical production and voice studies. Since 1994 it has been upgraded from three-year diploma status to an optional four-year degree. It has provided a solid practical grounding in the craft of theatre design and performance for many of the professional designers currently working in Australia. Peter Cooke (the current Head of Design) was himself a graduate of the course in its inaugural year in 1974. Many others, including Kim Carpenter, Victoria Feitscher, Allan Lees, Tom Lingwood, Jennie Tate, Brian Thomson and lighting designer Tony Youlden, have taught within the design course since that time, each bringing his or her own experience, flair and particular style of teaching to students.

The influence of NIDA and its teaching cannot be discounted in recent theatre design history. Many of the practising designers represented in this book are design or technical production graduates, and several are now back at their alma mater teaching future designers from their own industry experiences. More significantly, there are now many schools of theatre around the country using adaptations of the NIDA syllabus combined with their own teaching philosophies to train actors, directors, writers, technicians, stage managers and designers. The Western Australian Academy of Performing Arts (WAAPA) in Perth upgraded its technical theatre courses in 1990 to include a three-year design diploma in either sets and costumes or lighting. An optional degree upgrade was initiated in 1998. The Victorian College of the Arts (VCA) in Melbourne offers a huge range of related arts subjects through its different faculties — fine arts, visual arts, theatre, dance and music. Theatre design as a one-year postgraduate diploma in Performing Arts graduated its inaugural year in 1995 through the combined teaching of several departments. Flinders University in Adelaide has for a long time offered a combination of practical and theoretical study via the theatre and fine arts, as do James Cook University in far north Queensland, and the University of Western Sydney (Nepean) and the University of Wollongong in New South Wales.

Since the inclusion of theatre studies in the Higher School Certificate the number of students wishing to study design has increased. The financial need to gain students has encouraged universities to adopt a broader spectrum of courses, often without adequate training facilities or specialist teachers. This has diluted the market somewhat but it has also widened the focus on theatre training beyond Melbourne and Sydney. Although there are far too many designers (and actors) being trained now in relation to the number of jobs available, a culling process occurs when graduates hit the industry. It also forces theatre artists to stay one step ahead of theatre managements and producers when defining their role in performance.

▼ Figure 92 **A Dream Play**
A Western Australian Academy of Performing Arts student production
1993
see fig. 91
Costume concept for the Blindwoman.

The Blindwoman

Diversity

Design and technical training is broad enough, however, in its practical scope to allow graduates to find their way into a diverse range of careers not necessarily connected with 'performance design'. Only a few designers will continue in the same field for the rest of their working lives. The worlds of entertainment, performance, installation and interactive media are interacting and expanding, creating job opportunities for clever designers both here in Australia and overseas. Duncan Ord (former Dean of the School of Dramatic Arts, WAAPA) stresses the importance of staying ahead of the industry and providing students with a broad range of experiences in all areas of potential work:

One of the principles I would like to push at the Academy of Performing Arts is to broaden our canvas to include film and television so that the students who leave here have those options to cross boundaries and explore other artforms. One reason for that is that people's careers are largely changing; in the Australia of the future people are going to be more self-employed. I think it is inevitable that when you have things like work-place bargaining putting more emphasis on the individual contract, it is a very short step before management starts saying: 'The relationship we would like to have is with a whole lot of subcontractors and not necessarily as an employer with the implied responsibility to look after the employee for the long term'. I think we have seen [this process] move very quickly into theatre.

Most of the people we are graduating are going to be self-employed, then they are going to want to have their career opportunities grow and change, and not get bored doing the same thing. Most people change their line of work three or four times in their life, so I can see people being mobile between film, television, theatre, industrial arts and a whole range of related areas. If they are given a taste for it in their early education they can later specialise or find specialist skilling

▲ Plate 119 **The Glass Menagerie**
by Tennessee Williams
A Victorian College of the Arts student production
1992
venue: VCA studios, Melbourne
director: Robert Meldrum
set and costume designer: Scott Shaw
lighting design: VCA technical students
photographer: Scott Shaw

The set for *The Glass Menagerie* utilised the whole studio space, incorporating innovative ideas without a big budget.

when they need it. That is something I certainly didn't get the opportunity for in my training; it just didn't cross over. If you were a film or television person you would not have known the inside of a theatre at all. I don't believe that is the case now.[3]

This shifting between mediums can be seen in the career of Aubrey Mellor, who trained as a lighting designer and technician at NIDA before moving into directing. Another director-designer of Mellor's era, Kim Carpenter, has focused on the creation of visually based theatre forms with his company, the Theatre of Image. Brian Thomson has designed for all performance mediums, as well as directing for theatre and film. Stephen Curtis has similarly worked for film and theatre, as well as heading the design course at the Australian Film and Television School. Sue Nattrass took over the management of the Victorian Arts Centre after a long career in lighting design and production management. Wendy Dickson took her theatre skills into film and television design. Derek Nicholson, Eamon D'Arcy and Dennis del Favero formed Scenario Urbano, which explored the politics of architectural space and performance. Derrick Cox's company, R.E.D., has designed fashion shows, corporate events and commercial theatre. Inspiration (under the artistic direction of William Passmore) has specialised in casino and cabaret design, as well as film and television design. Geoff Cobham has been the production manager for several of the Festivals of Sydney, as well as actively supporting alternative theatre as a lighting designer. Andrew Carter, Michael Pearce and Mark Thompson work in the visual arts (paintings and sculpture), as well as in the theatre. John Rayment was the head of Technical Services at Expo '88, overseeing nearly two hundred staff and budgeting in the millions before joining the Sydney Dance Company as stage director and lighting designer. Michael Scott-Mitchell formed D4 Design with an architect and an interior designer, designed the award-winning Rockpool Restaurant in Sydney's historic Rocks area and was integral to the Sydney 2000 Olympics opening ceremony designs. For all these people performance design has been a stepping stone to other paths.

Tools of the trade

The standard way in which performance design is taught is by introducing students to the different areas that design encompasses, giving them practical experience in the making of things, before letting them design productions in a studio environment. Selection into a design course is by audition. Peter Cooke elaborated on what he personally looked for in an aspiring design student:

People bring in projects and portfolios but the key thing is: Do they have an imagination? Do they have something that can spark a discussion or develop an idea from what they have presented? Can I see that they can take on any thought and start developing and interpreting it? [Have they] a flexibility to change from what they thought the answer was, having been given a few other ingredients? Have they read a few books, been to a few exhibitions, had a certain amount of life experience or got something original about them? It can be aggressive, it could be dark, colourful, spooky or playful … something that makes me remember them when they leave the room, a unique quality at that point in time, which is very hard to define but has to do with language, imagination, visual information and literacy in the world of the arts.[4]

By the end of their second year students begin to design the public productions performed by the student actors, singers or dancers. Third year is spent consolidating skills, designing major school productions, working as assistants for professional designers and preparing their portfolios. By the time they graduate design students are considered to have all the necessary basic skills required by the entertainment and performance industry.

The areas that theatre design can move into are expanding constantly. Subjects that one can expect to learn when studying design and technical production cover a broad range of knowledge and craft: scenic painting, set and properties construction; lighting design, rigging, theatre technology, thermoplastics, welding and industry safety; basic tailoring, millinery, footwear, fabric technology, masks and make-up; model making, drawing, drafting and computer aided design (CAD); and theatre and costume history. Visiting designers are also brought in to conduct project-based workshops with students, pushing them into different areas of design.

In the practical world there is a changing emphasis on the mediums of design. No longer does performance design fit the stereotyped descriptions of theatre being all 'canvas and greasepaint'. The tools that are available to use, even in low-budget theatre, are changing our approach to theatre. One area that has grown in importance is the use of light and sound in design. Cooke is very aware of this and promotes design literacy in all areas of technical production:

The development of lighting and sound and the organisation of the stage space is now just a completely different activity to what it was twenty years ago. One used to talk in terms of scenery and costumes, now we speak of 'design of space and the creation of atmosphere'. There is such a mixture of technologies. The way we work here at NIDA is that lighting designers and set designers are working together continuously from the beginning of a project, contributing to each other's discussions and developing ideas.

Lighting is an awareness of seeing someone walk forward and how the space can change, of whether we see someone from here or from there. Is the lighting coming from the side, from behind or in front? What are the elements that can stop the space from being an inanimate black box and become a part of a living production that regenerates its atmosphere every few minutes? We have a space here that is always available to the lighting designers to take objects and fabrics into, to see what the lighting can do to it. You can only know by turning a lantern on and seeing how the colours and textures react. Our students are learning about electricity, how lanterns work and which lanterns do what. The course encourages project-based activities where lighting is used as the only design element.

All students work with lighting, though the actual lighting designers train in the technical production stream, not design. The only reason that lighting and sets are separate courses is that there is a huge body of work to teach in three years, and that is already pushed to the limit. You cannot think of one without the other ... The focus on lighting design is going to become more and more time-consuming [rather than becoming more compact and streamlined] and so the future of design will become a collaboration between two or three designers combining their skills.[5]

Ord spent many years as a lighting designer before teaching it, and agrees with Cooke that the combination of lighting with set and costume knowledge is essential. The technical production course at WAAPA provides students with the option of studying either sound technology or lighting design solely for three years, without needing to graduate as stage managers or backstage technicians. As with the course at NIDA, all technical and design students learn CAD in fully equipped computer studios, as well as working on short films. This encouragement of students to use new technology emphasises the adapting needs and growing reliance on electronic technology within the performing arts.

Practice versus theory

The design lecturers at institutions such as NIDA, WAAPA and VCA have a wealth of experience as practitioners, though they may not hold formal teaching qualifications. This has led to criticism by some that the teaching of stage design is by anecdote, not method. There exists no formal training for theatre design teachers in Australia however, and certainly no agreed methodology that could be taught. Even though many universities will offer theatre studies as part of their Arts degree curriculum, the emphasis is on the analytical study and discussion of theatre practice and theory rather than on training industry teachers. The spectrum of design teaching cannot help but grow as more and more graduates from all states enter the profession and begin to formulate ideas relating to the methodology and practice of performance design. It is an area that Cooke has been thinking about and his use of industry teachers and 'teachers of the industry' is important to NIDA's design programme. He asserts that the future of designers lies in increased professional collaboration and the development of a higher design profile within the industry:

Twenty years ago there were not [many] designers around who could teach. There were only a few practising designers like Yoshi Tosa, Anne Fraser and James Ridewood at The Old Tote who could contribute to the design training at NIDA. Now there is a whole range of people who can teach design at an extraordinarily high level. I draw on those people frequently. They are all working professionals and they are bringing knowledge and skills from the profession directly into the school.

There are two sorts of design teacher. Those who come in and bring with them the industry standards, developments and requirements. Often the industry is leading that area of design. Then there are those who are leading the industry, making the industry change and think about itself. They are not necessarily highly regarded within the industry because of being provocative characters. They are challenging the standards and asking difficult questions. The very best collaborators in the country do not necessarily get to where they should be because we have other people constantly looking over their shoulders at what has happened elsewhere.

At NIDA I want a mixture of highly professional standards, an understanding of what the industry's needs are, an understanding of where the profession could travel to and what the demands on a young designer may be in ten years time. I am always thinking: 'Where are these young people going to be in ten years time?'. A career takes five years to develop and five years to consolidate. One needs some kind of vision. What needs to change is that the industry must stop thinking of design as the people who turn up with all the chairs and a few interesting props. This is why there are a number of 'difficult' designers around; because they come with a broader range of opinions about a whole range of activities which in previous times they were not asked to be involved with.

I almost never separate design from the collaborative activity of 'doing theatre'. If there is a group of people heading in a direction, your contribution as a designer might be solely concerning the arrangement of chairs in space, but I encourage the students to have views on every aspect of a production. As part of their design ethos students are encouraged to talk about the writer just as much as the shape of the pot plants seen through the down-stage left windows. Let us talk about the casting, the venue, the budget, the director and their rehearsal methods as richly as we talk about the hem lengths in Act Three. For example, if you spoke to Catherine Martin, Angus Strathie or Dale Ferguson [all ex-students], they will have very strong ideas about what the company repertoire should be, which classics are more appropriate and which new writers should be encouraged. The days of just doing frocks and backdrops are well and truly over.[6]

These ideas mark an interesting departure from the theatre skills and craft-based syllabus that NIDA and other design schools have on paper. As a vocational training it has always reflected the practical needs of the industry and because the whole notion of stage, costume and lighting design only left the narrow boundaries of 'decoration' last century, very little analysis of the design role exists in written form. Unlike other artforms, performance design is nearly always an ephemeral response to a given environment, be it a text, a work-shop with actors or dancers, a performance or a piece of music. Given this, designers previously have not engaged in much phil-osophical debate and analysis of their role outside the confines of the production room, nor encour-

aged any other academic study of their work. In a caustic article published in *Age Monthly Review*, discussing the inadequacy of design thinking in Australia, designer-architect Michael Anderson argued that:

Traditionally, stage designers have not been expected to express themselves other than on the stage; they certainly have not been credited with the facility of talking or writing about what they might do. To judge from available evidence, costumes and settings spring from an intuitive, artistic response to the demands of the text and the director. As slaves to the stylistic and technical requirements of different productions, designers have not (historically speaking) enjoyed the opportunity of expressing their own ideological concerns or philosophical frameworks on stage.[7]

▼ Figure 93 **Season at Sarsaparilla**

by Patrick White

A Victorian College of the Arts student
production

1995

venue: Grant Street Theatre

director: Robert Draffin

set and costume designer: Gail
Thomlinson

lighting design: C. Mann

Costume renderings of the Pogson family.

Anderson is talking historically, but much of what he says is still relevant. Although Cooke is consciously pushing for his design graduates to be operating at the many levels within the industry and affecting the style and make-up of Australian theatre, it is still debatable whether most graduates will have the opportunity (or the necessary background knowledge of Australian and contemporary theatre history, writing, theory and practice) to be able to instigate lasting change. The formalised teaching of design by any theatre institution invariably keeps the designer (as well as the actors and directors) 'within' the institution of theatre. A notable exception to this is the work of designers who have become directors or writers, such as Kim Carpenter and Nigel Triffitt. They have both needed to create their own performance frameworks, since no existing theatre structures could contain their visions. The collaborative works of Brian Thomson with Jim Sharman, and Stephen Curtis with Neil Armfield have also had a strength of vision that has somewhat pushed the boundaries of Australian theatre and design. We have yet to see the effect of more recent graduates on the industry.

Disparity

Performance design as a tertiary subject has been given little academic weight by other institutions and professions which already have established means of communicating complex philosophical and political ideas. The worlds of architecture and the fine arts have developed lines of thought and language specific to their mediums. Performance design continues to use a hybrid language based on textual considerations, actors' syntax, technical theatre jargon and expressions borrowed from the fine arts. The disparity between academia, professionalism and practice in the performing arts is what Eamon D'Arcy encountered after studying design at NIDA:

> I got to the stage in my own work where I needed to investigate what design was and what theatre was, and because of the situation in Australia (in which the theatre world doesn't value theory) I had to find out how I could study theatre in a fairly disciplined, conventional and formal way. I decided to do some study via the visual arts. When you go into the world of visual arts you realise that within that world there are a lot of philosophies and theories that are written and talked about and it is all a part and parcel of their world. It is a real problem in the theatre, in that we do not ever approach our work with that rigour. A lot of designers are dismissive of theory but they haven't really thought through the issues. The key areas are teaching and the way we think about theatre, and therefore how it will re-inform our practices. That is something that directly affects all designers and theatre practitioners.

Burns' set was a fragmented brightly lit vision of Broadway, with Powell's handpainted fabrics and costumes

standing out — an explosion of riotous cartoon-like colours.

▲ Plate 121 **Guys and Dolls**

music and lyrics by Frank Loesser; based
on stories by Damon Runyon

A National Institute of Dramatic Art
student production

1995
venue: Parade Theatre, NIDA, Sydney

director: Tony Knight

choreographer: Nancye Hayes

set designer: Gordon Burns

costume designer: Andrew Powell

lighting designer: Tony Youlden

photographer: Branco Gaica

in photo: Acting students from the 1995
graduating class in performance

◀ Plate 122 **Tonight We Improvise**
based on a play by Luigi Pirandello
A West Australian Academy of Performing
Arts student production
1994
venue: Drama Studio, WAAPA, Perth
director: Marie-Louise Abatte
set and costume designer: Anne Kohler
lighting design: WAAPA lighting design
student
photographer: Peter Northcote

The set during rehearsals. Kohler used distorted perspectives, projections and mobiles to add to the surreal qualities of the workshop production.

Theatre design is an interesting training. I think it is taught by default, by the very nature of design and the nature of the theatre ... [However,] we have to establish some sort of base to work off or against and that's what we haven't done in theatre design. The intuitive aspect of design is vital but it is not the whole thing, and that's part of what is going wrong in our collective thinking.

I don't think we can change our position until we can develop a theoretical base and places like NIDA actually open themselves up as research institutes. You can't really talk about theatre design the way I'm talking about it unless you go back to the institutions of theatre [training]. Once you go back to the theatre schools you are going to realise that they are really falling behind in their teaching. Not only in how they teach but what they teach. I don't think the institutions are really defining their role.[8]

Performance design analysts such as Eamon D'Arcy, Derek Nicholson and Pamela Zeplin are calling upon NIDA to assume a broader role, in the belief that practice can inform theory, and theory in turn can inform practice. They suggest that NIDA should be encouraging and housing a national archive of performance documentation from around Australia; that videotapes and interviews with practitioners be constantly updated and available to students and professionals doing research; and that some sense of performance history and theory is fostered within the practice. Derek Nicholson speaks passionately about the growing need to document and discuss the theatre work that is occurring across Australia:

How is it possible to define an Australian style or process of making and designing theatre if there is no knowledge of what is happening in different states? Without a common view or a body of work that documents what is being done now, how do we record the language of Australian performance for future discussion? It will not happen on a state level because the funding and scope would not be enough. This kind of thinking needs to occur at a national level. NIDA would be the perfect place to start.[9]

An important point that comes up in this debate is the validity of choosing NIDA as the focus of criticism. As Cooke points out quite clearly, NIDA was set up by practitioners to be a vocational school of theatre. It is training theatre artists to enter the entertainment industry as skilled craftspeople, not as theatre theorists:

> NIDA is a vocational training school. We train people to act, design and direct. Though the study of the theatre is important (in a university sense), if needed we draw on the University of New South Wales theatre studies' staff for theoretical appreciation.[10]

It is very clear that the practical skills being taught to design students are suited to the demands of their profession as it currently exists. In three years they cover a broad range of subjects and studio exercises that prepare them for work in most areas of performance design. If they graduate to discover that their degree is not considered as highly as a

► Plate 123 **Zorr Benium Function**

A West Australian Academy of Performing Arts student production

1993

venue: Arts Theatre, WAAPA, Perth

choreographer: Timothy Gordon

set designer: Imogen Ross

costume designer: Felipe Reynolds

lighting design: WAAPA lighting design student

photographer: Peter Northcote

in photo: Dance students of the WAAPA

in performance. Gordon and his designers stripped the theatre bare and exposed all backstage workings to create a futurist, underground world. The dancers were costumed in rubber and silver plastics, and red dust swirled down through overhead air vents

composer: Steven Rae
librettist: Hilary Bell
The NIDA Company
1993
venue: Parade Theatre, NIDA, Sydney
director: Jim Sharman
set designer: Andrew Purvis
costume designer: Tess Schofield
lighting designer: Rory Dempster
photographer: Peter Holderness
'The Islanders' costume drawing.

The Wedding Song drew upon the skills of both professional and student designers/ technicians, which is a feature of NIDA Company productions. Schofield described in interview how the process came about: '*The Wedding Song* was a musical ... It started out in outback Australia and moved to the highlands of New Guinea ... It was an epic love story set against cultural conflict and tribal wars. Jim Sharman was very involved with both the writer and the composer, and as he's a strongly visual director he was very influential in the outcome of the actual design. There were certain things that he needed and wanted it to be, and there was a brief that I was given that was constantly being cross-checked. I didn't get to work with [the writers] conceptually, but they had been working on it for a long time so that by the time it actually got to us, the designers, it was a very well rounded piece ... A few of the students [from the vocational training courses at NIDA] also became involved in the project. There were students from the acting course who became part of the ensemble and there were some theatre craft students — a recent graduate became a supervisor, and other theatre craft students worked in the workshop creating special headpieces and [other] quite complex design elements. We drew heavily on their different skills'.

[T. Schofield, interview with author, 22 November 1993]

similar course in visual arts or architecture, or that there is no professional representative body, no standard contract of work, then perhaps the problem is inherent in the way the performance industry views design as a profession (and the ways in which designers view themselves), not just the ways in which designers are trained.

Can designers affect change? Debate and action should be encouraged among all theatre practitioners if the Australian theatre profession is to move forward. The place to begin is not only within the established schools of performing art, but also within government funding bodies, professional performance companies, university theatre departments and visual arts courses across the board. If collaborative action remains the undercurrent of all theatre, then collaborative play between theory, thought and practice must be encouraged in all facets of contemporary performance — design, direction, writing and action. The teaching will follow.

1   P. Cooke, interview with author, 23 October 1995.

2   K. Rowell, *Stage Design*, Studio Vista, London, 1968, p. 82.

3   D. Ord, interview with author, 29 November 1993.

4   Cooke, op. cit.

5   ibid.

6   ibid.

7   M. A. R. Anderson, 'Upstaging theatre — design for the unreal world', *Age Monthly Review*, Melbourne, September 1989, pp. 5–6.

8   E. D'Arcy, interview with author, 5 March 1995.

9   D. Nicholson, interview with author, February 1996.

10 Cooke, op. cit.

▼ Figures 94a, 94b, 94c and 94d
The Wedding Song
The NIDA Company
1993
see pl. 125
Schofield's initial drawings of the Islanders.

Design
constrictions [1]

An essay by Derek Nicholson

Although concepts of space have existed throughout recorded history, it has only been
during the twentieth century that any great attention has been given to the concept that
there might be more precise meanings inherent in spatial relationships in the theatre than
hitherto imagined. The study of stage design has become largely the study of changing spatial
relationships. [2]

◄ Plate 125 **The Magic Flute**

by Wolfgang Amadeus Mozart

West Australian Opera

1994

venue: His Majesty's Theatre, Perth

director: Lindy Hume

set designer: Richard Roberts

costume designer: Tracy Grant (from an
original New Zealand production)

lighting designer: Stephen Wickham

photographer: Stephen Wickham

in photo: The opposite prompt (OP) side
of the false proscenium, and part of the
back wall of the set.

'We wanted to create a ruined or
abandoned version of His Majesty's
Theatre as the environment in which the
opera would take place. The audience
would initially be confronted with a large
abandoned stage space, seemingly
stripped right back to the back wall of
the theatre. It was only when this wall
split apart and vanished to reveal an
infinite sky, and an enormous moon, that
it was clear that there was more to the
set than had initially been apparent.'

[notes — Richard Roberts, 1996]

Multi-dimensional space

In the classic rehearsal room exercise of changing the proxemics of two actors who are playing the *Romeo and Juliet* balcony scene we can ask: How does the scene play better — with the actors close or far apart? The actors playing on a raised or level plane? How do the proxemics change the kinetic relationship of the characters?

These questions are difficult to answer. They are difficult to discuss as there is yet to be established a language that describes how the manipulation of stage space can be perceived or transformed by the actor and the designer. Theatre creators 'intuitively' use stage spaces to communicate ideas and stories. That we may use a space without a rational, conscious and full understanding of how it functions is of interest to me. The consequences of understanding spatial dynamics can give us insights into what we call 'intuitive responses'.

My aim is to attempt to describe how three-dimensional space may be perceived, researched and legitimately recorded. I then apply this to the analysis of stage space, with specific reference to Sydney's theatres.

It would seem difficult for me to write a chapter of this kind from the front to the back. One virtually writes from back to front because of the result of years spent groping around in the dark — of working with many

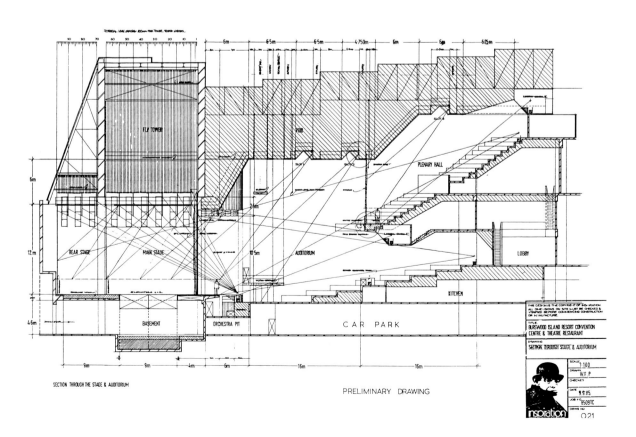

▶ Figure 95 **Burswood Casino**

Side elevation of theatre auditorium, designed and drawn by Passmore for Inspiration Design, as part of their theatre consultancy at the casino.

◀ Figure 96 **Remember Ronald Ryan**

by Barry Dickens

Playbox

1994

venue: Beckett Theatre, CUB Malthouse, Melbourne

director: Malcolm Robertson

set and lighting designer: John Beckett

costume designer: Laura Doheny

photo: Playbox archives

stage spaces and trying to interpret the experiences. At best, the primary research can only record a limited number of people's reactions to a series of presented phenomena in space, and try to bring order out of apparent disorder and 'intuition' in a written report.

The set under work lights in the Beckett Theatre during rehearsal.

One of the most potent elements of the theatre performance is that it is a transitory experience, and one of its most frustrating is its defiance of any attempt to document such an experience. As I begin to lay out some of the basic concepts, ideas and experiences, I ask that the reader takes many of these on trust. The results of my observations are not random guesswork. It is possible to recreate spatial phenomena that generate similar 'intuitive' reactions from different groups of people. I believe there is a common cultural base governing perception of space (and its usage) in a controlled event. In other words, I consider that we absorb spatial information and three-dimensional relationship patterns, triggering certain reactions that have a common cultural base.

In trying to define how the dynamics of a stage function we may need to develop a basic set of signs (not unlike that which has been invented for the recording of ballet moves), which we might call a stage language. During the process of learning, recording and defining a hierarchy of stage space we may develop ways of communicating more accurately the experience of the theatre event.

Utilising an equally diminutive space as that of Griffin's Stables Theatre in Sydney (see pl. 129), Red Shed highlighted the grimness and pain of the play's characters by placing them under an audience microscope in a stark, sterile environment. The enclosing walls and tight spaces were maximised, effectively suspending the audience in a reverberating mindscape. Tim Maddock described the design as: 'a steeply raked stage descended into black, the audience was seated on three sides on scaffolding two metres high. *All Souls* is a dense, poetic piece. I wanted to highlight the themes of dark and light, the highest point in white and the lowest in black. Everything was in threat of sliding down the rake into the black'.

(notes — Tim Maddock, February 1996)

▲ Figure 97 **All Souls**
by Daniel Keene
Red Shed
1993
venue: Red Shed Theatre, Adelaide
director: Cath McKinnon
set and costume designer: Tim Maddock
lighting designer: Karin Norris
photographer: David Wilson

To record for examination the relationships between our intuitive experiences of and reactions to a given space I use known 'tools' that require the reader to have some understanding of point, length, plane, area and volume. Embodied within these tools is the concept of 'distance'.

> A history of spatialisation in the theatre will thus be, in large part, a history of how different cultures have altered location, size, shape and exact relationship of acting and audience spaces according to changing ideas about the function of theatre, and its relationship to other cultural systems.[3]

Analysis shows us that theatre is not concerned with things, but with relationships. The artform is expressed in real time in three-dimensional space. The theatre artist creates the dramatic space with the tools of performance. The relationship between the performer, the space and the audience creates a multi-dimensional 'new space' in the imagination of the audience.

The extraordinary gift of stage language lies in the many levels at which it can be used, triggering deep responses within us, and enticing us to use our imaginations in ways not usually available in everyday life or through other media. It can open doors to new emotional responses and reactions, triggered by the associations implied or illustrated by the tools of performance.

The theatre space

The architecture of our theatre buildings has had, I believe, an important and restricting influence upon the style of theatre writing.[4]

The authority over the stage space of the architecture of a building has greatly influenced Australian scenographic practice. The building surrounding a performance exerts a powerful web of forces on how we perceive the event. It may be a purpose-built building (a theatre), a found space originally built for another use which is adapted or converted to suit the needs of a single production, or a place where a variety of theatre events can be mounted. If we accept that the built space has a significant influence on the performance, it follows that the shape and size of these stages can steer designers, directors, choreographers and performers into standardised ways of spatialising performance. This has a profound effect on how the 'dramatic space'[5] is interpreted and represented to our audiences.

Theatres generally have a viewing focus. With picture frame or proscenium arch staging (a commonly understood reference venue for theatre spaces) this focus is taken from the audience's centrally located viewing position in the auditorium, looking towards the stage platform. From the stage the focus is typically dominated by the existence of a 'zone of command'. From this location a performer feels in command of the space — stage and auditorium — and in control of the performer–audience relationship.

These directional forces are not so clearly identified in studio and open-space theatres. In these performance spaces it is the design which accords the focus to each production. In both theatre examples the viewing experience can be influenced by a network of interacting elements, fields, planes or lines. These elements act as 'volume rulers'[6] in which the event is contained.

The dramatic space

The three-dimensional space in which we live and communicate is focused and heightened in an immediate and sensual way by the theatre event. The imaginary world of the performance can and may be defined by a variety of elements — corporeal, aural, verbal and visual. These elements are used singly or in combination to create the dramatic space and this space stimulates the potential spaces in the imagination of the audience, both individually and collectively. The performer's vocal, corporeal skills with the interplay of kinesics and proxemics trigger the spectator's imagination to create the illusion of the dramatic world. For our performing arts practice to mature, this precious feature, this multi-dimensionality must be continually, accurately and creatively explored.

Theatre performance perpetually explores solutions for the representation of time through the manipulation of dimensional space and location of performers in time–space, both real and created. The space–time continuum is unique to the theatrical event and sets it apart from other forms of dramatic storytelling.

The availability of space, both on and off stage, not only defines and confines the use of three-dimensional built scenic pieces but also dictates how objects, props and clothing are utilised throughout a performance.[7] The performer is placed in a dramatic space by the written text and designed stage. The dramatic space functions to its full potential if it is informed, surrounded and serviced by 'other' spaces of equal or similar volume. Scale, distance, vertical and horizontal space then become the medium for a design language.

Sydney theatres

In Sydney few locally mounted theatre events are presented in purpose-built theatre buildings. The theatres which are used most frequently by government-fund-assisted companies and which have heavily influenced the styles of stage design are adapted or re-used buildings. Even the Sydney Opera House's opera and drama theatres are adapted theatre spaces:

When is Sydney going to face up to the harsh fact that its most treasured icon, its international symbol, its greatest tourist attraction — the Sydney Opera House — is not up to the job? This was made obvious once again last week when every review of the Australian Ballet's splendid new triple bill programme felt constrained to point out that the whole performance was constrained and distorted by the very inadequate stage area.[8]

The Opera Theatre in the Sydney Opera House is the home of Opera Australia and the Australian Ballet when in Sydney. It is also used by the Sydney Dance Company. It is a conventional proscenium-framed stage. Because of the quantity of theatre originating in Sydney and Melbourne the limitations at the Opera Theatre are controlling factors for designers who design for national tours.

Akwanso Fly South was an attempt by Moore to express a design viewpoint that was not necessarily western. In an article discussing gender and space she described it thus: '*Akwanso Fly South* was drawn from the lives of the four performers, all of whom were black women living in Australia ... The piece represented an unproblematic essentialist 'feminine' which emphasised the performers' similarity of experience despite their cultural diversity. The design echoed this commonality through the circle on the horizontal plane that defined the

playing space and its echo in the two pendulous semi-circles that were suspended in the vertical plane. The audiences' associations on shape led to the female body; their associations on texture and pattern led to weaving, basket weaving and traditional women's labour'.

[M. Moore, 'Sexing the space', in *Converging Realities*, ed. Peta Tait, Currency Press, Sydney, 1995, pp. 227–33]

▲ Plate 126 **Akwanso Fly South**
devised by Robyn Archer and the cast
Belvoir Street Theatre in association with
the Adelaide Festival Theatre Trust
1988
venue: Belvoir Street Theatre, Sydney
director: Robyn Archer

choreographer: Mary Barnett
set and costume designer: Mary Moore
lighting designer: John Comeadow
photographer: David Wilson
in photo: Dorinda Hafner, Rhoda Roberts,
Aku Kadogo and Jigsie Campbell

This series of six plays was originally performed at Griffin's home venue, the Stables, and was later developed into

▶ Figure 98 **PASSION** – Love Seen in Laundromat
by Lissa Benyon
Griffin Theatre Company
1994
venue: The Stables, Sydney
director: Monica Pellizzari
set and costume designer: Sue Field
lighting designer: Nigel Levings
photographer: Sue Field

a drama series for the ABC. Playing over a seven-week period, a minimum of three plays were performed per night. Field's ingenious designs facilitated quick set changes without sacrificing individual identities for each of the very different plays.

The Wharf Theatre (incorporating Wharf 1 and Wharf 2) is the home of the Sydney Theatre Company, and the Stables Theatre is the home of Griffin Theatre Company. The Belvoir Street Theatre is mainly used by Company B. The design and footprint of both the Wharf theatres and Belvoir Street Theatre were heavily influenced by the staging style developed by the Nimrod Theatre Company while at the Stables Theatre (then the Nimrod) in the late 1970s. The Nimrod theatre had a tiny stage contained by two walls meeting upstage in a corner. This footprint was repeated at the Belvoir and can be created in Wharf 1 when the movable seating units are arranged together on one side. These theatres are not traditional proscenium-framed spaces, nor do they have reasonable off-stage areas serving the performance space.[9] These factors have a definite impact on the ways in which productions are staged and designed.

Apart from the Drama Theatre at the Sydney Opera House, where to a confined extent conventional proscenium-framed staging techniques can be used, the designers who regularly use these spaces have developed a creative working process with their collaborators which could be considered as a Sydney method of staging design. The physical limitations of these theatres appears to have been a creative challenge to the directors, designers, choreographers and performers alike.

A brief description of the following three Sydney theatre spaces is necessary in order to illustrate this point, applying the notion of 'volume rulers'.

The Wharf Theatre: Wharf 1 at the Sydney Theatre Company

Wharf 1 is essentially a large rectangular room with the audience seated on steeply raked tiers on three sides facing the long wall, in front of which is a relatively small acting platform. The ceiling throughout is defined by a grid which is used for the stage lighting and is divided and dominated by a large metal beam.

The audience looks down and into the performance space; the performer faces and looks up and at a wall of audience. The audience and performers share the space.

The designs that are most effective in this space are those that raise the acting platform above the stage floor by at least a metre and re-orientate the focus of the room across one of the long diagonals; it is difficult to 'distance' the audience from the performers or the performers from the audience. Vertical placement of the dramatic space can be most effective. Audience reception of the performance varies considerably from seating position to seating position.

The Drama Theatre at the Sydney Opera House

The Drama Theatre is essentially an end-stage configuration with a single audience seating block at a right angle to the stage on a stepped, tiered, medium-raked incline, with the audience point of view looking down and at and into the stage space. The low auditorium ceiling emphasises the narrow vertical height of the stage opening into the stage space. The rectangular stage space at the end of the auditorium is framed by building limits of the auditorium with adjustable sides to the proscenium opening. Most audience members receive a similar stage picture.

The designs which deal with the low, narrow opening are most effective. The space tends to re-scale or subdue the human figure. Designs can counter this by clever use of scale and proportion. Vertical placement of the dramatic space is most difficult. Audience reception of the performance varies little except for the front three rows, where eye line is at stage-floor height.

Belvoir Street Theatre (upstairs)

The audience orientation to the performance space is in a tiered circular arc in three uneven-sized audience blocks. The audience point of view is looking down and across the acting space and is tiered on a medium-slope incline. The visual ceiling is created by the lighting grid, which extends across both the audience and acting area. The side walls meet at a right angle at the rear of the staging area and contain the acting area and audience seating. This corner is approximately at the centre of the total space. Seating is bench style, albeit with padding. Audience members receive three stage pictures — one from each of the three seating blocks.

The designs which are most effective in this space are those which define and background the action. The space has a natural 'theatrical' scale. Its dominant diagonal emphasis permits 'dramatic space' distance. Vertical placement of the dramatic space is most effective when against the long wall. Audience reception of the performance varies a little from the three blocks of seating, since the audiences on the seating blocks at the sides see a mirror image of themselves.

> I love the atmosphere at the Belvoir Street space. That corner stage has the feeling that you're looking into a space where people and behaviour are kind of cornered. It's so highly focused.
>
> Neil Armfield (artistic director of Company B)[10]

Towards an actor's solution-design method

The stages under discussion are variations of the open-stage format.[11] While these theatre buildings are an infliction which Sydney alone must take account of and bear, or change, this situation has forged a collaborative effort between performers, directors, designers and choreographers, resulting in powerful creative work. On the one hand, the theatre building's limitations have constrained development but, on the other, they have spawned a discernible 'method' of staging by encouraging a close working relationship between the performers, directors and designers during the rehearsal period. As there is a heavy reliance on the performer to carry the scenic information of a production, design work is regularly carried out in the rehearsal room by the director, designer and performers. This situation has contributed to the development of common problem-solving staging methods.

In attempting to identify common elements in the scenography of productions in these spaces I do not underestimate or simplify the complex design process through which the creative team passes in solving the staging problems of a production. Although the designer scenically defines the acting space in pre-production discussions with the director, these are then further manipulated and developed during the rehearsal process into functioning dramatic spaces. In this way the final design of the dramatic spaces required by the performers is created in the rehearsal room, not the model box, in a fluid and flexible manner befitting the needs of each space.

When using the open stage the challenge most often faced by the creative team is not so much how each individual scene is spatialised but how the team creates and re-creates the dramatic spaces into a seamless and fluid interpretation — in other words, creating a performance vernacular which brings into being a unified scenic style.

Designers and directors working in adapted theatre spaces do not have the luxury of solving scene-changing needs by simply moving scenic elements on and off stage as is the custom on better-equipped traditional stages. The open-stage design begs a certain simplicity and often requires direct intervention by the performers. Each production must invent the visual tools for the performers to use, evocatively indicating time and spatial boundaries.

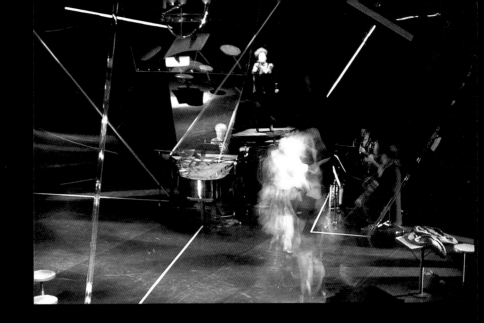

'Ingredients: a baby grand piano; 4 musicians; 1 singer; 4 dancers; 1 very small venue; a tour.

The idea:

Chrissie — "So I arranged to meet with her at this cafe in two years in Venice. I kept the appointment. I arrived but no cafe. It had vanished."

Robyn — "No, I reckon the environment needs to be somehow alienating, not romantic."

Me — "You mean like a fast-food joint?"

Process:

The four of us meet in Sydney and munch our way through french fries while I take photos. This is serious research. The glossy developed surfaces sum up the experience, fractured and reflected, the sign of the burger more sumptuous than the real thing. Back in my studio I start a model but the knife slips. Temporarily incapacitated, I read Frederick Jameson's article entitled "Architecture, Frank Gehry House, Santa Monica". As a consequence I become fascinated with the notion of multiple vanishing points (my thumb amongst them). Back to the cutting room and the model develops away from a unified, fixed, literal fast-food cafe to one of dislocated, disjointed, internal spaces; fractured worlds, multiple readings and split subject positions.'

(programme notes — Mary Moore, 1993)

▲ Plate 127 **See Ya Next Century**
by Robyn Archer
Chrissie Parrott Dance Collective
1993
venue: Belvoir Street Theatre, Sydney
director: Chrissie Parrott
composer: Cathie Travers
set and costume designer: Mary Moore
lighting designer: Mark Howett
photographer: Mary Moore

'Belvoir Street is a fantastic space. I think Neil Armfield once called it a "magical space". I think it is. The thing about working in spaces like Belvoir Street that I find so exciting is that the tasks of visibility are greatly reduced. See, if you're working at a big venue like the Capitol and you're trying to light a moody night scene so that people at the back of the circle, nearly 40 or 50 metres away can [still] see [the actors], then it's a difficult balance — the twenty people who are sitting in the front row might think that the whole thing is glaringly bright and has no mood or character to it, and the people who are sitting in the back row peering into the gloom [are] trying to detect who it is that's wandering around on stage. In purely practical terms, [in theatres] like Belvoir Street, for example, you could light with just one angled light and forget about the other side of the actor's face — there will be enough light that will bounce off the floor, or bounce light from the scenery, giving enough definition to the other side of the face so that the audience wouldn't lose the face entirely if the person turned away, faced in the other direction, or even turned straight on. Whereas if you're working in a big venue like the Capitol, you simply can't do that because the face just goes black and that degree of contact is then gone for the audience, and they lose that moment or whatever it is that the actor is doing.'

[Nigel Levings, interview with the author, 1 March 1998]

◄ Plate 128 **A View from the Bridge**
Arthur Miller
Belvoir Street Theatre
1996
venue: Belvoir Street Theatre, Sydney
director: Adam Cook
set designer: Justin Kurzel
costume designer: Justin Kurzel
lighting designer: Nigel Levings
photographer: Heidrun Lohr
Kurzel incorporated the architectural features of the venue and carried them through into the design. Steel girders stood and strutted the underbelly of the Brooklyn setting, allowing the actors to be concealed and revealed in their shadows.

The management model box

A second and considerable influence on the design process is the theatre company's management model, which brings together the creative team. How this team is governed and, in particular, at which point in the process the designer is included, is worthy of examination.

The rapid expansion of government-fund-assisted theatre companies from small enterprises into state theatre production companies has brought with it short-term organisational planning and the standardisation of a production management model.[12] As theatre matures and moves into the next phase of growth we should be closely examining this model. The most generously government-funded theatre is based on administrative production units which hire the artists to work on one-off productions. Even those enterprises that have a secure subscription base are repertory systems and not repertoire.[13] The exceptions to this are the national ballet and opera companies.

While the isolated solo designer may create a performance 'look' which advances the visual language of the stage, it is typically the case that new forms are born through the inspiration and stimulation of an interactive working process over the long term. In Australia few companies consider the establishment of a fully fledged design department with semi-permanent designers in residence as intrinsic to the artistic lifeblood of a theatre production company. Thus the majority of designers tend to be freelance workers. Yet the few state-funded performing arts companies with established design departments have benefited from the development of in-house design and enabled designers such as Stephen Curtis (STCSA), Kristian Fredrikson (MTC), Shaun Gurton (STCSA), Bill Haycock (QTC and QB) and Tony Tripp (MTC), among others, to mature in their craft while being engaged as resident designers.

Equally, directors who have nourished an ongoing relationship with a designer have not only greatly enhanced their work but

Rather than battling the balcony-style seating of the Space Theatre, Moore used the entire lower level as a promenade streetscape. Audience members were submerged in the energetic and intimate world of Jonah, a larrikin hunchback living in Cardigan Street and the back alleys of pre-First World War Sydney.

▼ Figure 99 **Jonah**

composed by Alan John with libretto by John Romeril, based on the novel by Louis Stone

State Theatre Company of South Australia

1991

venue: Space Theatre, Adelaide Festival Centre

director: Neil Armfield

set designer: Mary Moore

costume designer: Jennie Tate

lighting designer: Mark Howett

photographer: David Wilson

also advanced their audiences' understanding of performance design. Some examples of director–designer collaborations can be seen (or remembered) in the work of Rex Cramphorn with Melody Cooper and Eamon D'Arcy (the Centre for Performance Studies); Neil Armfield with Stephen Curtis and Brian Thomson (Lighthouse, STCSA and Company B); Baz Luhrmann with Catherine Martin (AO and Bazmark); Barrie Kosky with Peter Corrigan and Michael A. R. Anderson (AO, Bell Shakespeare and Gilgul); Elisabeth Burke with Pierre Thibaudeau (Entr'acte); Constantine Koukias with Anne Wulff (IHOS Opera); Cath McKinnon with Tim Maddock (Red Shed); Andrew Ross with Steve Nolan and Robert Juniper (Black Swan); and Grahame Gavin with Lou Westbury (Woolly Jumpers, Acting Out and Barking Gecko). All these directors have cultivated a close bond with the same designer over a sustained period of time with considerable success.

Funded dance companies are privileged with resources which allow permanent or semi-permanent groups of artists. The Sydney Dance Company and Meryl Tankard's Australian Dance Theatre in Adelaide have encouraged groups of artists, including designers, to develop long-term working relationships. There is an acceptance in the present funding culture that dance theatre ensembles need to work together on a semi-permanent basis to create performance whereas other theatre forms are able to put together a show without regular workshops and pre-rehearsals. There is also an inclination for smaller under-funded performance groups to seek to work open plan or along communal lines when rehearsing, rather than the commonly used 'vertical' authoritarian structure favoured by established performance managements.

For this reason dance, physical theatre and puppet theatre have been able to contribute more than conventional theatre forms to a progressive development of performance design in their work. Designers are involved for much longer periods of pre-production and must work within the rehearsal room in order to keep the design concept in line with the developing performance. Even when the ensemble group is unable to remain together for extended periods there is a marked tendency for the same group of performers and creative artists to re-form for each new season. This sets up a working visual language between collaborators and involves the entire group in design decisions. In larger production companies innovation in design can be constricted because old processes and management practices are not always appropriate to new ideas or new forms of exploring and expressing those ideas. As John McCallum puts it:

'The elaborate communal meeting processes required for consensus creativity ... are notoriously time-consuming and difficult, and in this country simply not funded'.[14]

The process of creating within a collaborative artform is complex because it does involve so many artists and craftspeople. To manage this process theatre companies tend to apply systems for management control rather than structures of facilitation in which artists are encouraged to create.

To develop that which is truly new takes time frames different from the common four- or six-week rehearsal period. For innovations to occur, particularly with the visualisation and spatialisation of the performance, the designer needs to be a full-time member of the artistic planning, pre-production/performance and the rehearsal process. As freelance designers tend to be engaged per show it is often not possible for them to devote time to all facets of the rehearsal process, and few Australian companies allocate design assistants on staff.

There are several factors at play here. The budgets made available for staging and design are comparatively low and there is no pre-production budget for the exploration of design ideas. Designers are required to present a finished design well before rehearsals begin in order to facilitate budgeting and planning. This prevents many designers from reworking their designs as new ideas become more appropriate during rehearsals. Although design management and implementation is considered by most managements to be a technical theatre function, seldom is the theatre space made available to designers or technicians before the production week for experimentation and exploration of new techniques. Often a company is locked into accepting an inappropriate design simply because it has been constructed or bought ahead of time, without allowing for the evolution of performance within a rehearsal room.

It may be argued that to sustain an ongoing management structure these management controls are necessary and are often the requirements of government grants. But creating and producing new performance is not only just a business, to be favoured with government assistance to enable it to operate in the quasi-commercial sector of the entertainment industry. Performance is an important aspect of our cultural life. It contributes to a fuller aesthetic appreciation of our created and creative worlds. The imagery of the stage space reflects and comments on our cultural identity. Visual thinking adds value to cultural well-being and awareness.

If Australian stage imagery is truly to reflect the present culture we need to look to reforming performance management systems. For theatre companies to utilise the designer's skills fully they need to be encouraged in the ongoing creative process at all levels — from pre-production discussions, to the rehearsal room workshops, to the performance venue and through to the post-production wrap. In this way, design will develop more fully from production to production.

While our mainstream theatre practice continues to rely clumsily on funded one-off projects it will remain very difficult for Australian performance designers to contribute fully to the artistic management of productions or to generate new ways of visualising performance.

It will remain difficult to distinguish if there is an emerging 'Australian style of performance design' until performing arts companies are prepared to commit artistically and financially to a progressive exploration of the process and practice of theatre making. Then an Australian way of 'seeing and re-presenting' may evolve.

Written theatre has a lot to learn from dance in terms of design.

Barry Moreland (artistic director of the West Australian Ballet) discussing the influence of the design work of Andrew Carter in dance performance.[15]

Geoff Cobham's restrained lighting and Jennie Tate's poetic yet frugal gathering of leaves, milk crates and a discarded bed converted the theatre into a shadowy playground of desolate souls.

◄ Plate 129 **All Souls**
by Daniel Keene
Griffin Theatre Company
1994
venue: The Stables, Sydney
director: Ros Horin
composer: Sarah de Jong
set and costume designer: Jennie Tate
lighting designer: Geoff Cobham
photo: Griffin archives
in photo: Rhonda Wilson as Phillipa

1 This chapter is an abridged version of Nicholson's thesis, submitted to NIDA in 1996 as part of the degree conversion programme.

2 D. Bablet, *Recent Trends in Scenic Design: 20 Years of Scenography*, Theatre Design and Technology, UK, 1989.

3 Helbo, Johansen, Pavis & Ubersfeld (eds), *Approaching Theatre*, Indiana University Press, 1991.

4 Katherine Brisbane in *New Currents in Australian Writing*, eds K. Brisbane, R. F. Brissenden & D. Malouf, Angus & Robertson, Sydney, 1978.

5 I consider the active spatial elements available to be:
(1) theatre space — architectural; (2) stage space — architecturally defined; (3) 'set' space — scenically defined; (4) dramatic space — space as used by the author of the work; (5) referred space — space as indicated by characters but not represented in the set space; (6) implied space — space as indicated by set, light, sound, but not seen; that is, placing the set space in a dramatic and/or scenic context. D. Nicholson, *Aspect, Art and Literature*, nos 32–3, 1985.

6 The critical elements are the rake or slope of the stepped seating tiers, the height of the ceiling above the audience, the nature and placement of the walls which frame or contain the performance platform and the audience, and the height and angle of the performance platform relative to the first rows of audience.

7 The support spaces to the performance platform — the so-called 'off-stage' spaces — function both as the performer's access to the 'dramatic space' and as places from where to indicate virtual 'dramatic spaces'. They also serve as locations to position supplementary stage technology.

8 Peter Robinson, 'Flaws in our Opera House', *Sun Herald*, 24 March 1996.

9 I take the description of a good stage to be that which is reasonably serviced by off-stage spaces, such as: stage left and stage right to be half the size of the performance area available on each side; up-stage space to be the same area as the performance area; access to under stage to be at least one-third of the acting area; and above the stage to have a minimum proportional volume equal to one-third the volume of the performance area.

In *Tristram Shandy — Gent*, the ruins of an eighteenth-century theatre spilled out and around the proscenium and into the auditorium of the small Russell Street venue. By knocking down parts of the wall separating the dressing rooms and the

auditorium, Roberts enlarged the acting space and created a second level with a balcony. He said of the production: 'I loved the challenge of finding ways to disguise the restrictions of this small venue'.

(R. Roberts, conversation with author, April 1996)

◄ ► Plates 130a and 130b **Tristram Shandy — Gent**

based on the novel by Laurence Sterne and adapted by Tim Robertson

Melbourne Theatre Company

1988

venue: Russell Street Theatre, Melbourne

director: Simon Phillips

composers: Gerry Hale and Richard Piper

set and costume designer: Richard Roberts

lighting designer: Jamieson Lewis

photo: MTC archives

10 *Sydney Morning Herald*, 13 December 1995.

11 Open stage is a configuration in which the audience and performer 'share' the same space without an architectural feature dividing them. The open-stage spaces that have given rise to much exploration in performance visualisation are: the Church Theatre, Melbourne; Downstairs at the Seymour Theatre, Sydney; The Performance Space, Sydney; the Fairfax Studio, Victorian Arts Centre, Melbourne; the Edward Street Community Arts Centre, Brisbane; Red Shed, Adelaide; and the Grant Street Theatre, Melbourne. There are also many companies that have used found spaces to explore performer–audience relationships. Some examples are: IHOS Opera, Hobart; Barrie Kosky's Gilgul Theatre, Melbourne; and IRAA, Melbourne.

12 Most Australian performing arts companies are governed through a committee or board of management which appoints an artistic director and an administrator. These two positions head the two operational units into which the management is divided — the artistic and the administrative.

13 A repertory system normally has one production in performance and another in rehearsal and may have several in different stages of planning, serviced by variously engaged artistic personnel. A repertoire system employs a permanent group of theatre artists and schedules different productions to perform over a season.

14 John McCallum, *Australian*, 2 April 1996.

15 Jo Litson, *Weekend Australian Review*, 11–12 May 1996.

Thea.tricks

A critique by Eamon D'Arcy

This chapter is dedicated to the memory of Australian theatre director Rex Cramphorn, who taught me that theory is practice and that practice is theory.

Lookout post

Look out — postmodernism is here.[1] Whether you like it or not it is having an undeniable effect on all of our cultural preconceptions and just about anything else you want to mention. Behind the buzzword lie new ways of reading, writing and thinking. It has begun to have an impact on our culture and it won't be long before it has an impact on theatre and design. As postmodernism confronts traditional notions of culture it forces us to rethink our very definition of Australian culture.

The year 2001 is not just a symbolic turning point but also a pivot for change. Philosophically, technologically and socially we are being forced to radically rethink ourselves. This change can be seen as either a crisis or an opportunity. Even those who are sceptical about the coming of postmodernism would have to agree that our world is changing. Technological advancement is now so fast that we are producing things well before we have time to think about their consequences. Our sense of self and our community are changing. We are now openly questioning issues raised decades ago by multiculturalism, feminism, gay rights and anti-colonialism. These issues are now part of mainstream political debate. The ideas formulated by these debates are now becoming part of our written (textual) theatre but unfortunately not part of our visual (imaged) theatre.

Our work as designers exists within the public sphere. All the designs shown in this book are for public consumption. This means that we should take responsibility for our actions. In a sense we have a civic duty to do so. We are never really involved in purely innocent entertainment. All the productions we work on are shaped by political rhetoric, cultural agendas and economic policies. Whatever we do has an impact on our culture and therefore our society.

Culture, as the word signifies, is based on growth.[2] Culture grows with the help of policies and strategies that are based on rich and diverse forms of thinking. This richness of thought allows us to assess our past decisions, to look at the present situation and to speculate about future directions. One area that concerns me as a professional theatre designer is our lack of theoretical enquiry. We must commit to the exploration of new ideas and get involved in any debates that affect our culture. In the development of culture there is much at stake and we in the theatre have much to declare.

Looking at theory

Theories are viewpoints. They help us to see issues in a new light. Theories help to analyse issues by focusing on our histories, languages and traditions. They give us the capacity to understand the issues at hand. Theories organise our thoughts and help make connections across different disciplines.

Our practices have histories. Whatever we do has a place within these histories. Theories expand our knowledge and we become better informed. We do this to learn more about our work. Theoretical enquiries probe beyond the surface. Designs are never accepted at face value but are examined and discussed. Practices which are informed by theoretical enquiry have the potential to add value to our cultural growth. One aspect of theory that is crucial to any form of growth is critique.

Critique examines all methods, positions, assumptions and interventions, including its own. Critique is a type of reflection committed to revision and development that allows an open, flexible and non-dogmatic approach. The German philosopher Immanuel Kant called this way of thinking 'reflective judgment'.[3] According to Kant, reflective judgment was a mode of thought that was not guided by rules for determining data but rather by showing itself as capable of developing such rules afterwards on the basis of results obtained reflectively. When designers say that it is their 'intuition' that produced the design, they are reflecting on a particular way of thinking and making. According to these designers they have had a particular insight into the production of a design.

This is the beginning of theoretical enquiry, albeit in a simplistic way. Designers do use their intuition but they forget that it has been shaped by various social and artistic forces. The designer might start a project with a blank page but not with a blank mind. No-one designs in isolation. We interact with other people such as directors, technicians, actors and writers. The designs shown in this book are the result of many people working together. Designing for the theatre involves collaborations of the most complex kind.

Critical insights

Theories can provide a language that talks about common experiences, discourses and practices. They help assess our institutions, individual practices and methodologies. Theories can point to emerging problems and

◄ page 228 **Hayden Orpheum, main auditorium (detail of curtain)**
photographer: Patrick Van Daele

provide resources with which to discuss them. When issues are discussed it is fundamental to effective communication that the languages used are common to all participants. Whatever we do or say should be open to all. Open discussion means that issues can and should be viewed from all angles.

Critique is a way of debating all the issues while acknowledging the debate itself. Therefore my outlook, my viewpoint, is not the only position of command. I cannot claim that I achieve maximum insight without any distortion. For example, a glance at the language I am using demonstrates the ubiquity of visual metaphors. Some commentators might say that my thinking is 'occularcentric'. This means that the way I am conditioned to think is based on a particular way of seeing. The language I use has an optical dynamic which impacts on the way I think. This is not uncommon, since traditional western philosophy is loaded with visual metaphors. It could then be inferred that I use traditional thinking as I depend on these metaphors when constructing an argument … if you 'see what I mean'.

We use various methods and different types of logic, and we speculate when designing. These are usually hidden well within the deep recesses of the filofax. Most designers are unaware of these layers building up within their work. However, their notes, sketches, models and plans actually construct viewpoints about design in the theatre. This says much about designers and how they think. Each designer represented within this book has a viewpoint about some facet of our culture. There is more at stake here than just the cut of a costume or the texture of scenery. Theoretical enquiry encourages us to think about how and why this is so.

The theatre, both as building and space, has a particular place within our society. Too often this point is ignored. We are implicated in this ignorance because theatre design is not recognised as a serious discipline within our academies or within our culture. This has ramifications.

At present, any thinking, planning or strategy about theatre design involves the importation of ideas from other disciplines. Our designs are never seen in their own light. Because we have devalued and neglected the role of theory we have set up a situation in which we cannot interact equally with others in the arts community. The lack of enquiry and the wilful ignorance of theoretical thinking reveals a theatre world that borders on the mundane, especially if we compare it with the world of art. We have not developed a common language that challenges assumptions others have about theatre design. Subsequently we avoid rigorous critical analysis, which results in the use of stereotypical language to describe our work.

Without theory it is very difficult to set up an environment in which we can grow intellectually. We do have a duty to participate within our intellectual community. Social problems are compounding and it is essential that we do something about them. Obviously the introduction of theory alone will not solve society's ills. However, the resources that it does give could help to point towards some practical solutions.

Seeing through the issues

It is extraordinary to find that we (as an industry/profession/community) have produced very little by way of substantial theoretical debate.[4] Critical debates do not seem to exist within the world of theatre design. It is a pathetic situation. This means that we are not prepared to think differently. It implies that we do not want to declare anything at all about our work. We have produced very few theoretical design projects. There are not many research-based projects occurring within our theatre training institutions. There are no postgraduate courses undertaking design research.

Unfortunately this must be expected. There is hardly a glimmer of rigorous thinking within our discipline. Instead, old-fashioned notions of art and design reign. Most of the talk is based on anecdotes and it never rises above personal opinion. Implied in many of these interviews is the notion of the designer as artist — a person who 'created' the designs using his or her 'emotions' and 'instincts' to achieve an 'imaginative' result. I highlight these words because they point to a number of problems which concern me. These words are untranslatable within their context. Whoever uses these words does so knowing that their meaning is inaccessible and thus cannot be criticised.

Using these words deliberately stops any form of enquiry. As I mentioned before, it is crucial that we remain open to ideas. When someone is scared they usually keep their eyes closed. Implicit in all of this is a fear of debate and, therefore, the fear of theory. Writing about the subject of theory, the Australian philosopher Elizabeth Grosz says that this fear 'verges on a psychosis, a paranoiac defensive reaction to an incursion from the outside by what is perceived as threatening … theory is a kind of control over the intoxication of art'.[5]

When debate about theory is stifled arguments are either black or white. It is easy to con people when they have their eyes closed. They start to believe that theory is the opposite of practice. Following on from this myopic view is the belief that theory is therefore uncreative and unimaginative. Without practice there would be no theory — it is as simple as that. The real bluff starts when theory is automatically deemed irrelevant. It is a game in which you keep going round in circles.[6]

Blind-man's b[l]uff

Blindman's buff is the game in which someone covers his or her eyes and pretends to be blind. The trick when blindfolded is to catch the others while being pushed around. It is a game that is acceptable in primary school. For many people, however, the game goes on into later life, and it becomes easy to 'bluff' themselves into believing anything. Some designers believe that 'creativity' is at the heart of designing. This is a word that constantly goes unchallenged. Of course to these designers it is a word that exists in some mystical world, and within this world only the initiated can find true significance. If you do not understand the meaning of the word you are 'uncreative'. Designers who are initiated seem to have insights into creativity that transcend ordinary human knowledge. They use words such as 'emotional' and 'instinctive' to infer that they inhabit an inner creative world that has nothing whatsoever to do with an outside real world. However, like most words in our language, these words have a history and are themselves shaped by theoretical practices.

Designers might think they do their work in non-theoretical ways, but they are bluffing themselves. Cultural issues are always at stake, whether intentionally or not. Most information comes to us via conceptual and theoretical materials (for example, by reading the latest theatre magazine from Germany).[7] It is romantic and naive to claim that art and design are about emotions and instincts that are privately accessible to the artist/designer, yet remain latent in the public display of the work itself. The ways theatre is practised and the processes necessary for its production are always implicated in the design work. To disown or distance the works shown in this book from theoretical and conceptual issues is simply to continue the ignorance about the commitments to which a theatre designer is bound.

Anyone who uses the word 'creativity' usually implies that they are artists first and foremost. But before rushing into accepting the mantle of artist, designers should realise what is happening within the visual arts. A student going through a visual arts training institution is now educated using methodologies usually associated with the humanities. In the humanities, knowledge is provisional and open to revision. Topics such as postmodernism are commonplace. Subjects are becoming cross-disciplinary. Today's arts students study a wide range of subjects, including film, television, painting, multimedia and music. Cultural studies are now an accepted part of their curriculum. The range of readings and writings now standard within these schools is very broad. There seems to be a commitment to developing an environment that encourages intellectual rigour. Most of these art schools are attached to universities which teach art theory. New types of thinking are encouraged. This impacts on the practices of art. Purely theoretical projects are nurtured and the results point towards a richer environment of diverse visual art culture.

Thea.tricks

How refreshing it would be if intellectual rigour were applied to designing for the theatre. If we did study the theatre in a rigorous way we would know that the words 'theatre' and 'theory' come from the same Greek word, *thea*, which means 'to see'.[8] Designers who play the game of 'bluff' would never believe this. It all sounds a bit tricky to them. Yet whether we want to admit it or not, the theatre is intrinsically linked to theory. I use the word 'intrinsically' because theatre and theory naturally belong to one another. Discovering the word *thea* is found not by some mystical flash of creativity but by applied research.

Much of the design work shown in this book was designed with 'imitation', 'artifice' and 'surface' in mind. In my interpretation of the designs, I tend to use words other than 'instinct' and 'creative' to describe the art of theatre designing.[9] As I mentioned before, words have histories and meanings. Each word we use has a meaning that can differ depending on the context. Within philosophy, and aesthetics, words such as imitation have fascinating histories that can go back to the ancient Greeks.

Designers who insist that they are not imitators and that their designs are original have very little knowledge of aesthetics. When aesthetics (for example) is not studied then 'artifice' is not part of the vocabulary. Interviewing a cross-section of visual artists on the other hand would soon lead you to questioning representation, immateriality or deconstruction.

Anyone who devalues theory acts in contempt of theatre practice. Devaluing theory causes a domino effect in which we start to devalue our languages and histories. Not to explore the practical and theoretical knowledge within our design work goes against all notions of culture. The desire to know and to think is the essence of our humanity. If we are not trained to develop enquiring minds then what are we trained to do? Why do we not acknowledge that words such as 'imitation', 'copy', 'mimesis' or 'representation' are part of our discipline? Even having to ask these questions means that we are failing to see that theatre has an important role to play in our society.

Speculations

I refuse to play the game of 'bluff'. I believe that what I do has value. I want designers to respond to what I am saying, to start to think differently, perhaps even to work in a new way. I wrote this chapter to begin a discourse about theatre design. Starting from a particular vantage point I looked around and allowed myself to be challenged by other viewpoints. I am communicating statements, mental images, associations and metaphors that give shape to various ideas. I am attempting to put things into perspective, trying to convince other people to accept my ideas. This sort of dialogue is simple and meaningful. Culture can only grow in a positive way when it is open to dialogue.

As we move into the next millennium we have to ask the question of whether there are fundamental changes in our contemporary world compared with past worlds. Our world is definitely changing, and at an extraordinary rate. The sheer force of technological progress proves this. Indeed, one development that we must face is the onslaught of the televisual and how that affects us. So where are we now?

To ignore the possibilities opened up by ideas such as postmodernism is to do so at one's peril. One good side to postmodernism is the way it breaks down barriers between all the artforms. Postmodernism is slowly rediscovering theatre and performance. We must set up opportunities to become involved in cultural debates. As this book shows, we have much to offer.

If we fail to look closely at our work, our theatre, our culture, then we will remain blind to other ways of thinking. Within our culture we have to decide what is at stake and we have to decide how much to declare. When asked to take a position on issues we want to be fully informed about the options, to be able to think through the details and to articulate responses that have positive meanings.

We must open our eyes, look around and develop some vision.

1   Postmodernism is an impossible term. Its meaning is always ambiguous and elusive. For an introduction to the term and the issues it covers see Jean François Lyotard's *The Postmodern Condition: A Report on Knowledge*, Manchester University Press, Manchester, 1984. In very simple terms, Lyotard says that the usually accepted grand narratives of our culture are no longer adequate for explaining the world, and that words and things no longer coincide.

2   Growth here implies a kind of nurturing. I am now aligning culture with nature, which is problematic in itself. Raymond Williams in his book *Keywords* (Fontana Press, UK, 1988) says that these two words are the two most complicated words in the English language.

3   I mention Kant not to make philosophical claims but rather to show that philosophy can engage with the day-to-day activities of us all. Some theorists need to be reminded of this as well. For an introduction to Kant see Gilles Deleuze, *Kant's Critical Philosophy*, trans. H. Tomlinson & B. Habberjam, University of Minnesota Press, Minneapolis, 1993.

4   I know of only three writers — Pam Zeplin, Tom Bannerman and Michael A. R. Anderson — who are interested in the theories of theatre design. Each of these writers comes from a discipline outside the theatre.

5   Elizabeth Grosz in 'Every picture tells a story' from the catalogue essay for the exhibition 'Shifting References', Artspace, Sydney, 1986.

6   It must be said in fairness to practitioners that it is common to find theorists defining 'practice' in condescending tones.

7   *Stage Design Now: Stage Design of the Future* (Cantz Publications, Karlsruhe, Germany, 1994) was the catalogue of an exhibition held at the Centre of Art and Media Technology, Karlsruhe, Germany. The four theatre designers highlighted in this catalogue are all professors of design: Achim Freyer, Dieter Hacker, Johannes Schutz and Erich Wonder.

8   For an introduction to the word *thea* used within this context see David M. Levin, *The Opening of Vision*, Routledge, London, 1988, pp. 98–100. Levin uses the work of German philosopher Martin Heidegger to develop this idea further.

9   See M. Livingstone, *David Hockney*, Thames & Hudson, London, 1996, for an insight into the use of different terminologies. The chapter on Hockney that deals with his designs for the theatre is called 'Invention and artifice'.

Selected Bibliography

Allen, John (ed.), *Entertainment Arts in Australia*, Paul Hamlyn, Sydney, 1968.

Anderson, M. A. R., 'Upstaging theatre — design for the unreal world', *Age Monthly Review*, Melbourne, September 1989, pp. 5–6.

Anderson, M. A. R., 'Pressing against ideas', in *Cities of Hope*, ed. Conrad Hamann, Oxford University Press, Melbourne, 1993, pp. 148–58.

Artaud, A., *The Theatre and its Double*, Grove Press, New York, 1958.

Bablet, D., 'Recent trends in scenic design: 20 years of scenography', *Theatre Design and Technology*, UK, 1989.

Bannerman, Tom, Australian stage design: A current direction put into an historical context, unpublished essay, Department of Theatre Studies, University of New South Wales, Sydney, 1990.

Bannerman, Tom, Brian Thomson: The enfant terrible, unpublished essay, Department of Theatre Studies, University of New South Wales, Sydney, 1990.

Bannerman, Tom, Image and scenographic considerations in Alma de Groens's *The Rivers of China*, unpublished essay, Department of Theatre Studies, University of New South Wales, Sydney, 1991.

Bannerman, Tom, Inanimate links in Kim Carpenter's theatre, unpublished essay, Department of Theatre Studies, University of New South Wales, Sydney, 1991.

Bannerman, T., Gurton, S. & Tate, J., Australian scenography since 1945, unpublished paper presented to the Asia Scenography Conference, Tokyo, 1993.

Bonney, Gabrielle, Critically injured: Designer vs critic, unpublished essay held by the author, Sydney, 1995.

Bramwell, Murray, 'Setting out the stages', *The Adelaide Review*, July 1988.

Branson, D. & Troy, P., 'Subtle spectacle', *RealTime 9*, Oct./Nov. 1995, p. 31.

Brisbane, K., Brissenden, R. F. & Malouf, D. (eds), *New Currents in Australian Writing*, Angus & Robertson, Sydney, 1978.

Brodsky, Isadore, *Sydney Takes the Stage*, Old Sydney Free Press, Sydney, 1963.

Brown, M., Morgan, F. & Wright, J., *Strategic Planning for Design Organisations*, Australian Institute of Landscape Architects, Australian Production Design Association and Design Institute of Australia, November 1987.

Burstall, B., Jones, L. & Garner, H., *La Mama: The Story of a Theatre*, McPhee Gribble/Penguin, Ringwood, Victoria, 1988.

Carroll, Dennis, *Australian Contemporary Drama*, revised edition, Currency Press, Sydney, 1995.

Cochrane, P., 'The Tate Gallery', *Sydney Morning Herald*, 23 April 1997, p. 12.

Cosic, M., 'Stage by stage', *Good Weekend*, *Sydney Morning Herald*, 12 August 1995, pp. 30–35.

Craig, Edward Gordon, *On the Art of the Theatre*, Mercury Books, London, 1962.

Deleuze, Gilles, *Kant's Critical Philosophy*, trans. H. Tomlinson & B. Habberjam, University of Minnesota Press, Minneapolis, 1993.

Freyer, A., Hacker, D., Schutz, J. & Wonder, E., *Stage Design Now: Stage Design of the Future*, catalogue essay, Cantz Publications, Karlsruhe, Germany, 1994.

Grosz, Elizabeth, 'Every picture tells a story', catalogue essay for the exhibition 'Shifting References', Artspace Gallery, Sydney, 1986.

Hamann, Conrad (ed.), *Cities of Hope*, Oxford University Press, Melbourne, 1993.

Helbo, Johansen, Pavis & Ubersfeld (eds), *Approaching Theatre*, Indiana University Press, Indiana, 1991.

Hutcheson, Ann, 'The photographic art of Regis Lansac', *Dance Australia*, Aug./Sept. 1991, pp. 23–26.

Jones, Robert Edmond, *The Dramatic Imagination*, Theatre Arts Books, New York, 1941.

Levin, David M., *The Opening of Vision*, Routledge, London, 1988.

Litson, Jo, 'Theatre's master builder', *Australian Weekend Review*, 21 November 1992, pp. 11–12.

Livingstone, M., *David Hockney*, Thames & Hudson, London, 1996.

Love, Harold (ed.), *The Australian Stage: A Documentary History*, University of New South Wales Press, Sydney, 1984.

Lyotard, Jean François, *The Postmodern Condition: A Report on Knowledge*, Manchester University Press, Manchester, 1984.

Marson, Linda & O'Neil, Kym, 'Analysing the design process: A consultative document', *Arts Training Australia*, Victoria, 1992.

Moore, Mary, 'Performance for non-theatre spaces', in *Australian Theatre Design*, ed. Kim Spinks, Australian Production and Design Association, Sydney, 1992, pp. 141–46.

Moore, Mary, 'Sexing the space', *Converging Realities*, ed. Peta Tait, Currency Press, Sydney, 1995, pp. 227–33.

Nicholson, D., 'Aspect', *Art and Literature*, no. 32–33, 1985.

Nicholson', D., Design constrictions, unpublished thesis, NIDA, Sydney, 1996.

Page, R., 'The evolution of a designer', *Theatre Australia*, July 1981, p. 27.

Parsons, Phillip (ed.), *Companion to Theatre in Australia*, Currency Press, Sydney, 1995.

Payne, Pamela, 'Offences of perspective', *The Bulletin*, 30 April 1991, pp. 108–9.

Robinson, Peter, 'Flaws in our Opera House', *Sun Herald*, 24 March 1996.

Roderick, C. (ed.), *Ralph Rashleigh or the Life of an Exile*, Angus & Robertson, Sydney, 1952.

Rowell, Kenneth, *Stage Design*, Studio Vista, London, 1968.

Shevtsova, M., Greek–Australian odysseys in a multi-cultural world, unpublished essay, University of Sydney, Sydney, 1995.

Spinks, Kim (ed.), *Australian Theatre Design*, Australian Production and Design Association, Sydney, 1992.

Tait, Peta (ed.), *Converging Realities*, Currency Press, Sydney, 1995.

Thorne, Ross, 'Theatres', *Companion to Theatre in Australia*, ed. Phillip Parsons, Currency Press, Sydney, 1995, pp. 589–95.

Walton, J. Michael (ed.), *Craig on Theatre*, Methuen, London, 1983.

West, John, *Theatre in Australia*, Cassel Australia, Sydney, 1978.

Williams, Raymond, *Keywords*, Fontana Press, UK, 1988.

Zeplin, Pamela, 'Literally a dumb situation', *Lowdown*, no. 6, December 1989, pp. 55–57.

Zeplin, Pamela, 'The space between: Political space and theatre artist', in *Australian Theatre Design*, ed. Kim Spinks, Australian Production and Design Association, Sydney, 1992, pp. 119–24.

Zeplin, Pamela, 'The brush-off syndrome: Stage design, history and visual art in Adelaide', *Artlink*, vol. 12, no. 3, Spring 1992, pp. 57–60.

Zeplin, Pamela, 'Stage design and effects', in *Companion to Theatre in Australia*, ed. Phillip Parsons, Currency Press, Sydney, 1995, pp. 545–50.

The following publications provided authors with performance reviews on a weekly, monthly or quarterly basis between 1993 and 1996.

Australian and New Zealand Theatre Record (ANZTR), quarterly periodical of the Department of Theatre Studies, University of New South Wales, Sydney

Adelaide Advertiser

The Age

The Australian

Australian Opera News, Opera Australia

The Bulletin magazine

Dance Australia

NIDA Newsclippings, NIDA, University of New South Wales, Sydney

RealTime, OpenCity, Sydney

The Sydney Morning Herald

Vive, Ansett inflight magazine

The West Australian

The following people were interviewed by the authors during their research for the book. The original recordings and transcripts of these interviews have been housed at the Performing Arts Museum of Victoria, Victorian Arts Centre, Melbourne.

W. Akers, 8 March 1995; B. Anderson, 3 May 1995; T. Bannerman, 2 March 1995; K. Barrett, 22 November 1993; H. Bell, 23 March 1995; J. Bell, 13 March 1995; R. Burke, 15 March 1995; D. Byrnes, 9 March 1995; K. Carpenter, 18 November 1993; A. Carter, 19 August 1993; J. Cobb, 24 August 1993; G. Cobham, 9 March 1995; H. Colman, 18 August 1993; P. Cooke, 23 October 1995; M. Cooper, 23 March 1995; P. Corrigan, 23 March 1995; D. Cox, 10 March 1995; T. Crea, 7 March 1995; S. Curtis, 15 November 1993; E. D'Arcy, 5 March 1995; R. Dempster, 10 March 1995; G. Elston, 26 March 1995; B. Evans, 5 April 1995; V. Feitscher, 13 March 1995; S. Field, 3 March 1995; L. Frank, 20 March 1995; A. Fraser, 26 June 1995; K. Fredrikson, 18 November 1993; A. French, 13 April 1995; S. Grey-Gardener, 22 March 1995; S. Gurton, 23 August 1993; B. Haycock, 7 March 1995; J. Hoddinott, 15 November 1993; J. Hoenig, 5 March 1995; D. Hough, 14 March 1995; L. Hume, 19 March 1995; R. Jeziorny, 21 March 1995; R. Juniper, 9 September 1993; J. Kemp, 31 January 1996; R. Kemp. 14 November 1993; T. Kobin, 8 March 1995; B. Kosky, 5 April 1994; C. Koukias, 20 March 1995; E. Kurzer, 26 March 1995; A. Lees, 18 December 1995; N. Levings, 1 March 1995; J. Litson, 15 March 1995; D. Longmuir, 11 March 1995; A. Lovejoy, 24 March 1995; 26 March 1996; L. McCarthy, 19 March 1995; G. Maclean, 9 March 1995; C. Martin, 4 April 1995; A. Mellor, 14 March 1995; C. Mitchell, 20 November 1993; P. Mitchell, 14 March 1995; G. Murphy, 30 March 1995; T. Newth, 22 March 1995; D. Nicholson, 12 October 1996; D. Ord, 29 November 1993; W. Osmond, 22 March 1995; M. Oxenbould, 29 March 1995; T. Parker, 11 August 1993; W. Passmore, 15 March 1995; P. Payne, 22 March 1995; M. Pearce, 11 December 1993; D. Potra, 22 November 1993; J. Rayment, 14 March 1995; R. Roberts, 23 November 1993; I. Robinson, 17 November 1993; A. Ross, 10 March 1995; K. Rowell, 18 December 1995; N. Schlieper, 12 March 1995; T. Schofield, November 1993; M. Scott-Mitchell, 20 November 1993; J. Senczuk, 11 March 1995; M. Shelton, 15 March 1995; E. Soropos, 23 November 1993; K. Sproul, 5 March 1995;

J. Stoddart, 23 October 1995; J. Tate, 23 November 1993; P. Thibaudeau, 21 November 1993; M. Thompson, 3 April 1995; B. Thomson, 18 November 1993; T. Tripp, 14 October 1993; L. Westbury, 30 August 1993; R. Wherrett, 17 February 1998; K. Wilby, 8 March 1995; P. L. Wilson, 3 and 20 March 1995; A. Wulff, 20 March 1995; T. Youlden, 17 March 1995; P. Zeplin, April 1996.

The resource libraries, programme archives and photographic catalogues of the following performance companies were used for reference information:
Australian Ballet (AB); Australian Dance Theatre (ADT); Australian and Islander Dance Theatre (AIDT); Australian Nouveau Theatre (ANThill); Bangarra Dance Theatre; Barking Gecko Theatre for Young Audiences (including archives for Acting Out Theatre for Young Audiences); Bell Shakespeare Company; Belvoir Street Theatre and Company B; Bizircus; Black Swan Theatre Company; Chamber Made Opera; Chrissie Parrott Dance Collective; Circus Oz; Entr'acte; Gilgul Theatre (archives housed in the office of Corrigan and Edmonson, Melbourne); Gordon/Frost Organisation; Griffin Theatre Company; Handspan Puppet Theatre; IHOS Opera; IRAA Theatre; Kickhouse Theatre Company; La Mama Theatre; Legs on the Wall; Lyric Opera of Queensland; Magpie Theatre Company (archives housed at the State Theatre Company of South Australia); Melbourne Theatre Company (MTC); National Institute of Dramatic Art (NIDA); Nimrod Theatre (archives housed in the State Library of New South Wales); Opera Australia (includes the archives of the Australian Opera); Playbox Theatre Company; Red Shed Theatre Company; Rock and Roll Circus; Royal Queensland Theatre Company (RQTC); Skylark Puppet Theatre; Spare Parts Puppet Theatre; Splinters Performance Group; State Opera of South Australia (SOSA); State Theatre Company of South Australia (STC SA); Sydney Theatre Company (STC); Theatre of Image; Victoria State Opera (VSO); West Australian Ballet (WAB); West Australian Opera (WAO); Western Australian Academy of Performing Arts (WAAPA).

All other images in the book were sourced directly from the personal collections of the designers interviewed and/or the archives of the photographers responsible.

Contributing photographers

Eric Algra, ph: 0411 227 301; Corrie Ancone; Frances Andrijich, ph: +61 8 9384 4089; Australian Ballet archives, ph: +61 3 9684 8600; Christobel Baranay; Barking Gecko archives, ph: +61 8 9388 2611; Belvoir Street Theatre archives, ph: +61 2 9698 3444; Marco Bok; Jeff Busby, ph: +61 3 9525 3585; Earl Carter, ph: +61 3 9525 5288; Jennie Carter; Kiren Chang; John Clutterbuck; Robert Colvin, ph: +61 3 9387 9249; Peter Corrigan, ph: + 61 3 9662 2651; David Dare Parker; Dennis Del Favero, ph: +61 2 9798 9102; Mathew Dwyer; Sandy Edwards, ph: +61 2 9332 1455; Entr'acte archives, ph: +61 2 9358 5483; Anthony Figallo; Branco Gaica, ph: +61 2 9698 7748; Gordon/Frost Organisation archives, ph: +61 2 9255 0088; Lorrie Graham, ph: +61 2 9516 1323; Griffin Theatre archives, ph: +61 2 9332 1052; Chris Ha Estate; Hugh Hamilton; Handspan archives, ph: +61 3 9645 5331; Phillipe Hargreaves; Ponch Hawkes, ph: +61 3 9416 2869; Brett Hilder, ph: 0411 281 638; Peter Holderness, ph: +61 2 9699 2910; Reina Irmer, ph: +61 7 3840 7943; Gerald Jenkins; Henry Jolles; Miki-Nobu Komatsu; Joseph Lafferty; La Mama Theatre archives, ph: +61 3 9347 6948; Regis Lansac, ph: +61 8 8212 2084; Elise Lockwood, ph: +61 2 9960 8889; Heidrun Lohr, ph: +61 2 9290 1928; James McFarlane; Robert McFarlane, ph: 0412 210 988; George Mackintosh; David McMicken; Don McMurdo, ph: +61 2 9452 1674; Harry M. Miller archives, ph: +61 2 9357 3077; Moomba Festival archives, ph: +61 3 9650 9744; Melbourne Theatre Company archives, ph: +61 3 9684 4500; Derek Nicholson, ph: +61 2 9361 5263; Greg Noakes, ph: +61 3 9808 1482; Peter Northcote, ph: +61 8 9273 8287; Opera Australia archives (includes Australian Opera archives), ph: +61 2 9699 1099; David Parker, ph: +61 3 9646 4022; Playbox Theatre archives, ph: +61 3 9685 5100; Bill Plowman; Sesh Raman; Neil Roberts; Andrew Samson; Scenic Studios archive, ph: +61 3 9329 4811; Dean Sewell; State Theatre Company of South Australia(including Magpie Theatre Company images) archives, ph: +61 8 8231 5151; Sydney Theatre Company archives, ph: +61 2 9250 1700; Lisa Tomasetti; Sally Tsoutis, ph: +61 2 9388 8754; Sven Ulsa; Patrick Van Daele, ph: +61 2 9665 1165; VIC Perrier archives; Robert Walker, ph: +61 2 9698 8280; West Australian Ballet archives, ph: +61 8 9481 0707; Gary Willis; David Wilson, ph: +61 8 8278 6265; Ann Wulff; William Yang, ph: +61 2 9365 5876.

Index

Illustrations indicated by *italic* numerals.
Major reference indicated by **bold** numerals.